TAKING AMERICA BACK FOR GOD

TAKING AMERICA BACK FOR GOD

CHRISTIAN NATIONALISM IN THE UNITED STATES

ANDREW L. WHITEHEAD
AND
SAMUEL L. PERRY

OXFORD
UNIVERSITY PRESS

OXFORD
UNIVERSITY PRESS

Oxford University Press is a department of the University of Oxford. It furthers
the University's objective of excellence in research, scholarship, and education
by publishing worldwide. Oxford is a registered trade mark of Oxford University
Press in the UK and certain other countries.

Published in the United States of America by Oxford University Press
198 Madison Avenue, New York, NY 10016, United States of America.

Library of Congress Cataloging-in-Publication Data
Names: Whitehead, Andrew L., author. | Perry, Samuel L., author.
Title: Taking America back for God : Christian nationalism in the United States /
Andrew L. Whitehead, Samuel L. Perry.
Description: New York, NY, United States of America. :
Oxford University Press, 2020. | Includes bibliographical references. |
Identifiers: LCCN 2019031330 (print) | LCCN 2019031331 (ebook) |
ISBN 9780190057886 (hardback) | ISBN 9780190057909 (epub) |
ISBN 9780190057893 (updf) | ISBN 9780190057916 (online)
Subjects: LCSH: Christianity and politics—United States—History—21st century. |
Nationalism—Religious aspects—Christianity—History—20th century. |
Nationalism—United States—History—20th century. |
Christianity and culture—United States—History—21st century. |
Christianity—Influence.
Classification: LCC BR516 .W438 2020 (print) | LCC BR516 (ebook) |
DDC 261.70973—dc23
LC record available at https://lccn.loc.gov/2019031330
LC ebook record available at https://lccn.loc.gov/2019031331

3 5 7 9 8 6 4

Printed by Sheridan Books, Inc., United States of America

To Kelly,
You know I would.
~ Andrew

To Ryan, Beau, and Whitman,
You are the reason we need to get this right.
~ Sam

In the imagination of the simple patriot the nation is not a society but Society. Though its values are relative they appear, from his naïve perspective, to be absolute . . . . The nation is always endowed with an aura of the sacred, which is one reason why religions, which claim universality, are so easily captured and tamed by national sentiment, religion and patriotism merging in the process.

—Reinhold Niebuhr, *Moral Man and Immoral Society*, 1936:96–97

See to it that no one takes you captive through hollow and deceptive philosophy, which depends on human tradition and the basic principles of this world rather than on Christ.

—Colossians 2:8 (NIV)

CONTENTS

PREFACE

Most Americans who watch the news or scroll through social media could quickly list the most salient cultural and political issues currently driving a wedge down the middle of the United States: immigration reform, mass shootings, climate change, military spending, terrorism, gun control, travel bans, refugees, political correctness, opioid addiction, public education, racial injustice in policing, redefinitions of "marriage" and "the family," secularism, transgender rights, single-parent households, and, of course, Donald Trump.

It doesn't take a social scientist to identify the sticking points in our country. The more contentious debate, rather, is over what connects those dots. What has us so increasingly and uniformly divided on those issues? Ask ten social scientists to explain that to you, and you may get ten different theories. There aren't any simple answers to that question, unfortunately. There are a myriad of historical, demographic, economic, and technological factors contributing to our increasing polarization on issues of race, family, religion, gender, human rights, the environment, taxes, and so on. There is no silver-bullet explanation, and we don't intend to offer one here. Our goal in this book is to thoroughly explore one factor that, as we will show, plays a large, unique, but often unrecognized (and at times, *mis*recognized) role in our nation's current cultural and political conflicts. That factor is Christian nationalism.

Some conceptual clarifications would be helpful at the onset. Though journalists and historians have bandied about the term a good deal in the past decade, we mean "Christian nationalism" to describe an ideology that idealizes and advocates a fusion of American civic life with a particular type of Christian identity and culture. We use "Christian" here in a specific sense. We are not referring to doctrinal orthodoxy or personal piety. (In fact, we find some Christian nationalists can be quite secular.) Rather, the explicit ideological content of *Christian* nationalism comprises beliefs about historical identity, cultural preeminence, and political influence. But just as important, it also contains ideological content that is often implicit. This includes symbolic boundaries that conceptually blur and conflate religious identity (Christian, preferably Protestant) with race (white), nativity (born in the United States), citizenship (American), and political ideology (social and fiscal conservative). Christian nationalism, then, provides a complex of explicit and implicit ideals, values, and myths—what we call a "cultural framework"—through which Americans perceive and navigate their social world.

What do we *not* mean by Christian nationalism? First—and this may surprise (or disappoint) some readers—this isn't a book about white evangelicals. Certainly, we will address the considerable overlap between Christian nationalism and white evangelicalism. But the two concepts are not at all synonymous. Christian nationalism is a framework that orients Americans' perspectives on national identity, belonging, and social hierarchies. American evangelicalism, strictly speaking, is a theological tradition prioritizing certain doctrinal commitments including biblical inerrancy and conversionism. While a large percentage of Christian nationalists are affiliated with evangelical Protestant denominations and hold characteristically evangelical beliefs, many non-evangelicals (or non-Christians, for that matter) also hold strong Christian nationalist beliefs. Conversely, many white evangelicals in surveys unequivocally reject Christian nationalism, including a number of the white evangelicals we interviewed for this book.

Second, occasionally people have been confused by the term *nationalism*, which we do not strictly mean in the chauvinistic sense of blindly believing that one's nation is superior to others. Though strong Christian nationalists would no doubt hold that sentiment about America (Christian nationalists do tend to be more "nationalistic"), we mean something more like "Christian nation-ism" or what sociologist Rogers Brubaker calls "Christianism," a commitment to a vision of American civic life and polity as closely intertwined with an indentitarian, politically conservative strain of Christianity.[1]

We also want to distinguish Christian nationalism from "theocracy" as people commonly think of that term. (Reformed camps of evangelicals debate different philosophies of church–state relations using terms like *theonomy*, and *two-kingdom theology*, and *neo-Kyperianism*, but these are fights among theological elites.[2] Those views are not wide-spread like the more populist Christian nationalism.) While there is indeed some technical overlap between the goals of strong Christian nationalists and theocrats, some key distinctions deserve mention. Strictly theocratic Christians would want the Bible principally to inform our national laws. To the contrary, some Christian nationalists are not only fond of our founding documents, many believe they are "divinely inspired," not quite as authoritative as the Bible but still supernaturally revealed to Christian men with intentions to preference Christianity.[3] Moreover, while theocracy often implies that religious leaders, even clergy in some manifestations, play a central role in governance, Christian nationalists, it turns out, are quite willing to elect notoriously impious heads of state if they happen to support right-wing causes. One staunch Christian nationalist, in fact, famously articulated what has become a popular refrain used to defend the religious vote for Donald Trump: "[W]e're electing a president, a commander-in-chief, not a pastor-in-chief."[4]

Two more points of clarification. This book will provide the first empirical examination of *contemporary* Christian nationalism in the *United States*. The italicized words further qualify our focus.

Dozens of books written by sober-minded historians, political scientists, and historical-comparative sociologists trace the "Christian America" narrative from when Europeans set foot on the continent, to the American revolution and subsequent attempts to redefine and institutionalize America's collective identity as a "Christian nation," to modern-day movements to make the "founding fathers" seem like card-carrying members of the Religious Right. The literature is massive and growing. We have no intention of adding another historical analysis, as we feel our greater contribution will be to document, analyze, and understand Christian nationalism in its most recent manifestation. Consequently, we will only reference the long history of Christian nationalism to the extent that it directly informs our national situation within the past decade. Readers interested in more historical background should follow our notes.

Along with our contemporary focus, we also limit our analyses to *American* Christian nationalism. Sociologists like Rogers Brubaker, Lydia Bean, and Bart Bonikowski, and political scientists J. Christopher Soper and Joel Fetzer, have produced vital comparative analyses of nationalism, religion, and populism. These scholars and others continue to document nationalist movements across the world in response to perceived demographic and cultural threats from a variety of sources. These movements have incorporated, among other things, a narrative about national religious identities in order to draw symbolic boundaries around cultural membership, similar to what we will observe among Christian nationalists in the United States.[5] We acknowledge at the outset there are many international parallels to what we observe in these pages. However, we also believe that an exclusive focus on American Christian nationalism is not unjustified, because there is such an historic and enduring connection between conservative Christianity and American civic life and polity—one that is almost wholly denuded in most of Europe. We encourage readers to consider our work in conversation with these other important studies.

A brief word about the examples we cite. Throughout the book we illustrate our arguments about Christian nationalism by drawing upon events on the national stage and quotes from political and religious leaders. We fully expect that some of the examples we provide may appear older or outdated by the time readers are able to hold this volume. It seems as though the news cycle continues to contract, and what was once front page news is almost forgotten a week later, let alone months later. This places us at a disadvantage when writing a book. We would ask readers to keep in mind, however, that our goal is not to illustrate our points using the latest breaking news. Our journalist friends and colleagues already do that quite well. We endeavor to show how our underlying arguments about Christian nationalism can be applied to those events that are breaking news, whatever they may be and whenever they may have happened. We hope the examples we use that took place while we were writing this book equip readers to look and listen for Christian nationalist rhetoric and understand its dramatic influence on the actions, decision, and speech of those around us in the present moment.

Finally, in the pages that follow we present findings concerning Christian nationalism that may cause consternation among some readers. As social scientists, our goal is to use high-quality and transparent methods to gather and analyze data, and then truthfully present what we find in the data. We are confident that what we present isn't a fluke. In Appendix B we share dozens of tables so readers can check our work. For those readers who find themselves troubled by what support for the core tenets of Christian nationalism is associated with, we encourage them to think deeply with us about why that is, and consider if there is a better way forward. We hope all begin to consider if and how the dictates of the Christian religion may stand in opposition to those used to defend a "Christian nation." Finally, we caution against writing off most of those on the "other" side, whichever side that may be. In the hours we spent talking with American men and women from around the country, we were reminded that beneath the quantitative findings are people with complicated histories, desires, and viewpoints. The more we can talk, and work to truly listen, the greater the chances of building a civil society where all can flourish, not just a few.

ACKNOWLEDGMENTS

There are a number of people who deserve recognition for the work you now hold in your hands. We are deeply grateful to those who agreed to share with us their views of the religious heritage of the United States and the current state of our nation. As you will soon find out, we spoke with fellow Americans all across the spectrum. Each interview helped us sharpen our arguments as well as question some of our preconceived notions. We're sincerely indebted to each of you. Thank you. In the end, we were struck by how much common ground exists. And while there are significant barriers to finding that common ground, speaking with so many fellow Americans instilled in us a hope that there is a way forward.

We are also indebted to our sociology of religion friends and colleagues at Baylor University, especially Paul Froese and Carson Mencken, who have each directed the Baylor Religion Surveys that form the quantitative cornerstone of this work and much of our previous work on Christian nationalism. It is no understatement to say that without their foresight in asking these types of questions in 2007, and then providing us space to include them again in 2017, we would all know much less about Christian nationalism in the present-day United States. Thank you for sharing your data with us. Special thanks as well to the Association for the Sociology of Religion's Fichter Grant Program, the Society for the Scientific Study of Religion's Jack Shand Grant Program, as well as to (then chair) Ellen Granberg of the Department of Sociology & Anthropology and the (now defunct) College of Business and Behavioral Science at Clemson University for providing monetary support to the first author for placing several batteries of questions on the 2017 Baylor Religion Survey.

We are also grateful to our friends and colleagues within the sociology of religion subfield and beyond. A number of you have shaped our thinking on Christian nationalism at various stages or offered incisive feedback regarding what is found in this book specifically or in our previous published work. Chief among these is Joseph Baker, who graciously provided comments and encouragement from when this book was merely an idea to what you hold in your hands. Many thanks as well to Lydia Bean, Ruth Braunstein, Joe Burgett, David Cramer, Joshua Davis, Jack Delehanty, Kevin Dougherty, Scott Draper, Penny Edgell, Phil Gorski, Dan Greene, Jeff Guhin, Andrew Mannheimer, Gerardo Marti, Landon Schnabel, Buster Smith, Evan Stewart, and Sam Stroope.

We must also recognize the support provided by our home departments. Thank you to our department chairs—Katy Weisensee (Clemson University) and Loretta Bass (University of Oklahoma)—and colleagues who asked how the work was progressing and encouraged us that it would indeed see the light of day. And many thanks to those we've interacted with consistently through social media who have shown us new angles to pursue and underscored the importance of this work in general. Special thanks to Jack Jenkins not only for his great work on Christian nationalism but for being one of the first journalists to provide a platform for our work in this area. There are many more we would like to name, but fear leaving anyone out. So to our Twitter/Facebook friends, followers, and frequent commenters—thank you!

Our editor, Theo Calderara, saw the potential in this project from the beginning and has helped us move efficiently through each stage. He and his staff at OUP are consummate professionals, and we are grateful for their partnership on this project.

Finally, to our families we will each speak directly.

Sam: I owe an unpayable debt to my parents and my in-laws for the support they've given me during this long journey to and through academia. For this book in particular, I want to thank my mother-in-law, Melinda Jobe-Palvado, and my aunt-in-law, Ann Wynia, for the stimulating conversations regarding religion and politics over the years. I have recognized your influence in these pages more than once!

To my wife, Jill, I'm not sure how I could make it without you. You are stronger, smarter, and generally more capable than I will ever be. I am so grateful you are in my life. Thanks for putting up with yet another book. At least *this* one's not about porn!

Lastly, to my wonderful daughter, Ryan, and my sons, Beau and Whitman, I dedicate this book to you three. Your mom and I are daily amazed at the potential we see in each one of you. Our greatest hope is that you each develop and use that potential to make this world better, for everyone.

Andrew: To Monica, Chandra, Shawn, Alex, Sarah, Jill, Brian, and Kent—thank you. I am so grateful for each of you and the love and support you offer me and my family through every step of our journey. You all inspire me and I'm so proud to be your brother.

To my parents, Cathy and Kim Whitehead and to Deb and Tom Van Abeele—my father and mother "in-love"—thank you. Thank you for moving us all over the country, believing in me at every step of this journey, and for always offering your unwavering support.

To my kiddos, Joel, Natalie, and Theo—daddy loves you more than he can bear. Joel and Theo, you each teach me so much about what it means to love. Let's go read about sharks and watch helicopter videos on YouTube. Natalie, I can't believe how fortunate I am to have you as my daughter. I believe in you more than you'll ever know and I am so thankful that you are mine. I am incredibly proud of each of you.

To my spouse, best friend, and partner-in-life, Kelly—I love you. There really are no words. All of our tears, laughter, pain, and joy are so precious to me. You're the only one I would want to walk with through the valleys or to stand with on the mountaintops. You're my hero. Everything I do, including this book, will always and forever be for you. It is always for you.

INTRODUCTION

A HOUSE DIVIDING

The sanctuary was bursting with stars and stripes—draped from the balcony, lining the stage, printed on the identical ties and scarves worn by the 100-person choir and full orchestra. An image of the Bible resting on Old Glory was displayed on all the screens throughout this conservative Baptist church in South Carolina, including in the overflow area, which was quickly filling up. The balcony and ground floor of the sanctuary were already at capacity. The "God and Country Celebration" would be starting soon, and it was clear that both God and country were equally sacred in this place. After one particularly rousing part of the worship service in which the choir and orchestra performed anthems from each branch of the Armed Forces, the emcee—in full military uniform—intoned, "We would be remiss if we did not mention God, author and perfecter of our faith. He's guided and protected this country throughout its history. Any victories we claim are all because of him and his faithfulness, and in the good times and bad, *he's always been on our side.*"

Earlier in the day, across town, a much larger Baptist congregation held a similar "Celebrate America" service. During this service the entire congregation pledged allegiance, *first*, to the United States flag, then to the Christian flag, and third to the Holy Bible. Actors representing various founding fathers and decked out in historically themed costumes recited lines proclaiming America's special relationship with God. Throughout the service, the leaders and congregants lamented that the United States failed in its devotion to God's laws and principles. This backsliding had caused God to withdraw his hand of blessing. But out of this darkness, they declared, there shines a bright light. As the emcee, also in military uniform, exclaimed, "Jesus alone has the power to change our nation, he gave the ultimate sacrifice for our lives *and for our nation.*"

Halfway across the country in Oklahoma, on the same day, a similar "Freedom Celebration" service was in full swing. The senior pastor began his message, entitled "America—An Exceptional Nation," by confronting the pernicious myth about the country's secular roots. Referencing political operative and self-proclaimed historian David Barton, whose ministry, WallBuilders, supplies quotes and factoids for services just like this one, the pastor proclaimed that anyone who questions the Christian heritage of the United States would need to ignore scores of original letters and documents from the founding fathers. Deniers of our heritage would also have to "go to Washington, D.C. and take a sandblaster and remove the Scriptures from the monuments and the buildings. It's all there!" Beaming with pride, the pastor boasted that his church frequently hosts a "Reclaiming America for Jesus Christ" conference, though he'd begun to wonder recently whether America really *can* be reclaimed. For that to happen, he proposed, Americans must remember their Christian past while living like Christians in the present. Only *then* would God make their country prosperous: "America has to be 'blessable' for God to shed his grace on thee." He closed his sermon with a solemn charge, citing an Old Testament verse upon which Dwight D. Eisenhower placed his hand while taking his inaugural oath, 2 Chronicles 7:14: "If my people, who are called by my name, will humble themselves and pray and seek my face and turn from their wicked ways, then I will hear from heaven, and I will forgive their sin and I will heal their land."[1] The pastor then whispered, "The key word here in this promise is that word '*If.*' "

These July 4th worship services reflect more than a particular understanding of American history. The symbols they hold sacred, the narratives they retell, the charges they make—all express a specific vision of Christianity's relationship to American identity and civic life.

And it is one that seems to be increasingly at odds with the views of the rest of the nation, and self-consciously so. To be sure, most Americans are somewhere in the fuzzy middle on these issues. They recognize America's vaguely Judeo-Christian past and Christianity's numerical dominance in the United States. But they also celebrate the ideal of religious freedom and believe church–state separation to be a good thing. And yet it sometimes appears that Americans are gravitating toward extremes on these topics.[2]

A growing number of more secular Americans, for example, maintain that both Christianity and America's public institutions are at their best when the two function like considerate neighbors—friendly in their interactions but always respecting the boundaries between them. Toward the other end of the spectrum, however, an equally large group of Americans, the kind who attend services like those we just described, insist that since its inception the United States has been married to Christianity. As these services we attended made clear, the Christian God has "always been on our side," his son Jesus gave his life "for our nation," and our prosperity is contingent upon our returning to him. Those who hold this opinion are often quick to cite evidence of this covenantal relationship in America's founding ideals, historic documents, sacred symbols, policies, and elsewhere. Most importantly, both America and Christianity, they argue, have benefited greatly from that union, and consequently, those who wish to dissolve the marriage want nothing less than to destroy America.

This book is about the underlying causes and social consequences of this latter view, what we and others call "Christian nationalism."[3]

IS AMERICA A "CHRISTIAN NATION"? WHY THE ANSWER DOES AND DOESN'T MATTER

What *is* Christianity's relationship to American identity and civic life? What *should* it be?

While these are interesting historical, theological, and political questions, they aren't necessarily questions social science can or should answer. Many books seek to test particular claims about the Christian

3

heritage of the United States.[4] However, the answer to whether the United States ever was or still is a "Christian nation" is not the focus of *this* book. Rather, we focus on how these beliefs, whether strongly held or barely acknowledged, influence the lives of those who hold them, as well as those who do not. Taking this angle, it becomes clear that it does not even matter whether the United States *is* or *ever was* a Christian nation. What matters is that a significant number of Americans *believe* that it is. And a significant number believes the opposite. The particular stance people take on this issue is strongly associated with how they see the world, as well as how they act to preserve or change that world. Therefore, the contention that the United States is a Christian nation has implications for us all, even for those Americans who reject such interpretations.[5]

The stakes are high. For example, a large percentage of Americans who favor Christian nationalist views (which we will detail further below) believe that the American government should unapologetically privilege Christianity. Robert Jeffress, a megachurch pastor and member of Donald Trump's evangelical advisory board, argues, "The framers of the Constitution and the earliest jurists demonstrated a clear preference for Christianity. They did not hesitate to declare that America was a Christian nation . . . the government can (and for more than 150 years did) show a preference for the Christian faith."[6] To the extent that such views become reflected in public policy, the growing percentage of Americans who are not Christian will undoubtedly feel ostracized, treated as though they are not *fully* American. These groups fear that explicitly privileging Christian identity, symbols, and "doctrines" (according to any number of interpretations) will threaten their access to civil society in more tangible ways.[7] And they would be right, as we will see. Further, it is not just religious minorities who have something to fear. Christian nationalism is linked to prejudice toward numerous minority groups.

But strong Christian nationalists are declining in number, and this also has important implications. More and more Americans collectively agree that the United States should not favor Christianity formally. Consequently, the sizeable portion of Americans who pine for

Christianity's former prominence in American civic life feel threatened and marginalized. They fear that their values and priorities will, at best, no longer be dominant, and at worst, that their freedom to preach their moral values and share their religion with others would be outlawed. But readers should not mistake these fears as limited solely to *religious* identity. There is more to the "us" that Christian nationalists wish to defend and more to the "them" that Christian nationalists wish to oppose. Throughout the book, we will show that the degree to which Americans seek to impose Christianity on the public sphere often operates as a powerful indicator of their commitment to a specific social order—with boundaries and hierarchies among natives and foreigners, whites and nonwhites, men and women, heterosexuals and others—an order they recognize is also being threatened.

How Do We Study Christian Nationalism and Christian Nationalists?

Several important books—to which we are greatly indebted—have recently addressed the phenomenon of Christian nationalism (though not always by that name) in the United States.[8] But to date, there have been no attempts to systematically and empirically examine Christian nationalism and its influence in American social, cultural, and political life. This is precisely what we do in this book, using large-scale quantitative data to develop more reliable answers to questions about who Christian nationalists are and how Christian nationalism influences their lives. Each of the datasets we use includes important sociodemographic measures that allow us to isolate the unique influence of Christian nationalism, along with scores of questions concerning politics, religious and racial/ethnic diversity, and family life and values. Several of the surveys also allow for comparisons over time. So in addition to demonstrating Christian nationalism's significance in the current cultural moment, we will also explore shifts in its prevalence and importance.

But numbers can only get us so far in understanding *narratives* of Christian nationalism. To better understand Christian nationalism and

5

how people articulate and apply it, we draw on 50 in-depth interviews with Americans who—to varying degrees—endorse or challenge the privileging of Christianity in the civic life of the United States. We also engaged in participant observation at large events in Texas, Oklahoma, and South Carolina where Christian nationalists and their beliefs were prominently represented. For more discussion of the specific datasets we use and how we conducted the interviews and participant observation, see Appendices A and C.

So how do we measure Christian national*ism* and Christian national*ists* in our data? Definitions matter a great deal. Consider how narrowly or broadly we could define a "Christian nationalist" depending on the measures we use. Data from the 2017 Baylor Religion Survey (BRS) shows that 29 percent of Americans agree that "the federal government should declare the United States a Christian nation." Even more Americans, 46 percent, agree that "the federal government should advocate Christian values." Depending on the question we use, then, we could estimate that a quarter to half of Americans to some extent agree that the United States is a Christian nation and the government should recognize this either formally or informally. In addition, in the same survey 42 percent of Americans agreed that "the success of the United States is a part of God's plan." Using slightly older data from 2013, almost two-thirds of Americans either mostly or completely agreed with the statement, "God has granted America a special role in human history." At the very least we would conclude that a sizeable proportion of Americans embrace the idea of a special relationship between God and the United States. Yet the picture of what Christian nationalism is, and who Christian nationalists are, is still rather fuzzy.

Let's see whether, by adding more detail, we can paint a clearer picture. In the 2017 BRS, 26 percent of Americans agreed that the United States has always been and currently is a Christian nation. Nearly one-third of Americans (32 percent) believe that at some point in its past the United States was a Christian nation, but is not anymore. A smaller number of Americans, 20 percent, report that America has never been a Christian nation. And still another fifth (21 percent) couldn't say either way (see Figure I.1). The responses could be combined in several ways

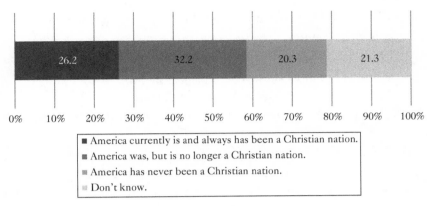

FIGURE I.I.
Americans' Beliefs Regarding the Christian Nation Narrative
Source: 2017 Baylor Religion Survey.

depending on the story one would like to tell. If you define a Christian nationalist as anyone who believes the United States is currently or ever was a Christian nation, more than three out of every five Americans reside in this category. If it includes only those who currently see America as a Christian nation, the number is less than three in 10.

While the question we use in Figure I.1 is useful in that it gives us a general idea of where Americans stand on the Christian nation narrative, it doesn't tell us how strongly Americans embrace Christian nationalism.[9] Furthermore, "Christian nationalism" is not a single idea that can be measured solely by agreement with a founding myth, but rather a more dynamic ideology incorporating a number of beliefs and values. We want to know if Americans believe the United States *should* be a Christian nation, not just whether they think it is or was a Christian nation. Thus, to measure the concept as comprehensively as possible, we primarily use a composite measure created from multiple BRS survey questions from 2007 and 2017 that asked Americans to rate their levels of agreement with the following six statements:

1. "The federal government should declare the United States a Christian nation."

2. "The federal government should advocate Christian values."

7

3. "The federal government should enforce strict separation of church and state."

4. "The federal government should allow the display of religious symbols in public spaces."

5. "The success of the United States is part of God's plan."

6. "The federal government should allow prayer in public schools."

For each statement, respondents could strongly disagree, disagree, agree, strongly agree, or indicate that they are undecided.[10]

Americans who believe the federal government should declare the United States a Christian nation, or who want the federal government to advocate explicitly Christian values, are obviously signaling a belief that Christianity and civil society should be intimately intertwined. These measures also tap into some of the cultural touchstone moments that have occurred in the recent past. For instance, various rulings from the United States Supreme Court on prayer in public schools or the display of religious symbols in public spaces have generated a great deal of response from the American public.[11] Figure I.2 displays how Americans responded to each of these questions in the 2017 BRS.

Comparing responses to these individual measures highlights that while 50 to 60 percent of Americans may agree or strongly agree with

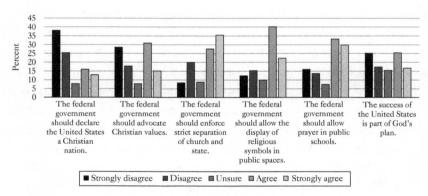

FIGURE I.2.

Variation in Level of Agreement across Six Christian Nationalism Measures

Source: 2017 Baylor Religion Survey.

one of the six questions, fewer will answer consistently across all six.[12] In order to create the scale, we scored every answer on a scale from zero (strongly disagree) to four (strongly agree). Therefore, any respondent who "strongly agrees" on all the measures would score a 24 on the Christian nationalism scale, and anyone who "strongly disagrees" with each of the statements would receive a 0 on the scale. (Keep in mind responses to the third statement are reverse-coded.) As readers can clearly see in Figure I.3 below, Americans are widely distributed all along the scale, meaning there is a great deal of variation across the population.

There are several other observations that we can make about Americans' support for Christian nationalism. First, just over seven percent of the population strongly disagrees on every question. This shows that there is a subset of Americans who completely reject the idea of a close, symbiotic relationship between Christianity and American society. There are not, however, as many Americans who completely affirm this idea. Only one percent of Americans strongly agree with all the statements. Second, most Americans fall somewhere in the middle of the distribution. While a significant number place themselves at the upper and lower ends of the distribution, a majority are neither strongly opposed to nor strongly supportive of Christian nationalism. Third, Americans are not unevenly clumped at either end of the scale, their support for Christian nationalism is widely distributed along the scale.

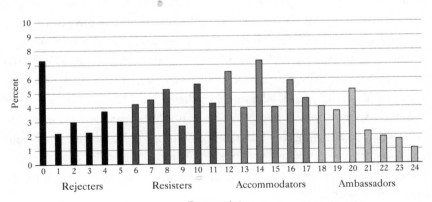

FIGURE I.3.

Distribution of Americans on Christian Nationalism Scale

Source: 2017 Baylor Religion Survey.

Using this scale as a guide, we propose there are four main orientations toward Christian nationalism in the United States. Americans are either *Rejecters, Resisters, Accommodators,* or *Ambassadors*.[13] We use these categories—intended as rough guidelines, not a rigid taxonomy—to explore patterns in Americans' diverse responses to Christian nationalism and the consequences of that ideology for public opinion and political behavior.[14]

Before we define these categories in the next chapter, though, we want to clearly define Christian nationalism and why we think it is different from both "civil religion" and religion writ large.

UNDERSTANDING CHRISTIAN NATIONALISM AND ITS CONSEQUENCES

Simply put, Christian nationalism is a cultural framework—a collection of myths, traditions, symbols, narratives, and value systems—that idealizes and advocates a fusion of Christianity with American civic life. But the "Christianity" of Christian nationalism is of a particular sort. We do not mean Christianity here as a general, meta-category including all expressions of orthodox Christian theology. Nor will we use terms such as "evangelicalism" or "white conservative Protestantism" (to the extent that these represent certain theological-interpretive positions) as synonyms for Christian nationalism. On the contrary, the "Christianity" of Christian nationalism represents something more than religion. As we will show, it includes assumptions of nativism, white supremacy, patriarchy, and heteronormativity, along with divine sanction for authoritarian control and militarism. It is as ethnic and political as it is religious. Understood in this light, Christian nationalism contends that America has been and should always be distinctively "Christian" (reflecting this fuller, more nuanced sense of the term) from top to bottom—in its self-identity, interpretations of its own history, sacred symbols, cherished values, and public policies—and it aims to keep it that way.[15]

Several theological and ideological tributaries have shaped Christian nationalism into what we see today. Here it is helpful to draw some critical distinctions between Christian nationalism and what has traditionally been thought of as America's "civil religion." Civil religion represents America's dominant self-understanding and ethical lodestar. Its religious influences come primarily from the prophetic Old Testament tradition in which God demands justice, mercy, and humility from his people, and from civic republicanism, a dynamic political philosophy emphasizing that civic virtue and a strong constitution that separates institutional powers are critical for maintaining free human societies.[16]

Though it has existed for just as long as America's civil religious tradition, Christian nationalism has been informed by different parts of the Bible.[17] While civil religion has held that "Providence," the "Creator," or "Nature's God" demands our exemplary fairness, beneficence, and faithful stewardship if we are to retain our blessed inheritance, the Christian nationalist tradition by contrast views God's demands more in terms of allegiance to our national—almost ethnic—Christian identity. Christian nationalism is rarely concerned with instituting explicitly "Christ-like" policies, or even policies reflecting New Testament ethics at all. Rather, Christian nationalists view God's expectations of America as akin to his commands to Old Testament Israel. Like Israel, then, America should fear God's wrath for unfaithfulness while assuming God's blessing—or even mandate—for subduing the continent by force if necessary.[18]

Finally, proponents of Christian nationalism have consistently viewed their mission through the lens of apocalyptic Christianity. A number of influential advocates of Christian nationalism could be characterized as "postmillennial," meaning that they believe that Christ's kingdom is already established on earth, and thus his followers should bring every aspect of American civic life under his reign. Others—including many influential Christian nationalists in recent decades—are better described as "premillennial," meaning that they believe the world will become increasingly corrupt until Christ returns to rescue the faithful, followed by his millennial reign on earth.[19] The former group—led by thinkers like Abraham Kuyper, Cornelius Van Til, Rousas John Rushdoony, and Gary North—believed Christ's followers could ultimately "reconstruct" civilization as they established Christ's "dominion" over all things.[20]

Premillennial Christian nationalists have seen their role as "delaying" the world's eventual destruction, ostensibly so that more unbelievers can be won to Christ.[21]

But what about average Americans? Do we see evidence that these ideological tributaries inform contemporary Christian nationalism in the general population? In fact, we do.

The 2007 wave of the BRS contained questions that allow us to assess whether certain theological or ideological beliefs predict higher scores on our Christian nationalism scale, even after accounting for factors like gender, age, income, education, race, region of the country, and so on. Table I.1 shows the top ten predictors of higher scores on our Christian nationalism scale, ordered from strongest to weakest, though all the relationships are statistically significant. Importantly, almost all socio-demographic factors appear nowhere on the list because many—including race, income, age, or even whether people consider

Table I.1. Top Predictors of Stronger Adherence to Christian Nationalism

Predictor (ordered from strongest predictor to weakest)	Direction
1. Identifying with Political Conservatism	+
2. Identify as "Bible-Believing"	+
3. Bible is the literal word of God [a]	+
4. Bible is perfectly true, though not literally interpreted [a]	+
5. Religiously Unaffiliated [b]	−
6. Religious Practice [c]	+
7. Believe that the nation is on the brink of moral decay	+
8. Believe that God requires the faithful to wage wars for good	+
9. Believe in "the Rapture"	+
10. Education	−

Note: See Table B.1 in Appendix for full model.

All variables are statistically significant predictors of Christian nationalism beyond the .001 level. + = positively correlated; − = negatively correlated. [a] Compared to believing the Bible is a book of history and legends. [b] Compared to being an evangelical Protestant. [c] A scale made up of three questions asking how frequently respondents attend religious services, prayer, and read their sacred scriptures.

Source: 2007 Baylor Religion Survey.

themselves Republicans or Democrats—paled in comparison to the ideological commitments shown here.[22]

Far and away the strongest predictor of Christian nationalism is identifying oneself with political conservatism. This shouldn't be surprising, since both political conservatism and Christian nationalism are interested in preserving an older order or restoring the past, reflected in clear boundaries and hierarchies and perceived to be closer to America's founding ideals. The two factors are not synonymous, however. As we will show throughout this book, Christian nationalism is often a *stronger* predictor of Americans' attitudes about race, gender, immigration, gun rights, Islam, and family/sexuality issues than political ideology.

The next three strongest predictors after political conservatism all involve identification with a particular view of the Bible, most prominently a belief that it should be interpreted literally and characterizing oneself as "Bible-Believing." As sociologist Philip Gorski has argued, Christian nationalists have historically built their ideological foundation on a narrow, literalist interpretation of God's commands to Old Testament Israel, applying them to their contemporary national situation.

Following Bible beliefs, the next strongest predictors have to do with religious practice and affiliation. Americans who are religiously unaffiliated are obviously less likely than evangelical Protestants to embrace Christian nationalism. But it is important to note that this isn't the strongest predictor of Christian nationalism. This suggests that, as we will show more concretely later, Christian nationalism isn't localized primarily within particular religious traditions but is undergirded by a combination of conservative political ideology, belief in the Bible, apocalyptic visions of societal decline, and divine militarism.

Though religious practice is a positive predictor of Christian nationalism, the fact that it is no stronger a predictor in comparison to other ideological/theological commitments suggests there is substantial discontinuity between the two. In fact—and this is something we wish to underscore throughout the book—religious commitment and Christian nationalism appear to foster distinct moral worldviews that differ in critical ways.

Next are fears about the moral decay of the nation and belief that, following this decline into depravity, Jesus will literally whisk Christians to heaven, an event known as the Rapture. This affirms that contemporary Christian nationalism is more characterized by a "premillennial" worldview, one that interprets Christians' responsibility as delaying America's inevitable decline, as opposed to a more optimistic "postmillennial" view that sees Christians as victorious in the here and now. Sandwiched between these views is Americans' belief that "God requires the faithful to wage wars for good." This is entirely consistent with Philip Gorski's observation that Christian nationalism has historically been used to justify bloody conquests, often taking the form of imperialist and jingoist projects under the banner of God's blessing and mandate for his people.[23]

One way we can further distinguish Christian nationalism from religious commitment in general is by comparing the moral content of both. The 2007 BRS also includes a battery of questions asking, "How important is it to do the following if one wishes to be a good person?" Respondents were then presented with a list of seven behaviors. When we predict whether respondents believe a certain behavior is important for being a good person, we find that Christian nationalism and religious practice influence Americans' views differently in key ways (see Table I.2).[24]

While both Christian nationalism and religious practice are positively associated with views of morality that emphasize fidelity to one's religious faith (believing in God, teaching others about one's moral values, evangelizing), only Christian nationalism predicts that Americans see serving in the military as important to being "a good person." Religious practice, on the other hand, is negatively associated with this view, meaning devoutly religious Americans are *less* likely to say that serving in the military is important to being a good person. Furthermore, religious practice is powerfully related to views of morality that emphasize ideas of care for the vulnerable, social justice, and even reducing one's consumption patterns for the sake of environmental stewardship. Christian nationalism, however, is unrelated to taking care of the sick and needy and consuming fewer goods. In fact,

Table I.2. Ideas of Morality, Christian Nationalism, and Religious Practice

How important is it to do the following if one wishes to be a good person?	Christian Nationalism	Religious Practice
Care and Justice		
"Take care of the sick and needy"	NS	+
"Actively seek social and economic justice"	−	+
Stewardship		
"Consume or use fewer goods"	NS	+
Fidelity to the Religion		
"Have faith in God"	+	+
"Teach others your morals"	+	+
"Convert others to your religious faith"	+	+
Fidelity to the Nation		
"Serve in the military"	+	−

Note: See Table B.2 in Appendix for full model.

NS = not a statistically significant predictor of this moral belief; + = positive and statistically significant; − = negative and statistically significant. [a] Christian Nationalism scale. [b] A scale made up of three questions asking how frequently respondents attend religious services, prayer, and read their sacred scriptures.

Source: 2007 Baylor Religion Survey

Americans who embrace Christian nationalism are *less* likely to believe actively seeking social and economic justice is important to being a good person.

These initial analyses establish some broad characteristics of contemporary Christian nationalism that will guide our discussion throughout the book. Christian nationalism is a cultural framework that blurs distinctions between Christian identity and American identity, viewing the two as closely related and seeking to enhance and preserve their union. It is undergirded by identification with a conservative political orientation (though not necessarily a political party), Bible belief, premillennial visions of moral decay, and divine sanction for conquest. Finally, its conception of morality centers *exclusively* on fidelity to religion and fidelity to the nation.

Our Three Main Arguments

In this book we lay out three main arguments, each building on the preceding one. First, we argue that understanding Christian nationalism, its content and its consequences, is essential for understanding much of the polarization in American popular discourse.[25] That includes such pressing national questions such as:

- *Why did so many conservative Christians vote for, and continue to support, Donald Trump despite his many overt moral failings?* Contrary to the dominant narrative offered by pollsters and pundits, the answer isn't simply "white evangelicalism" or "conservative Christianity." Rather, we will show that Christian nationalism motivates Americans—whether they are evangelical or not—to see Trump as the defender of the power and values they perceive are being threatened.

- *Why do many Americans advocate so vehemently for xenophobic policies, such as a border wall with Mexico?* The answer isn't primarily about political allegiances. Rather, Christian nationalism, especially when it is held strongly by white Americans, appears to reinforce boundaries around national group membership, encouraging antipathy and mistrust toward those who do not meet the membership requirements of *native-born, Christian, and white*—namely, racial minorities, nonwhite immigrants, and Muslims. Christian nationalism expresses a particular racialized understanding of national identity. It allows those who embrace it to express a racialized identity *without resorting to racialized terms*.

- *Why do many Americans seem so unwilling to acknowledge the injustices that ethnic and racial minorities experience in the United States?* For instance, the responses of prominent conservative Christian commentators toward dozens of instances of police violence against black Americans that have been caught on camera has been largely cold, sometimes even engaging in victim-blaming. More troubling than this, their responses reflect the sentiments of millions of Americans. The cause has little to do with religion per se. Rather Christian nationalism, we will show, tends to promote defenses of authoritarian control, especially when the target population of that control is nonwhite.

- *Despite the progress made in women's equality in the workplace and in the home, why do a sizeable proportion of Americans continue to hold attitudes suggesting women are unfit for politics? Or that healthy families require that women stay home?* While the answer to this question has traditionally been conservative religion, or perhaps conservative political ideology, we show that these factors pale in comparison to the power of Christian nationalism for predicting Americans' attitudes toward gender (in)equality. Christian nationalism advocates for a particular social order that lionizes hierarchies between men and women. The society that strong Christian nationalists wish to live in—whether they are theologically conservative Christians or not—is a society in which families are "traditional," and men and women are in their "proper place."

Other factors are involved in these issues, of course. But Christian nationalism, we will show, plays a powerful role that is essential to understanding the seemingly intractable debates and divisions plaguing American politics and society. In short, we cannot fully understand these issues without considering Christian nationalism.

We also want to stress that we are focused on Christian national*ism*, which is not synonymous with the Christian nation narrative. The American Christian nation narrative is potent because it enlists traditions and symbolism from Christianity and intertwines them with the United States' national story. Narratives and origin stories are vital aspects of cultural frameworks—telling us about where we come from, where we should be going, and how we should get there. But the Christian nation narrative can be—and indeed has been—invoked in the service of the disempowered demanding justice as well as those who wish to preserve their own cultural power. Black Protestants and white evangelicals, for example, throughout America's history have drawn upon the Christian nation narrative, but to very different ends. Frederick Douglass and

Martin Luther King Jr. cited America's so-called Christian heritage as a form of rebuke, to challenge an unjust social order. White evangelicals in the South, by contrast, have more often cited the Christian nation narrative not to contest the unjust social order but to preserve it. The difference is not the Christian nation narrative but Christian national*ism*, which again includes not only narratives, but a particular set of symbols, value systems, and moral requirements intertwined with implicit boundaries and hierarchies.

Furthermore, throughout the book we are focused on examining Christian national*ism*, not just Christian national*ists*. Clearly, we will learn a lot about Americans who strongly embrace Christian nationalism. But we will also hear from those who reject or resist Christian nationalism, and their views and stories are equally important. So instead of writing about a specific social group—Christian nationalists—we aim to examine the cultural framework of Christian nationalism as a whole, including reactions against it. We hope to show how Christian nationalism has thoroughly permeated American society and culture.[26] It is a lens through which all Americans experience and interpret the social world, and the rejection or embrace of it motivates them toward very different ends.

Our second argument is that to understand Christian nationalism, it must be examined on its own terms. Christian nationalism is necessarily part of a complex web of ideologies. We are not arguing that it is *the* single reason why certain Americans act or believe in a particular way. Rather, it works alongside and serves to prop up other ideologies in such a way that various Americans, whether religious and political elites or rank-and-file citizens, can effectively ignore discussions of economic, gender, sexual, or racial inequality. To be sure, it is related to many other important social factors and phenomena. As we will show, it is consistently and strongly associated with certain theological beliefs, political loyalties and behaviors, gender, race, sexuality, and so on. Yet it is not *synonymous with, reducible to,* or *a byproduct of* any of those things.

Let's use racism as an example. Approval of Christian nationalism, we will show, is a strong predictor of whether someone holds racially intolerant attitudes, especially if that person is white. But being white is not synonymous with being a Christian nationalist, nor is being a Christian nationalist synonymous with being racially prejudiced (though the two are powerfully related). Christian nationalism is also not reducible to racism. In other words, we cannot claim that Christian nationalism is "really just about racism when you get down to it." On the contrary, in some instances being a member of a racial minority group and holding certain Christian nationalist views is associated with having a stronger racial justice orientation, the exact opposite of what we see in white Americans. In this sense it is the *intersection* of race and Christian nationalism that matters. Lastly, Christian nationalism is not simply a by-product or manifestation of racism or racial prejudice. If we were to miraculously eliminate racism, Christian nationalism would still be with us.

The same goes for "right-wing authoritarianism" (RWA) or "authoritarian personality." These terms generally refer to certain personality tendencies that incline individuals toward intolerance of outsiders and toward highly conservative religious and political stances. Some might assume that Christian nationalism is really just another measure of authoritarian personality or RWA. However, they are not synonymous. We consistently find that even when we account for Americans' authoritarian leanings, Christian nationalism maintains a distinct and powerful influence on a variety of beliefs and behaviors. Nor is Christian nationalism reducible to RWA or merely a symptom of an authoritarian impulse. While they are strongly correlated, Christian nationalism exhibits an independent and important effect that is distinct from authoritarianism. For instance, when we examined what factors inclined Americans to vote for Donald Trump in 2016, we included measures of ethnocentrism, racial prejudice, and a variety of indicators that psychologists often use to measure RWA: sexist beliefs, intolerance toward ethnic and religious others, and religious literalism.[27] Chapter 2 explores this in greater detail. Yet even when controlling for each of these well-established concepts, Christian nationalism was among the strongest predictors of voting for Trump. Thus, despite knowing that people who hold more strongly to Christian nationalism are also more likely to be authoritarian, ethnocentric, racially prejudiced, Christian nationalism represents a *unique* cultural framework. It is simultaneously related to other beliefs, attitudes, prejudices, and behaviors—like racism and authoritarianism—but it is also distinct and must be addressed as such.[28] Christian nationalism is not just repackaged ethnocentrism, racial resentment, or authoritarianism.

Related to this, Christian nationalism should not be thought of as synonymous with "evangelicalism" or even "white evangelicalism." In fact, we intend for this clarification to undo a tremendous amount of confusion regarding American evangelicals and their political behavior — confusion that, we fear, polling results perpetuate. Stated simply: being an evangelical, or even a white evangelical as pollsters often define that category, tells us almost nothing about a person's social attitudes or behavior once Christian nationalism has been considered. The two categories often overlap, to be sure. Roughly half of evangelicals (by some definitions) embrace Christian nationalism to some degree. And yet what is *really* influencing Americans' behavior? Being affiliated with evangelicalism? Holding to traditional views about the Bible? Or advocating Christian nationalism? As it turns out, being an evangelical does not lead one to enthusiastically support border walls with Mexico; favoring Christian nationalism does. Being an evangelical does not seem to sour Americans' attitudes toward stronger gun control legislation; endorsing Christian nationalism does. Being an evangelical was not an important predictor of which Americans voted for Donald Trump in 2016; supporting Christian nationalism was. Readers should keep this in mind throughout.[29]

Following from our second claim that Christian nationalism should be examined on its own terms, our third argument is that Christian nationalism is not "Christianity" or even "religion" properly speaking. We mentioned this earlier, but we wish to elaborate a bit more. A commitment to Christian nationalism is not in any way similar to "religious commitment" as sociologists often conceptualize it. This is not merely semantics. In fact, we will show that Christian nationalism often influences Americans' opinions and behaviors in the *exact opposite direction* than traditional religious commitment does.[30]

Take, for example, showing respect for America's traditions. As we show in Chapter 2, those who hold more strongly to Christian nationalism are more likely to agree that people should be made to show respect for America's traditions (as one might expect from the church services we described above). By contrast, people who frequently attend church, pray, or read their sacred scriptures are actually *less* likely to agree with such a sentiment. Or consider attitudes toward race and policing, which we explore in Chapter 3. The more Americans adhere to Christian nationalist views, the less willing they are to acknowledge police discrimination against black Americans. But as people more frequently attend church, pray, or read their sacred scriptures, they become *more* likely to recognize racial discrimination in policing. We find these same patterns when it comes to Americans' attitudes toward immigration, environmentalism, refugees, and Muslims, as well as expanding the fight against terrorism, and so on. Thus, while Christian nationalism is a significant part of American Christianity, the two are not one and the same. Where Christian nationalists seek to defend particular group boundaries and privileges using Christian language, other religious Americans and fellow Christians who reject Christian nationalism tend to oppose such boundaries and privileges. In sociologist Philip Gorski's words, "[Christian nationalism] is political idolatry dressed up as religious orthodoxy."[31] In the final analysis, this should give us all hope, religious and secular alike. To condemn Christian nationalism as we define it is not to condemn Christianity or religion per se.[32]

So far we've only scratched the surface of these issues. The following chapter will describe exactly who Rejecters, Resisters, Accommodators, and Ambassadors are. It will also further delineate the characteristics of contemporary Christian nationalism in the United States, documenting its diversity, demographics, and growth in recent decades.

CHAPTER 1

FOUR AMERICANS

I believe we were founded on Christian principles, so, yes, I believe that, in essence, how we were created was the principle of Christianity. It's Christian beliefs. That's where we come from.

—Trina, *Ambassador*

I would agree that it was founded on Christian values, and maybe it was founded as a Christian nation. But today, presently, I don't know . . . That's a harder question to answer, right?

—Luke, *Accommodator*

I don't feel comfortable identifying the United States as a Christian nation even though I know that Christianity has been a major part of the history of this nation.

—Deb, *Resister*

No, I do not think the United States is a Christian nation. We are founded on a godless and secular Constitution.

—Donald, *Rejecter*

In the weeks leading up to the "Freedom Sunday" service at First Baptist Church, Dallas, on June 24, 2018, senior pastor Robert Jeffress arranged for two billboards advertising the event to be posted on the North Dallas Tollway. While it is certainly not uncommon for churches to hold events like this around Independence Day, what ignited some controversy was his "special message" for the occasion, prominently displayed in all caps: "AMERICA IS A CHRISTIAN NATION."

Within a few days, a Jewish columnist at the *Dallas Morning News*, Robert Wilonsky, blasted the billboards, arguing that Jeffress "is among this city's most divisive voices" and "preaches a gospel that has been repeatedly debated—and disproved—by scholars and researchers." Jeffress's "gospel," in his own words, is that "the vast majority of men that founded our nation were evangelical Christians." Wilonsky also reported comments from Dallas Mayor Mike Rawlings. An outspoken Christian and the grandchild of Nazarene ministers, Rawlings also criticized the billboards. "I don't mind someone being proud of the Christian tradition in America—it's obviously there. But one of the strengths of Dallas is our faith-based community [and] it's the strength that makes us a city of love verses a city of hate." He went on to distance himself further from Jeffress: "That's not the Christ that I follow. It's not the Dallas I want to be—to say things that do not unite us but divide us. I never heard those words, that voice come out of Christ. Just the opposite. I was brought up to believe: Be proud of yours [religious heritage], but do not diminish mine."[1] Shortly after Wilonsky's column was published, the billboard company informed First Baptist Church that they were taking the billboards down. A visibly indignant Robert Jeffress immediately went on Fox News (for whom he is a near-weekly contributor) and the Christian Broadcasting Network to publicly excoriate Mayor Rawlings for what he called a blatant example of liberal government suppression of religious freedom that was potentially "illegal." Less than a week before the event, Jeffress boasted to the *Dallas Observer* that he planned to put up not just two but *twenty* new billboards advertising the event, having reached an agreement with another billboard company.[2]

This incident depicts a variety of orientations toward the interweaving of Christianity and American civil society that reflects where many Americans find themselves. Like Robert Jeffress, some Americans endorse the idea that Christianity and our national identity are inextricably bound together. Those who disagree with him are "seculars" and "liberals" blinded to the truth and out to suppress religious freedom. Robert Wilonsky, a man of Jewish heritage, represents another subset of Americans who flatly reject the idea that the United States is somehow distinctly Christian. Wilonsky and others also reject what Jeffress's gospel implies—that America has some sort of obligation to privilege its Christian heritage and population while other non-Christian groups are merely tolerated as an afterthought. Finally, Mike Rawlings, a professing Christian who is quick to affirm that America has a "Christian tradition" that is "obviously there" exemplifies many other Americans. But unlike Jeffress, Rawlings is clearly uncomfortable with pronouncements that Christianity holds an exclusive claim to America's national self-concept. Rather, he sees his Dallas community, and America by extension, as fundamentally built upon principles of unity and acceptance of others.

In this chapter, we explore the variation in Americans' orientations toward Christian nationalism. While Americans hold diverse views on this question, we can sort them into four broad categories: Ambassadors, Accommodators, Resisters, or Rejecters, based on our 24-point Christian nationalism scale (see Figure 1.1).

Around 21.5 percent of Americans are *Rejecters*, most likely either disagreeing or strongly disagreeing with each statement on the Christian nationalism scale.[3] As we touched on in the previous chapter, a substantial percentage of respondents answered "Strongly Disagree" to each of the six questions, resulting in an overall score of zero on the Christian nationalism scale.[4] That is, more than seven percent of Americans—over a quarter of the Rejecters—oppose Christian nationalist ideology as strongly as possible. *Resisters* are the second-largest

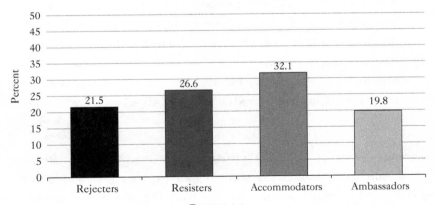

FIGURE 1.1.
Percent of Americans who are Ambassadors, Accommodators, Resisters, or Rejecters of Christian Nationalism
Source: 2017 Baylor Religion Survey.

of the four groups at around 27 percent of the population. Resisters are those who score between 6 and 11 (the average) on the Christian nationalism scale. *Accommodators* are the largest of the four groups, encompassing almost a third of all Americans (32.1 percent). Accommodators range from a score of 12 to a score of 17. Lastly, on the far right of the spectrum, *Ambassadors* make up about a fifth of the United States population (19.8 percent). They are the smallest group, consisting of respondents whose score ranges from 18 to 24 overall.

Are Ambassadors precisely who we are talking about when we refer to "Christian nationalists" in our study? Yes and no. On the one hand, these are indeed the Americans who appear to espouse Christian nationalist views most fervently. Yet on the other hand, we found that many men and women who scored as "Accommodators" often espoused strong Christian nationalist beliefs when they were able to explain themselves. These four categories are meant to be useful shorthand. Each is highly predictive of different views on various social and political issues. But to be clear, no system of categorization can perfectly capture the diversity of Americans' views on this subject.

REJECTERS

Is the United States a Christian nation? No. It explicitly states that the United States was founded in no way on the Christian religion in the Treaty of Tripoli.[5] Christianity is not mentioned in the Constitution. The major movers and shakers, when it comes to creating our governing structures, were mostly deists. Thomas Jefferson cut everything out that he didn't like from the Bible, and there wasn't a whole lot of it left.

—Patrick, *Rejecter*

Rejecters generally believe there should be no connection between Christianity and politics. As Donald told us, "We are founded on a godless and secular Constitution. We were the first nation in history to refuse to acknowledge a deity in that Constitution and to separate state and church." Rejecters oppose declaring the United States a Christian nation or favoring Christian values in public policy. One

Rejecter told us that in a pluralist democratic society like the United States, Christianity shouldn't shape social policies *at all*. Rejecters object to any efforts to institute the official practice of religious behaviors in public schools or allow the display of Christian religious symbols in public places. Rick, a professing evangelical Christian and Rejecter, told us how fights over displaying the Ten Commandments in courthouses is a "false battle" that the church likes to fight. "I think as a believer I should be more concerned about what a Muslim feels when he sees that [the 10 Commandments], because I'm not sure how that affects my faith one way or the other." Rejecters do not recognize any narrative that proposes a special relationship between the United States and the Christian God or some other higher power. For Rejecters, the wall of separation between church and state is high and impenetrable—or at least should be.

Rejecters display some interesting socio-demographic characteristics (Table 1.1). Rejecters are younger than the overall sample—43 years old versus 49. They are disproportionately male. Whites make up three-quarters of this group, while African Americans compose only four percent, even though they are 10 percent of the whole sample.

Rejecters are more highly educated than the three other groups. A third have engaged in some level of postgraduate studies, well above each of the other groups. In total, 80 percent of Rejecters have at least some post–high school education. Rejecters also report higher yearly earnings than the sample as a whole. Rejecters are most likely to be found in cities and suburbs, as well as in the Northeast or West regions of the country.

It would be easy to assume that Rejecters are completely nonreligious and politically liberal.[6] However, when we examine the religious and political contours of this group we see a slightly more complicated story.

One-third of Rejecters affiliate with a Christian religious tradition, either Protestant or Catholic, while one-half are unaffiliated (see Table 1.2). Half of Rejecters believe in some form of higher power, with one-quarter believing in God and a third identifying as atheist. Rejecters, as a group, do not completely reject common expressions of religious behavior, even though most Rejecters never attend religious services, pray,

Table 1.1. Socio-demographic Characteristics of Ambassadors, Accommodators, Resisters, and Rejecters

	Rejecters (21.5%)	Resisters (26.6%)	Accommodators (32.1%)	Ambassadors (19.8%)	Whole Sample
Age					
Average age (years)	43.2 [b,c]	45.3 [b,c]	49.8 [a,b,c]	54.3	48.8
Gender (%)					
Women	45.4 [b,c]	48.6 [b]	57.4	55.3	52.0
Men	54.6	51.4	42.6	44.7	48.0
Race (%)					
White	75.0 [a,b]	61.3 [c]	63.1	69.9	64.8
Black	4.2 [a,b,c]	9.5 [b]	14.5	11.0	10.1
Hispanic	10.3 [a,b]	20.1	15.7 [c]	11.4	15.0
Other race	10.5	9.1	6.8	7.7	10.1
Marital Status (%)					
Percent married	49.0 [a]	45.2 [b]	56.0	52.2	50.2
Education (%)					
Less than high school	4.4 [b]	8.6	9.4	7.2	9.1
High school graduate	15.2 [a,b,c]	24.6 [b,c]	32.3	38.7	27.6
Some college	26.9 [c]	32.7	28.8 [c]	37.1	31.6
College graduate	20.9 [c]	16.0 [c]	17.2 [c]	7.2	15.2
Postgraduate	32.6 [a,b,c]	18.1 [b,c]	12.3	9.8	17.5
Income					
<$20k	13.5 [a,b,c]	22.3	23.1	20.2	21.0
$20–35k	9.1 [b,c]	10.1 [b]	14.0	19.4	13.6
$35–50k	13.3	16.8	16.5	16.8	15.0
$50–100k	24.8	27.0	27.3	30.3	27.1
>$100k	39.2 [a,b,c]	23.8 [c]	19.1 [c]	13.4	23.3

Table 1.1.   Continued

	Rejecters (21.5%)	Resisters (26.6%)	Accommodators (32.1%)	Ambassadors (19.8%)	Whole Sample
Size of Place					
City	26.2 [c]	24.6 [c]	27.1 [c]	16.2	24.1
Suburb	35.0 [b,c]	31.0 [c]	25.9	23.7	28.6
Town	29.6 [c]	34.4	32.0 [c]	39.5	33.7
Rural	9.2 [b,c]	10.0 [b,c]	15.0	20.6	13.6
Region					
Northeast	28.2 [a,b,c]	18.4 [c]	13.4	10.1	17.5
Midwest	16.2 [b]	19.8 [b]	27.8 [c]	20.6	21.5
South	26.7 [b,c]	32.3	38.7 [c]	49.9	37.2
West	28.9 [b,c]	29.6 [b,c]	20.1	19.5	23.8

[a] Significant difference compared to Resisters.

[b] Significant difference compared to Accommodators.

[c] Significant difference compared to Ambassadors.

or read sacred texts. However, one in 10 report attending religious services at least once a month, and close to a quarter pray at least once a week. While majorities identify as politically liberal or align themselves with the Democratic Party, 40 percent classify themselves as Independents, and a quarter respond that they are politically moderate (see Table 1.3).

RESISTERS

> Is it a Christian nation? I'm trying to think. I would say no. I think of it more as the melting pot right now, right? With all religious beliefs, creeds, colors of people, right? Everyone's welcome. So, I think it was founded on a lot of the beliefs, but I don't know if that's what defines it.
>
> —Brett, *Resister*

This quote from Brett, a 38-year-old Baptist from South Carolina, exemplifies the attitudes of the Resisters. While Rejecters completely repudiate the notion that the United States is a Christian nation, Resisters

Table 1.2. Religious Affiliations, Beliefs, and Behaviors of Ambassadors, Accommodators, Resisters, and Rejecters

	Rejecters (21.5%)	Resisters (26.6%)	Accommodators (32.1%)	Ambassadors (19.8%)	Whole Sample
Religious Tradition					
Evangelical Protestant	7.4 [a,b,c]	17.6 [b,c]	33.0 [c]	54.9	28.8
Mainline Protestant	10.4	13.4	12.5	11.3	12.4
Black Protestant	2.2 [a,b,c]	6.9	8.7	9.9	7.2
Catholic	14.2 [a,b]	30.8 [c]	31.9 [c]	18.6	25.1
Jewish	3.4 [a,b,c]	1.1	.8	.1	1.2
Other	11.1 [c]	7.6 [c]	7.5 [c]	3.2	7.3
No affiliation	51.1 [a,b,c]	21.9 [b,c]	6.2 [c]	2.3	18.1
Belief in God					
God exists, no doubts	12.6 [a,b,c]	43.9 [b,c]	77.5 [c]	94.4	59.5
God exists, some doubts	12.1 [a,c]	19.4 [b,c]	13.7 [c]	3.6	12.5
Higher power	25.4 [b,c]	19.9 [b,c]	6.6 [c]	1.4	13.1
Agnostic	13.3 [a,b,c]	8.0 [b,c]	.4	.4	4.8
Atheist	36.5 [a,b,c]	8.8 [b,c]	1.7 [c]	.2	10.2
Bible Views					
Biblical literalist	1.4 [a,b,c]	3.9 [b,c]	20.0 [c]	49.4	19.0
Bible inspired word of God	10.9 [a,b,c]	28.9 [b,c]	47.2 [c]	38.4	32.6
Bible contains human errors	7.7 [a,b]	17.9 [c]	13.4 [c]	6.9	11.9
Bible is book of legends	71.2 [a,b,c]	28.9 [b,c]	7.5	4.5	25.1
Don't know	8.8 [a,c]	20.4 [b,c]	11.9 [c]	.9	11.4
Religious Service Attendance					
Never	59.9 [a,b,c]	34.9 [b,c]	17.3 [c]	9.5	28.0
Several times a year	30.5 [a,c]	38.8 [b,c]	30.7 [c]	19.5	30.6
Several times a month	8.7 [a,b,c]	24.9 [b,c]	43.5	48.4	33.3
Weekly or more	.8 [b,c]	1.4 [b,c]	9.4 [c]	22.6	8.2

Table 1.2. Continued

	Rejecters (21.5%)	Resisters (26.6%)	Accommodators (32.1%)	Ambassadors (19.8%)	Whole Sample
Prayer Frequency					
Never	54.3 [a,b,c]	24.0 [b,c]	3.3 [c]	1.1	18.1
Rarely	23.2 [c]	26.7 [c]	21.0 [c]	7.1	20.5
Once a week	9.3 [a,b,c]	24.2 [c]	21.8	17.5	19.0
Once a day	8.5 [b,c]	12.9 [b,c]	25.4	25.7	18.8
Multiple times a day	4.7 [a,b,c]	12.2 [b,c]	28.5 [c]	48.6	23.7
Read Sacred Scriptures					
Never	69.6 [a,b,c]	48.9 [b,c]	26.6 [c]	9.8	37.2
Several times a year	24.9 [b]	30.1 [c]	31.5 [c]	22.8	28.3
Several times a month	1.4 [a,b,c]	8.1 [b]	12.4	8.5	8.0
Weekly or more	4.1 [a,b,c]	12.9 [b,c]	29.4 [c]	58.8	26.5

[a] Significant difference compared to Resisters.

[b] Significant difference compared to Accommodators.

[c] Significant difference compared to Ambassadors.

signal a bit more indecision. They may disagree that prayer should be instituted in public schools and believe that the government should not officially declare the United States a Christian nation, but they may be undecided about allowing the display of religious symbols in public places. In short, they lean toward opposing Christian nationalism.

Resisters share some clear demographic similarities with Rejecters: the average age, the gender distribution, or the size of place where Resisters live is not significantly different from Rejecters.[7] Whites make up 61 percent of Resisters, a much smaller proportion than Rejecters. The share of Resisters who are black (10 percent) or Hispanic (20 percent) is double the size for Rejecters. Forty-five percent of Resisters are married, which is significantly less among Rejecters.

The percent of Resisters in the various education or income categories is similar to Rejecters except in the proportion who are high school

Table 1.3. Political Ideology and Party of Ambassadors, Accommodators, Resisters, and Rejecters

	Rejecters (21.5%)	Resisters (26.6%)	Accommodators (32.1%)	Ambassadors (19.8%e)	Whole Sample
Political Ideology					
Conservative	7.4 [a,b,c]	20.4 [b,c]	43.8 [c]	68.8	35.3
Moderate	24.3 [a,b]	47.2 [c]	44.1 [c]	27.3	37.0
Liberal	68.4 [a,b,c]	32.4 [b,c]	12.0 [c]	3.9	27.7
Political Party					
Republican	5.9 [a,b,c]	16.9 [b,c]	40.3 [c]	55.7	29.5
Independent	40.0 [b,c]	42.1 [b,c]	29.2	23.9	33.7
Democrat	54.1 [a,b,c]	41.0 [b,c]	30.6 [c]	20.4	36.8

[a] Significant difference compared to Accommodators.

[b] Significant difference compared to Resisters.

[c] Significant difference compared to Rejecters.

graduates (25 percent) or who have completed postgraduate work (18 percent). Resisters, it appears, are slightly less well-educated than Rejecters. Compared to Rejecters, a larger share of Resisters are found at the lower end of the income distribution, while a smaller share occupy the highest end of the income distribution. Similar percentages of Resisters and Rejecters live in the various regions of the country, except in the Northeast, where significantly fewer Resisters live (18 percent).

The biggest difference between Resisters and Rejecters, however, is in their religious characteristics. Resisters are actually quite religious. More than two-thirds of Resisters identify with a Christian religious tradition, with over 30 percent of Resisters being Catholic and 18 percent affiliating with an evangelical Protestant denomination. The size of the unaffiliated group of Resisters (22 percent) is significantly smaller than that of the Rejecters (51 percent). Clearly, resisting Christian nationalism does not mean that one is completely disengaged from religion. This trend was visible in those we interviewed. Of the 12 Resisters we talked with, eight said religion was "very important" to them.

Resisters are also less likely than Rejecters to renounce common measures of religious belief. A clear majority of Resisters believe in a God or higher power (80 percent), much higher than Rejecters. Significantly fewer Resisters identify as agnostic or atheist than do Rejecters. One-third of Resisters say the Bible is either the literal or inspired word of God. A quarter attend religious services several times a month or more, or pray at least once a day, while over one-fifth read their sacred text at least several times a month.

Politically, Resisters of Christian nationalism are quite diverse. One-fifth (20 percent) identify as politically conservative, nearly a third (32 percent) as liberal, and almost half (47 percent) as moderate. Seventeen percent of Resisters claim they are Republican, while almost equal percentages identify as Independent (42 percent) or Democrat (41 percent).

Taken together, Resisters and Rejecters make up almost 48 percent of the US population.

ACCOMMODATORS

I think . . . maybe lessons taught through Christianity can be good foundational value points for the government as they're creating law and as they're enforcing law. I think Christian values are important in that I think the values that Christians cherish are important. And not so much because of the religious symbology itself, but just because of the general golden rule, "Let's be good to each other. Let's follow a value system."

—Luke, *Accommodator*

Accommodators are in many ways a mirror image of Resisters. While Resisters are somewhat undecided but lean toward opposing Christian nationalism, Accommodators show comparable levels of indecision but lean toward accepting it. While perhaps agreeing that the federal government should advocate Christian values, Accommodators might be undecided about the federal government officially declaring the United States a Christian nation. The quote from Luke above is a perfect example. Luke and other Accommodators see much to admire about Christianity and believe it can be a positive influence on

American society. But it is the *values* of Christianity, which they agree can be found in other world religions, too, that are key. It isn't that these things are found in Christianity *alone*. So Accommodators might support the government allowing the display of religious symbols in public spaces but may (paradoxically) be less certain about whether the government should weaken the separation of church and state in order to do so. This group is generally comfortable with the idea of America's Christian foundations, and is amenable to the idea of a society where Christianity is conspicuous. They stop short, however, of fully and completely favoring Christianity alone in the public sphere. Their support is undeniable, but it is not unequivocal.

Accommodators are older than Resisters and Rejecters, with an average age of about 50. Accommodators also consist of many more women than men, which is a distinct difference from the previous two groups. Racially, Accommodators are quite similar to Resisters. While a greater proportion of Accommodators are black compared to Resisters and Rejecters, equal shares of Accommodators are white, Hispanic, or of another race. A significantly higher percentage of Accommodators are married compared to Resisters, but there is no significant difference between Accommodators and Rejecters regarding marriage rates.

Accommodators are almost identical to Resisters when it comes to income and are mostly similar to them on education. Similar shares of Accommodators and Resisters live in cities, suburbs, and towns, but many more Accommodators live in rural areas compared to Rejecters and Resisters, and larger numbers of Accommodators live in the Midwest and South, with fewer on the coasts.

A third of Accommodators affiliate with evangelical Protestantism, while another third identify as Catholic. Much higher percentages of Accommodators espouse belief in God and have a higher view of the Bible than Resisters and Rejecters. More Accommodators than Resisters and Rejecters report attending religious services several times a month or more, praying once a day or more, or reading scriptures several times a month or more.

Forty-four percent of Accommodators say they are politically conservative and only 12 percent say they are liberal. These are

significant departures from Resisters and Rejecters. An equal proportion of Accommodators and Resisters, though, say they are political
moderates (44 and 47 percent). The Accommodators we interviewed
mirrored these findings. The vast majority considered themselves either
"moderate," "fairly," or "mostly" conservative politically. Regarding
political party, more Accommodators than Rejecters or Resisters align
with the Republican Party, while fewer say they are Independent or a
part of the Democratic Party. However, 60 percent of Accommodators
are either Independents (29 percent) or Democrats (30.6 percent).

AMBASSADORS

> I think that if we fail to acknowledge the Lord's work in the founding of
> our country . . . if we as believers fail to give credit where credit is due,
> the Lord may take his hand of blessing off our country. And I think that's
> exactly what it is. I think that we were founded on Christian principles,
> as one nation under God. And our country has steadily strayed from that.
> —Ashlyn, *Ambassador*

Those we call Ambassadors are wholly supportive of Christian nationalism. As one Ambassador we interviewed simply declared: "Our
country was definitely founded on Christian principles . . . I believe the
Constitution was following biblical principles, and that our laws should
follow the same principles." In fact, when asked if the United States was
a Christian nation, Ambassadors thought there was very little to discuss: We are a Christian nation. Todd, from Oklahoma, elaborated: "I
do believe [America] was founded on Christian principles and influence.
And I believe most of the founders had strong Christian belief. Most of
the laws were founded off of Christian principles. Just about every law
in every state, and most of the federal government's initial laws were
founded off of Christian principles." In the minds of Ambassadors like
Todd, the founding fathers were indeed establishing a Christian nation
and merely refrained from choosing a specific denomination. The assumption, however, was always that Americans would be "Christian."
One Ambassador living in the Midwest illustrates this well:

35

While I don't have a problem with Muslims in the country practicing their religion, I don't want it forced on me or to be told I now live in a Muslim country, or a Buddhist country or anything. I believe our framers founded on Judeo-Christian principles, as I said before, and that is . . . their intention was not to define, "We're Baptists. We're Catholic. We're Protestant. We're Lutheran." It was just, "We're Christian."

Ambassadors also tie our prosperity as a nation to our heritage of obedience to God's commandments as laid out in the Christian Scriptures. An Ambassador from Oklahoma, Matthew, after some conversation about Christian nationalism, actually embraced the label, seeing it merely as a recognition of our country's historic dependence on the Bible.

I would probably be identified from my beliefs as a Christian nationalist. But I don't see Christian nationalism as a bad thing . . . I'm by no means an expert, but I do consider myself decently well read in American history. And I think my Christian nationalism is more recognizing the profound impact the Bible has had on America from the 1500s and 1600s to the present. Has America ever been perfect? Absolutely not! Will America ever be perfect? No. [But] I think it is quite possible that the prosperity America has enjoyed is in large part due to America's embracing the Bible more so than any other country in history with the exception of Israel.

Ambassadors believe the United States has a special relationship with God, and thus, the federal government should formally declare the United States a Christian nation and advocate for Christian values. Ambassadors support returning formal prayers to public schools and allowing the display of religious symbols in public spaces. When we asked Betsy, a 56-year-old Ambassador, how she felt about displaying the 10 Commandments in courthouses, even if not everyone participating in the legal system is Christian, she told us, "Absolutely, the Ten Commandments should be displayed in the courthouse. Again, when you're in a courthouse, if you're there charged with murder, what do the Ten Commandments say? You know? I guess there's not a whole lot [more] to say on that one. It's just a big, fat yes."

On the topic of church–state separation, Ambassadors we spoke with were largely unified in their opinion that the First Amendment was intended *solely* to keep the state out of the church's business, not to keep religion from influencing politics, as if that were possible.[8] Todd "strongly disagreed" that the government should enforce a strict separation of church and state, explaining, "Having most of your laws in the US founded on Christian principles, I find it very difficult to separate church and state. I believe that God's word has the final say in everything, how we live, the laws that we make, how we treat people." Similarly, Trina in Texas argued that the idea of separation of church and state was like "asking me to separate myself from who I see myself as."

Ambassadors are the oldest of the four categories by a wide margin, with an average age of 54 years. Women make up a greater share of Ambassadors. Ambassadors are also 70 percent white, 11 percent black, and 11 percent Hispanic. Compared to the three other groups, fewer Ambassadors have postgraduate educations or college degrees. A much smaller proportion of Ambassadors are high earners compared to each of the other groups.

Only 16 percent of Ambassadors reside in cities, which is significantly lower than any other groups. Almost two-thirds live in towns or rural areas. Almost half of all Ambassadors reside in the South, the highest proportion by far across each of the four groups.

Over half (55 percent) of Ambassadors identify as evangelical Protestant. Similar to Rejecters, fewer Ambassadors are Catholic (19 percent) compared to Accommodators or Resisters. Only six percent of Ambassadors are not affiliated with a Christian tradition. Large proportions of Ambassadors report holding traditional Christian beliefs. They overwhelmingly believe in God without any doubts at all and hold the Bible in high esteem. Ambassadors consistently report attending religious services more frequently, praying more frequently, and reading sacred scriptures more frequently than those in other groups. While Ambassadors can be found at the lowest levels of both public and private religious behavior, there is a clear linear trend toward more religious activity among those who fully support Christian nationalism.

Being an Ambassador of Christian nationalism is closely related to political views and political party. Two-thirds of Ambassadors (69 percent) identify as politically conservative, while four percent identify as politically liberal. On both accounts, Ambassadors are significantly different from each of the other groups. Interestingly, though, just over a quarter (27 percent) claim to be politically moderate, which is significantly less than Accommodators and Resisters but very similar to Rejecters. Finally, 56 percent of Ambassadors align with the Republican Party, with 24 percent saying they are Independents. Importantly, however, one out of five Ambassadors are Democrats. It is essential to note that despite the clear relationship between fully supporting Christian nationalism and one's politics, Ambassadors are found at both ends of the spectrum.

DISTRIBUTION OF AMBASSADORS, ACCOMMODATORS, RESISTERS, AND REJECTERS ACROSS SOCIAL GROUPS

Now that we have a clearer statistical socio-demographic portrait of Ambassadors, Accommodators, Resisters, and Rejecters, we need to consider how these four orientations are represented across various demographic, religious, and political groups. Here we're looking at the other side of the coin, with questions like, "What percent of evangelicals are Accommodators or Resisters?" or "What proportion of those living in the South are Ambassadors or Rejecters?" As it turns out, variation in support for Christian nationalism cuts across American civil society. No group is a monolith.

For instance, we see in Figure 1.2 that while over 65 percent of those Americans with a postgraduate education are either Resisters (27 percent) or Rejecters (40 percent), a significant minority are also Accommodators and Ambassadors. The same is true for college graduates. So, while at the highest level of education, Americans' support for Christian nationalism is quite low, more education does not seem to preclude someone from supporting Christian nationalism.

Or consider region (Figure 1.3). Ambassadors are found within every region of the United States but are not the majority anywhere. Rejecters are the largest group in the Northeast. Resisters are the largest group

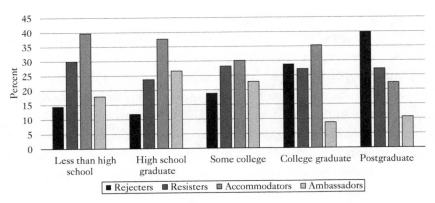

FIGURE 1.2.

Percent of Americans with Different Education Levels Who are
Ambassadors, Accommodators, Resisters, or Rejecters

Source: 2017 Baylor Religion Survey.

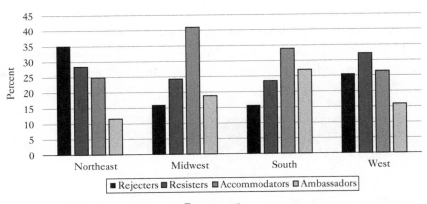

FIGURE 1.3.

Percent of Americans in Each Region of the U.S. Who are Ambassadors,
Accommodators, Resisters, or Rejecters

Source: 2017 Baylor Religion Survey.

in the West. In the Midwest and South, Accommodators are most prevalent. The key, however, is that each response is found in every region.
So, while a majority of residents from the South are Ambassadors or
Accommodators, two out of five Southerners oppose Christian nationalism to some extent. In fact, Accommodators and Resisters are each

at least a quarter of the population *on their own* in every region of the United States. Variation in support for Christian nationalism thus clearly exists across geographic space.

Figure 1.4 provides us with another way to view regional variation in Christian nationalism. The 2017 BRS included information about each respondent's state of residence. Using this information, we imputed the average score on our Christian nationalism scale for each state in the union. Unfortunately, even with a survey sample of over 1,600, some states had very few respondents, so we grouped states together into the nine major divisions used by the US Census Bureau and then averaged their scores. Darker shading indicates higher average scores on the Christian nationalism scale. The regional distribution of stronger adherence to Christian nationalism is just as we might expect: concentrated primarily (though not exclusively) in the Bible Belt and Midwest. Americans on either coast, and particularly in the New England area, appear far less favorable toward this cultural framework.[9]

Throughout the history of the United States, Christian nationalism has shifted according to the cultural context that surrounds it. This has

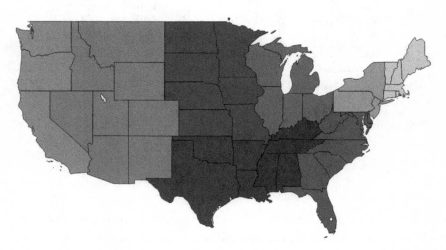

FIGURE 1.4.

Map of the United States Showing Average Christian Nationalism Score Across Nine Major Census Divisions

Source: 2017 Baylor Religion Survey.

been especially true regarding views toward race and how different racial groups respond to racial injustice. White Americans in different eras have drawn on Christian nationalism to both support and oppose slavery and Jim Crow laws. African Americans have also drawn on certain Christian nationalist ideals and narratives to oppose their unequal treatment in American society.[10] Understanding that Christian nationalism is perceived through the "prism" of racial identity, the flexible character of Christian nationalism suggests that we should see each of the different responses present across racial groups. In Figure 1.5, we find this to be true.

Among white Americans we find almost equal numbers of Ambassadors, Accommodators, Resisters, and Rejecters. For African Americans, however, a different relationship exists. While each of the four orientations is present, Accommodators are by far the largest group. Sixty-five percent of African Americans are supportive of Christian nationalism, which is the largest proportion of any racial group. Hispanic Americans are evenly split with similar percentages both supporting and opposing Christian nationalism. However, most Hispanic Americans are found in the more moderate groups, Accommodators and Resisters. Overall, we see that the four orientations toward Christian nationalism

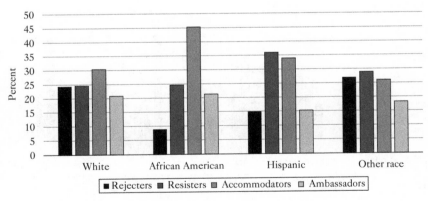

FIGURE 1.5.

Percent of Americans Across Racial Groups Who Are Ambassadors, Accommodators, Resisters, or Rejecters

Source: 2017 Baylor Religion Survey.

are represented across racial groups in the United States, with some interesting variation between the different racial groups.

The four orientations toward Christian nationalism are also found among Americans in different religious traditions. Figure 1.6 displays the percentage of various religious traditions who are Ambassadors, Accommodators, Resisters, and Rejecters. Most evangelical Protestants are Ambassadors (40 percent) or Accommodators (38 percent). This is unsurprising given the Christian nationalist rhetoric used by the Religious Right, whose leaders are largely located within evangelical Protestantism. Yet nearly a quarter (23 percent) of evangelicals are Resisters or Rejecters.[11] The current political climate and the high levels of support among evangelicals for the Trump administration has led to greater visibility among evangelicals who are opposed to Christian nationalism. For example, soon after exit polls showed 81 percent of white evangelicals voted for Donald Trump in 2016, a segment of evangelicals began labeling themselves "the 19 percent" to declare their opposition to the reactionary politics espoused by others in their faith tradition.[12] As these data affirm, not all evangelicals are Christian nationalists, and a substantial minority reject it.

Another important point is that Accommodators are the largest group within each of the Christian traditions except for

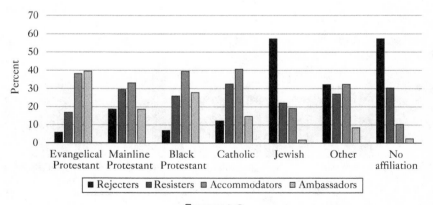

FIGURE 1.6.
Percent of Americans Across Religious Traditions Who Are Ambassadors, Accommodators, Resisters, or Rejecters
Source: 2017 Baylor Religion Survey.

evangelical Protestantism, where Ambassadors barely outnumber them. Accommodators even make up almost a third of the "Other" category, which includes all non-Judeo-Christian religions. Resisters are also well represented across each faith tradition, ranging from a low of 17 percent among evangelicals to a high of 33 percent among Catholics. Unsurprisingly, large proportions of Americans in non-Christian traditions are Rejecters of Christian nationalism. But Rejecters exist in significant numbers within Christian traditions. Clearly, Americans' orientations toward Christian nationalism are dependent on the religious tradition with which they affiliate. But only to a point.

Finally, let's examine whether any Democrats are Ambassadors or Republicans are Resisters, or if a person's politics completely accounts for their stance toward Christian nationalism. Figure 1.7 displays the percentages of each political party that are either Ambassadors, Accommodators, Resisters, or Rejecters. Republicans are clearly much more supportive of Christian nationalism, with four out of five being either Ambassadors or Accommodators. Much more variation exists among Independents and Democrats. Among Democrats, over one-third are either Ambassadors or Accommodators while 30 percent are Resisters and 32 percent are Rejecters. Among Independents, each orientation toward Christian nationalism can be found in

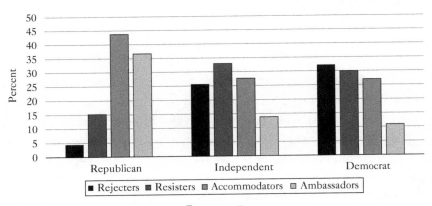

FIGURE I.7.

Percent of Americans Across Political Party Who Are Ambassadors, Accommodators, Resisters, or Rejecters

Source: 2017 Baylor Religion Survey.

numbers similar to Democrats. It is clear that political party itself does not fully account for Americans' orientations toward Christian nationalism.

Overall, these data show that the four orientations toward Christian nationalism can be found across the socio-demographic, religious, and political make-up of the United States. This is crucial to grasp. It is inaccurate to assume, as many have done recently, that "white evangelical" is synonymous with Christian nationalism or that all Democrats want religion banished from the public sphere. Rather, each of the four orientations toward Christian nationalism are present within all of these various groups. In the 1980s, Princeton sociologist Robert Wuthnow proposed that American religion had experienced a "restructuring." One of the main axes upon which the shift took place concerned the public expression of religion, especially the intersection of Christianity and American identity and civic life.[13] Now Americans of different religious traditions and even political persuasions could be organized by how much they support ideologies like Christian nationalism. Simply put, knowing you are an Ambassador or Rejecter of Christian nationalism can now tell us far more about your social and political views than knowing what denomination you affiliate with, how often you attend church, and even whether you identify as Democrat or Republican.

IS CHRISTIAN NATIONALISM GROWING OR DECLINING?

A significant and consistent trend in American religion is the growth of the religiously "unaffiliated" or religious "nones" (those who check "none" for religious affiliation on surveys). Throughout the 1970s and 1980s, this group ranged in size from five to almost eight percent of the population. However, in the mid-1990s this group began to grow quickly, reaching 14 percent by 2000 and 22 percent by 2017. The growth of the unaffiliated corresponds to the decline in the percentage of the population that identifies with a Christian tradition (Protestant or Catholic). Throughout the 1970s around 90 percent of the population identified as Christian. In the 1980s the average hovered around

89 percent. In the 1990s we see a slight dip to an average of 85 percent of the population identifying as Christian. This dropped further to an average of 74 percent from 2000 to 2016. In 2017, 71 percent of the population identified with a Christian tradition.

In *The End of White Christian America* (2016), Robert Jones thoroughly demonstrates not only this demographic decline and the reasons for it, but also the implications of such a decline for the broader culture. While Christians still wield considerable political power, they no longer dominate the cultural and social context like they used to. Therefore, it could be that the growth in the nonreligious and corresponding decline of the Christian population influences the proportion of the population that supports an ideology like Christian nationalism.

Let's first compare the sizes of the four orientations toward Christian nationalism over time. Because the questions comprising our Christian nationalism scale were asked in both the 2007 and 2017 BRS, we can determine if the relative sizes of the four orientations have changed in the last decade. For reference, in 2007, 16 percent of Americans identified as unaffiliated, while in 2017 this number increased to 22 percent. In 2007, 77 percent of Americans identified with a Christian religious tradition, which decreased to 71 percent by 2017. Clearly, from 2007 to 2017 there is an overall trend of Americans disaffiliating with Christianity. But is this decrease in affiliation matched by a similar decrease in Christian nationalism?

Figure 1.8 displays the percent of Americans who are Ambassadors, Accommodators, Resisters, or Rejecters of Christian nationalism in both 2007 and 2017. Beginning with Ambassadors, it is clear that fewer Americans are in this group now than a decade ago, a statistically significant difference. Accommodators also declined in size from 34.9 to 32.1. This difference, however, is not statistically significant. Accommodators are essentially the same size today as they were in 2007. Both Resisters and Rejecters have actually increased in size, and both reflect statistically significant changes. In 2007, Resisters made up 22 percent of the population but are now close to 27 percent of Americans. And in 2017 Rejecters are about 21.5 percent of the United States population, a three percent increase from 2007.

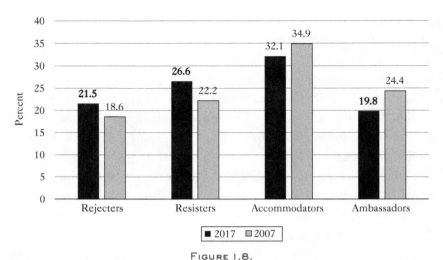

FIGURE 1.8.

Percent of Americans Who Are Ambassadors, Accommodators, Resisters, or Rejecters of Christian Nationalism, 2007–2017

Note: Bold indicates a significant difference between years.

Source: 2007 and 2017 Baylor Religion Surveys.

Combining the Resisters and Rejecters shows that over the last 10 years there has been an eight percent increase in the number of Americans who oppose Christian nationalism to some extent. And while Accommodators are about the same size, the number of Americans who are wholly supportive of Christian nationalism has decreased by almost five percent. It appears that as Americans have moved away from organized religion over the last 10 years, they have begun to make small shifts toward a more oppositional response to Christian nationalism as well.

Data sources that use a single-item measure of adults' views on America's Christian heritage also show a decline in viewing the United States as a Christian nation (see Figure 1.9). In 2012, a survey asked Americans to choose among four responses regarding whether they think the United States is a Christian nation. Two out of five Americans (40 percent) reported believing that "America has always been and is currently a Christian nation."[14] Only five years later, one out of four Americans (26 percent) chose this same response. In 2012, two out of

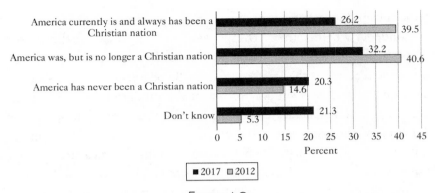

Figure 1.9.
Americans' Views Toward United States as a Christian Nation,
2012–2017
Sources: 2012 Religion, Class, and Culture Survey & 2017 Baylor Religion Survey.

five (40 percent) agreed that "America was a Christian nation in the past, but is not now." Half a decade later just 32 percent of Americans answered similarly. Back in 2012, 15 percent of Americans reportedly believed that "America has never been a Christian nation" and only five percent were undecided. By 2017, 20 percent of Americans claimed the United States has never been a Christian nation, and over 21 percent said they were undecided.

It is important to note that from 2012 to 2017 the percentage of Americans who did not affiliate with a religious tradition increased from 20 percent to 22 percent. However, during this same time period the percent of Americans who affiliated with a Christian religious tradition also increased a slight amount, from 69 percent to 71 percent.[15] These data, taken over a five-year span rather than 10 years, suggest a similar story with Christian nationalism. The proportion of Americans who believe the United States ever was or still is a Christian nation is declining. More Americans now believe that America has never been a Christian nation. And somewhat surprisingly, there has been a dramatic increase in the proportion of Americans who do not know what they believe about the Christian heritage of the United States.[16]

A final piece of evidence points to a long-term trend of slow but stable decline in the past 30 years regarding support for Christian nationalism. Since 1974 the General Social Surveys (GSS) have asked respondents whether they "Disapprove" or "Approve" of the United States Supreme Court ruling that no state or local government may require the reading of the Lord's Prayer or Bible verses in public schools. This question is very similar to one of the measures included in our Christian nationalism scale, and the wording (essentially tapping into Americans' thoughts about the government restricting Christianity's influence in public institutions) makes it a useful measure for our purposes. Figure 1.10 displays the results from 1974 to 2018. While in the 1970s less than 32 percent of Americans approved of this ruling, roughly 48 percent of Americans feel that same way today. Likewise, nearly 70 percent disapproved 40 years ago while only 52 percent respond similarly today. Since the mid-1980s, however, there is little evidence of shifts in either group despite small variations across survey years. This long-term trend suggests two things. First, there is mostly stability with some evidence of growth in resistance to Christianity in public life. Second, though, a *majority* of Americans (52 percent) still

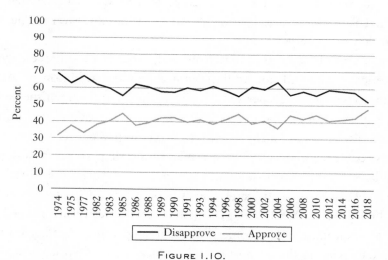

FIGURE 1.10.
Percent of Americans Who Disapprove or Approve of U.S. Supreme Court Ruling that No State or Local Government May Require the Reading of the Lord's Prayer or Bible Verses in Public Schools

Source: 1974–2018 General Social Surveys.

disapprove of this Supreme Court ruling, meaning most Americans are at the very least accommodating of a key Christian nationalist belief.

Will there continue to be a decline in support for Christian nationalism across the culture? Or, will recent events cause Americans to pine for a more intimate intertwining of Christianity and civic life? Two broader trends, one demographic and one religious, would lead us to predict that Ambassadors will continue to decline in size while Resisters and Rejecters will slowly grow their ranks.

First, as we discussed already, Americans continue to disaffiliate from the Christian tradition and Protestantism more specifically. Americans who are not connected to a Christian tradition will be much less likely to be exposed to Christian nationalism. Furthermore, their social networks will offer much lower levels of social support for those beliefs in the event that they hold them. The number of Christians in the United States will most likely continue to decline, and this could foreshadow changes in the levels of support for Christian nationalism. This decline does not mean, however, that Ambassadors will grow less fervent. Rather, this committed core of true believers will most likely maintain their intensity of support for Christian nationalism, especially as they continue to see themselves as a persecuted minority.

A second reason why decline is probable is that Americans who support Christian nationalism are getting older and older. Cohort replacement will lead to a continued decline in their numbers. Consider the following evidence. As Table 1.1 shows, the average age of Ambassadors (54 years) is significantly higher than each of the other three groups. The average age of Accommodators (50 years), while lower than the average age for Ambassadors, is significantly higher than Resisters (45 years) or Rejecters (43 years). However, looking at the average ages in 2017 alone could lead one to argue that these differences in age are merely due to the fact that as people age, they are more likely to become more supportive of Christian nationalism. This would lead us to predict that these groups might not shift in size over time.

However, the differences in average age across the four groups have changed significantly since 2007. Then, Ambassadors were actually *significantly younger* than Accommodators (47 years versus 49 years) and not significantly older than Resisters (45 years) or Rejecters (45 years). If Americans were more likely to support Christian nationalism as they age, we would expect this same relationship to be apparent in both 2007 and 2017. Rather, a decade on, we see that Ambassadors are much older on average and are now significantly older than Accommodators.

Using the arbitrary generational divides common in popular discourse, we can see that Ambassadors are much less prevalent among Millennials and make up a much larger proportion of the Greatest Generation (see Figure 1.11). Among Millennials, more than 60 percent resist or reject Christian nationalism. Over half of those in Gen X support Christian nationalism to one extent or the other, but overall many more Gen Xers are opposed to Christian nationalism than Baby Boomers or the Greatest Generation. The reality of a much older set of Americans supporting Christian nationalism implies it may continue to decline across the population. It is also difficult to see any reason why strong support for Christian nationalism would reverse the aging trend of the last decade and somehow become even more prevalent.

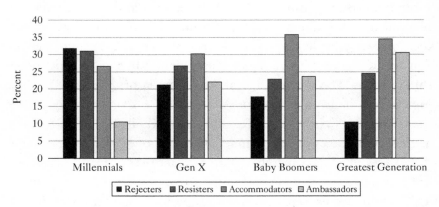

FIGURE 1.11.

Percent of Americans Across Generational Divides Who Are Ambassadors, Accommodators, Resisters, or Rejecters

Source: 2017 Baylor Religion Survey.

While it is difficult to predict future trends for Ambassadors, Accommodators, Resisters, and Rejecters given that we only have two data points spanning the last decade, this evidence would lead us to question anyone who believes a large-scale increase in support for Christian nationalism is imminent. Rather, these trends suggest that while ebbs and flows will occur, overall, high levels of support for Christian nationalism will slowly decrease, while the accommodation of it could continue indefinitely.

But there is an alternate possibility. Though the data points we've shared thus far suggest a steady decline in Christian nationalism over the last few decades, other data shows that Christian nationalism, by certain measures at least, may wax and wane in response to certain societal tensions. In 1996, 2004, and 2014, the GSS asked how important Americans believe being a Christian is for being "truly American." Though it is only a single-item measure, at the very least it indicates how much Americans conflate Christian identity with American civic belonging and corresponds quite well with our Christian nationalism measure in the BRS.

Figure 1.12 shows us two important trends. First, there was an obvious increase in the purported importance of being Christian to being truly American from 1996 to 2004. Second, this was followed by a similarly sized decline from 2004 to 2014.[17] In their 2010 study, sociologists Jeremy Straughn and Scott Feld sought to explain the jump from 1996 to 2004 by proposing a theory of "symbolic boundary alignment" where religious nationalism is used to designate who is "in" and who is "out." They contend that symbolic boundaries become more salient in times of social unrest. Given the events of 9/11 in 2001, by 2004 Americans were still looking for ways to clearly indicate who they were as a group by highlighting who they were not. For these reasons, there was an *increase* in the percentage of the population that believed being Christian is vital to being a true American *in spite of* a decrease in the proportion of the population that is Christian over that same time period.

Building on Straughn and Feld's work with the 2014 GSS data, a more recent study found that as 9/11 slipped further into the rearview

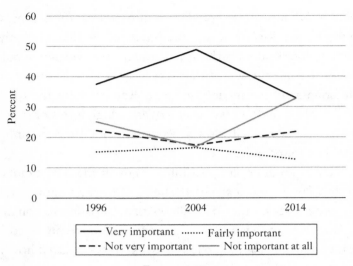

FIGURE 1.12.
Variation in Percent of Americans Who Believe It Is Important to Be a
Christian to Be Truly American
Source: 1996, 2004, 2014 General Social Surveys.

mirror, Americans did not continue to view being Christian as "very important" for being a true American. In fact, in 2014 the percent that believed it to be very or fairly important dropped below the 1996 levels. Now, an equal number of Americans believe it is either not important at all or very important to be a Christian in order to be a true American. This suggests that historical events and shifts in the culture may alter the salience of the Christian religion as a symbolic boundary marker.[18]

Depending on the context, Christianity may not always be fundamental to the boundaries Americans draw around their national identity. Yet historians argue that Christianity can quite easily be made salient as a vital aspect of American identity by reactionary movements and leaders during periods of cultural, political, or economic unrest. This underscores the importance of the rhetoric used in the public sphere, especially from social and political leaders. It could very well be that since 2014, following the rise of Donald Trump to the presidency, there has been another significant increase in the number of Americans who believe it is "very important" to be Christian in order to be "truly American."

* * *

So what does all this mean? What does one's support for Christian nationalism—or lack thereof—tell us about a person, their politics, their willingness to include outsiders, their beliefs about what makes a good society? We answer these questions in the next three chapters.

CHAPTER 2

POWER

"Don't forget your flag!" a kindly, silver-haired woman reminded attendees meandering toward the sanctuary doors. Many were understandably a bit distracted. The cavernous lobby of First Baptist Dallas, which normally looked like that of a nondescript convention center, had been converted into a dazzling spectacle of patriotic symbolism, its columns festooned from floor to ceiling with balloons of red, white, and blue. Civilian attendees were decked out in stars and stripes, while military veterans were in full dress uniform. A veritable army of smiling ushers passed out American flags as we filed into the sanctuary. The much-advertised "Freedom Sunday" service at the 10,000 member megachurch was a finely woven tapestry of Christian nationalism. There were patriotic hymns (e.g., "When the Saints Go Marching In," "The Battle Hymn of the Republic") accompanied by pyrotechnics and lasers, throughout which attendees enthusiastically waved their little flags. There were prayers from army chaplains. There was a call to recognize veterans in attendance. A choir performed the "Armed Forces Medley," recognizing each branch of the military.

All these coordinated elements were ultimately building toward the crescendo of the service—pastor Robert Jeffress's controversially titled message, "America is a Christian Nation." Jeffress preceded his sermon by reading a letter from Vice President Mike Pence, which Jeffress said he had received the day before. Pence offered encouragement and commended the worshippers: "As President Trump and I both know, America's strength ultimately comes from our freedom and from the foundation of faith in this nation. We know that no podium we ever stand behind will be as important as the pulpits that pastors stand behind every Sunday. And no policy we ever advance will be as important as the message that you faithfully carry—a message of hope that is changing lives." After reading the letter, Jeffress asked his audience, "Aren't you glad we have a man like Mike Pence standing behind our great president Donald Trump?!" The crowd responded with uproarious applause.

The service's program contained a detailed outline of Jeffress's sermon, including a litany of quotes he would draw upon. He began by presenting two competing narratives about the country's founding:

> Listen long enough to organizations like the American Civil Liberties Union or the Freedom from Religion Foundation or any other left-wing group and you will come to believe this history of America: that America was founded by men of a wide diversity of religious beliefs, some deists, some atheists, and a few Christians. But they were all united by one dream: they wanted to build a completely secular nation that was devoid of any religious, especially Christian, influence. Their goal was to build an unscalable wall around this country that would protect this country from any religious influence seeping into public life.

The purpose of such narratives, according to Jeffress, is political, not historical. "*That* version of American history," Jeffress quickly assured his audience, "belongs in the same category as the story of George Washington and the cherry tree. It is a complete myth." Instead, Jeffress put forth an alternative narrative, one he would spend the entire sermon defending:

> America was founded predominantly, not exclusively, but predominantly, by Christians who wanted to build a Christian nation on the foundation of God's will [interrupted by applause]. And furthermore, these men believed that the future success of our country depended on our fidelity to the Christian beliefs. And that's why we can say, though it's politically incorrect to do so, we say without hesitation or apology that America was founded as a *Christian* nation [pounds pulpit], and

our future success depends on our country being faithful to those eternal truths of God's word [thunderous applause].

The remaining 45 minutes of the sermon included no key biblical text—rare for a conservative Protestant expositor like Jeffress. Instead, he leaned almost exclusively on quotes from "founding fathers," founding documents, and court decisions, all ostensibly suggesting the centrality of (evangelical) Christianity to America's core identity. But *that* America is under attack, Jeffress explained. In the final few minutes, he recounted how "secular Supreme Court justices" in the early 1960s had removed prayer and Bible reading from public schools. This led inexorably to a retreat from America's founding, biblical ideals. Instead, Jeffress argued, we are spiraling toward a dystopian future of homicide, single-parent households, and sexual depravity. As he wrapped up his message, Jeffress called his listeners to action:

> Now here's the question: What has changed? In these hundred and fifty years has the Constitution changed and nobody told us? Is that what happened? Of course not. What has happened is we've allowed the secularists, the humanists, the atheists, the infidels to pervert our Constitution into something our founding fathers never intended. And it is time for Americans to stand up and say, "Enough! We're not going to allow this in our Christian country anymore!" It is time to put an end to this.

This was in fact the *only* point of application in the entire sermon. No pleas for personal piety. No calls to be "good Samaritans" to our neighbors. Rather, faithful Christians must stand up and confront the "secularists," "humanists," "atheists," and "infidels" who are taking control of "*our* Christian country."

This Land Is Our Land

Twenty years ago sociologist Christian Smith argued that scholars and journalists had got white evangelicals all wrong—specifically, those evangelicals who were seemingly sympathetic to Christian nationalist rhetoric and ideals. First and foremost, Smith explained, white evangelicals are not a monolithic group. They hold diverse opinions about the nation's Christian heritage and should not be stereotyped as staunch Christian nationalists. But more than this, Smith argued, the use of "Christian nation" language, for most rank and file evangelicals, was not intended to mobilize *political* action, but to shore up their identity *as Christians* and to mobilize *religious* action. Their primary interest is not to "take America back for God" through political force, but simply to live as faithful Christians, redeeming their increasingly secular society through interpersonal influence. While certain evangelical elites and events—like Robert Jeffress and similar "Freedom Sunday" services—may have partisan goals in mind, Smith concluded that those sorts of rallying calls to political action ultimately had little influence in believers' lives.[1]

To some degree, we think Smith was correct. Average evangelicals in the pews have diverse views. Many who are amenable to the narrative of America being "founded on Christian principles," like many Accommodators we met, are more concerned with religious faithfulness than political power. But while Smith was careful to argue that not all evangelicals are Christian nationalists, he failed to point out that not all Christian nationalists are evangelicals. This has led to some unfortunate conceptual confusion. As we have shown, nearly half (45 percent) of "Ambassadors," those who are most favorable toward Christian nationalism, are not white evangelicals. More than 15 percent are black Protestants, Jewish, unaffiliated, or of a non-Christian faith. Christian nationalism, simply put, is not an exclusively evangelical ideology. It exists independently.[2]

Herein lies the potential misunderstanding: while many white evangelicals, as Christian Smith argued, may indeed often have *religious* goals in mind when they appeal to a "Christian nation" narrative—though we think Smith may underestimate white evangelicals' collective desire to protect their cultural-political turf—evangelicalism is not synonymous with Christian nationalism. Rather, those Americans who adhere most strongly to Christian nationalist ideals have *political* interests primarily in mind. Religious interests rank second, if they rank at all. Like Jeffress's sermon suggests, faithfulness to "our Christian country," in the minds of Ambassadors and many Accommodators, has little to do with personal piety; it is about political influence. That is because Christian nationalism is rooted in claims about who "we" are as a people and, more importantly, whose preferences should be reflected in "our" cultural symbols and implemented in "our" public policies.[3] Christian identity may play a part in that, but it is only a part. In this chapter we examine how Christian nationalism powerfully and uniquely influences Americans' political attitudes and activity in ways that are (1) above and beyond theological and political conservatism as traditionally measured, and (2) often diametrically opposed to Christian ethics.

For The Love of God, Why Trump?

The 2016 Election

Most Americans were surprised at the outcome of the 2016 presidential election, even Donald Trump.[4] While national polls were quite accurate in predicting a slight edge to Clinton in the popular vote (where she met expectations), statewide polls were less precise.[5] This was especially true in areas dominated by white, non-college-educated voters. Vote analyses show that Trump's narrow victories in a handful of counties in Wisconsin, Michigan, and Pennsylvania were why he was able to secure the necessary electoral college votes to ultimately win the election.[6] Soon after his victory, a barrage of columns, op-eds, and studies tried to determine the various reasons why that particular population of Americans—a considerable number of whom had voted for Obama in the two previous elections—helped put Donald Trump in the White House. A number of initial explanations appeared, often emphasizing single factors. Some stressed economic anxiety. Some racism or xenophobia. Others, sexism. And still others culture war factors like religious freedom, homophobia, or abortion.[7] Uniting these seemingly disparate explanations is the thread of *insecurity*—economic to some extent, but mostly cultural and political. Essentially, those in a traditionally high-status or dominant group (white Christian males in particular) who perceived a certain degree of threat to their status by some minority group (e.g., racial minorities, immigrants, Muslims, feminists, the LGBTQ community, secular elites) were much more likely to vote for Trump.[8]

But a more interesting storyline emerged in the media regarding who put Trump in the White House, namely, the role of white evangelical Christians. Though initially reluctant to support Trump as a candidate—in mid-2015 Trump's favorability ratings among white evangelicals hovered between 39 and 49 percent—once it was clear he would win the Republican nomination in mid-2016, those numbers began to climb.[9] It seemed the primary narrative in the coverage of Trump support among evangelicals was the hypocrisy angle. Why would white evangelical Christians, who had historically emphasized family values and pious devotion among their leaders, vote in such overwhelming numbers for a thrice-married, adulterous, unrepentant, self-styled playboy billionaire?

Indeed, white evangelical support for Trump seemed completely impervious to any new revelations about his moral character. When *The Washington Post* published an audio recording that captured candidate Trump boasting that he could kiss beautiful women without their invitation and "grab them by the pussy," many believed his chances of winning the election would plummet. Surely white evangelical Christians who had long emphasized voting for family-values candidates would withdraw support from Trump.[10] Soon after, however, Jerry Falwell Jr., the president of Liberty University—one of the largest Christian universities in the United States—defended Trump on national television. Reminding viewers that "we're all sinners," Falwell said he still believed Trump was "the best qualified to be President of the United States."[11] Similarly, Wayne Grudem, a widely respected evangelical theologian, echoed Falwell. While denouncing Trump's lewd remark, Grudem argued that being able to vote for Trump was an "answer to our prayers that [God] would deliver us from the increasing opposition to Christian values brought on by the Democratic Party and the

Obama administration."[12] Grudem's thoughts clearly reflected those of many white evangelicals. The day after the presidential election, *The New York Times* exit polls indicated that some 80 percent of voters who identified as white evangelical or born-again Christians ultimately voted for Trump over Hilary Clinton.[13]

But is religion's influence on the 2016 election as straightforward as "white evangelicals put Trump in the White House?" We think a better explanation of what happened in 2016 can be found in the cultural framework many Americans—evangelical or not—happen to share: Christian nationalism.[14] With the 2017 Baylor Religion Survey (BRS) we can rank the relative influence of the most popular explanations for why Americans voted for Donald Trump—such as economic dissatisfaction, racism, xenophobia, Islamophobia, sexism, being an evangelical—alongside our Christian nationalism measures. First, the two strongest factors in predicting who voted for Trump were self-identifying as a Republican and as a political conservative. This should be unsurprising, as most Americans vote with their political tribe rather than for specific candidates or issues.[15] The next two strongest predictors of voting Trump, however, were Islamophobia and Christian nationalism. Figure 2.1 shows the percentage of Americans within each

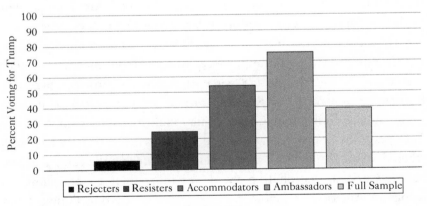

FIGURE 2.1.

Voting for Trump in the 2016 Presidential Election Across Ambassadors, Accommodators, Resisters, and Rejecters

Source: 2017 Baylor Religion Survey.

orientation to Christian nationalism who voted for Trump. It is clear that support for Trump among Ambassadors was greater than among Resisters or Rejecters. In fact, even when we account for a host of demographic measures, political party and political ideology, various measures of religion, and the handful of cultural explanations like economic dissatisfaction, Islamophobia, racism, xenophobia, or sexism that we mentioned above, Christian nationalism is still a significant and powerful predictor of voting for Trump.[16] To put this in perspective, two people could both be from the same region of the country, worship in the same denomination, identify with the same political party, but still significantly diverge in their likelihood of voting for Trump depending on their orientation toward Christian nationalism.

But perhaps what is just as significant is the fact that affiliating with evangelicalism, believing in a literal Bible, or even Americans' frequency of religious practice were all *unrelated* to voting for Donald Trump. Christian nationalism, in other words, explained almost all of the "religious vote" for Trump. In fact, Christian nationalism influenced the Trump vote across other social categories including Christian traditions, political parties, levels of education, or particular regions of the country (see Table 2.1). While on the whole more evangelicals than Catholics voted for Trump, many fewer evangelicals who are Resisters (32.8 percent) or Rejecters (27.3 percent) voted for Trump than Catholics who are Ambassadors (78.9 percent) or Accommodators (55.4 percent). While Republicans and Democrats were quite fixed in whether they voted for Trump, we see that for Independents, whether they were an Ambassador (78 percent), Accommodator (51 percent), Resister (27.6 percent), or Rejecter (11 percent) mattered a great deal.

But how exactly does Christian nationalism animate support for Trump? While Trump repeatedly and transparently pandered to voters when discussing America's Christian heritage during the campaign, we believe Christian nationalism stands for more than a mere pining to recognize America's religious heritage. One fascinating finding from our analyses of Trump support in the 2017 BRS is that Christian nationalism seemed to influence Americans to vote for Trump *through*

Table 2.1. Percent of Ambassadors, Accommodators, Resisters, and Rejecters Who Voted for Trump by Religious Tradition, Political Party, Education, and White Rurality

	Ambassador	Accommodator	Resister	Rejecter	Full Sample
Evangelical Protestant	85.7	59.6	32.8	27.3	63.1
Mainline Protestant	83.7	54.8	26.6	0	40.2
Catholic	78.9	55.4	21.7	4.4	42.3
Republican	92.0	88.7	75.0	30.7	86.1
Independent	78.1	51.1	27.6	11.4	36.9
Democrat	16.1	7.5	4.5	0	4.3
Bachelor's degree or more	81.0	56.9	14.7	4.4	28.9
White & rural	86.8	62.5	35.9	26.8	58.9

Source: 2017 Baylor Religion Survey.

its connection to other factors like Islamophobia and prejudice toward Mexican immigrants. In other words, for many Americans, Christian nationalism captures a cultural vision of whose country the United States *really* is ("ours"), and consequently who are the "others" or "outsiders" ("Muslim terrorists" and "violent Mexican immigrants"). Americans who sensed a threat in the form of ethnic and religious outsiders encroaching on their privileged position most likely envisioned a Trump presidency as a "return" to a better time. He would make America great again by making it *their* America again—at least for a little while longer.[17]

Speaking to Trump voters allowed us to see how explicit Christian nationalism could often hide more subtle prejudices.[18] Matthew is a married father of three in his late thirties. A Texas native and a staunch supporter of a border wall with Mexico, Matthew said that he would have preferred a more squarely evangelical candidate, but nonetheless threw his enthusiastic support behind Trump and still supports him today. Listing the reasons he voted for Trump, Matthew explained, "I saw [Trump] as the best, only option to hold to America's traditional Christian identity. I see America's traditional Christian identity as the only thing that has made America *America*. It also made Western Civilization. But America more strongly and for longer embraced Judeo-Christian principles and so has enjoyed greater freedom and prosperity than any other Western country."

Matthew contrasted this vision of America's identity and heritage—the preservation of which he sees as essential to civilization and prosperity—with Obama's subtle efforts to remove Christianity's influence.

> I saw Obama as trying to remove our Christian foundation, not necessarily the values. Obama made very clear that we are not a Christian nation and at the same time repeatedly applauded all the contributions of Muslims and Islam . . . There is a video of Obama basically making fun of those that believe the Bible. He quotes a passage and then says "people haven't been reading their Bibles" because the Bible says this and it doesn't work if we live that way. Which to me just shows that he doesn't understand the Bible.

Other Ambassadors of Christian nationalism shared similar thoughts. David, a 58-year-old from the Midwest, shared that Trump is "standing up for the Christian faith, Christian believers. He's bringing our country back to the way it should be." David's quote underscores his belief that the United States was moving away from this ideal in recent years. He also believes that Hillary Clinton would have continued to move the United States from its founding principles, that she was more "about control and socialism rather than individual freedoms and rights."

Returning to his explanation for why he voted for Trump, Matthew stressed the need to return America to her Christian foundations, lest it become corrupted like *other* nations. "An embrace of the Bible and Christian values created a country that millions from all over the world have flocked to. But people don't realize that if we throw off Christianity and instead embrace the values of the countries they have fled from, we will cease to be 'America' and instead will become like the countries they have fled from." In Matthew's view, "America" is defined by its Christian cultural values. And these Christian values—unless corrupted by external influences—are static because they are based on the unchanging Bible. Matthew also assumes other countries' values (likely by virtue of them simply being *other* countries) are not Christian, and thus inferior. Interestingly, however, Matthew does not consider the possibility that the values of other nations might somehow augment or improve America's core values. Rather, he sees the situation in terms of purity and corruption. To embrace the cultural values of other nations is inherently polluting, making our society just like the societies from which refugees flee. In light of the context of our conversation—which included immigration, border walls, and terrorism—Matthew's reference to nations from which refugees "have fled" almost certainly denotes Muslim-majority countries and Latin American countries.

Ambassadors and Accommodators like Matthew specifically saw in Trump an opportunity not only to restore their political and cultural influence, which they felt was threatened under Obama, but to fortify America's supremacy among other nations, which they believed to be rooted in fidelity to Christian principles and values. As Trump advisor and televangelist Paula White wrote, "What makes America great is that we were founded [as] a Judeo-Christian nation. That's very important for us to understand. He [Trump] understands it. It is personal to him . . . you will not understand democracy if you don't understand the biblical foundations and traditions and foundation of Christianity and of our faith."[19] According to White, Trump always knew that making America great again necessarily begins by making it Christian again.

WHY DO WHITE EVANGELICALS KEEP SUPPORTING TRUMP?

Understanding Christian nationalism's role in the 2016 election also gives us insight into the continued support for President Trump throughout his presidency. Despite a number of scandals and recurring instances of behavior that do not align with traditional Christian values, a significant minority of Americans still strongly approve of Trump. This is especially true among white conservative Christians.[20] At the time of Trump's inauguration, his approval among white evangelicals was 74 percent, and through the first year of his presidency it hovered between 65 and 75 percent. Despite a number of episodes that many thought could crater white evangelicals' support, nothing Trump says or does seems to move the needle. For example, in their Summer 2018 polls, both Pew Research Center and Gallup independently reported that 68 percent of white evangelicals approve of the way Trump is handling his job as president. A Fall 2018 Public Religion Research Institute poll had Trump's approval among white evangelicals at 71 percent.[21]

Knowing that "evangelical" support for Trump is more explicitly about Christian nationalism helps make sense of these trends. It also helps us understand the rhetoric of Trump's most vocal evangelical supporters. For instance, in early 2018 the news broke that right before the 2016 election, Stormy Daniels, an adult film actress, was paid $130,000 to stay silent about an alleged affair she had with Trump in 2006, four months after Trump's wife Melania gave birth to their son. Responding to these allegations of lurid affairs and hush-money payoffs, the Reverend Franklin Graham, president and CEO of Samaritan's Purse and son of famed evangelist Billy Graham, defended Trump. Admitting that he did not want Trump to be "pastor of this nation," he stressed, "But I appreciate the fact that [Trump] does have a concern for Christian values, he does have a concern to protect Christians." And, he added, "I appreciate the fact that he protects religious liberty and freedom."[22] Tony Perkins, former politician and head of The Family Research Council—a powerful evangelical lobbying group—also defended Trump, declaring that he and other conservative Christians were giving Trump a "mulligan" on these and other past sins. His justification was telling. "[Conservative Christians] were tired of getting kicked around by Barack Obama and his leftists. And I think they are finally glad that there's somebody on the playground that is willing to punch the bully." Asked about "turning the other cheek," Perkins replied, "You know, we only have two cheeks.

Look, Christianity is not all about being a welcome mat which people can just stomp their feet on."[23]

These defenses of Trump have nothing to do with defending Christian morality—just the opposite, it would seem. For Ambassadors and Accommodators, if Trump (or other politicians) can espouse Christian nationalist rhetoric and signal their willingness to restore conservative Christian influence in American cultural and political life, personal piety is of little concern. For Christian nationalists, the ends justify the means. We saw this in our interviews as well. Many people we spoke with expressed some misgivings about the things they hear about Trump, while maintaining he is still doing what is right for America. Brandon, an Accommodator and lifelong Southerner remarked, "I don't like his antics. I don't like the way he talks. Behind the scenes, I think he means well. I think he's trying to do good things for our country, putting us first . . . I do believe somewhere in there he's got a good heart and he does mean well." Others chalked up the negativity to "fake news," or said that Trump is being persecuted by those who don't like what he's trying to do.

How can we be sure Christian nationalism is the cognitive mechanism linking white evangelicals to Trump support? There are two ways. First, even when we remove the effects of race and religious affiliation, Christian nationalism predicts voting for Trump.[24] This means that it isn't the difference between being an evangelical and any other religious affiliation that truly matters. Rather, it is the degree to which Americans differ in their orientation toward Christian nationalism. It is the fact that there are more Ambassadors and Accommodators among white evangelicals that creates those differences between religious traditions.

Second, when we break down white evangelicals by their adherence to Christian nationalism (Figure 2.2), it is the Ambassadors and Accommodators who overwhelmingly supported Trump, not the Rejecters or Resisters. Similar to the findings in Table 2.1 where there is significant variation within each religious tradition across the four Christian nationalism groups, here again we see that preference for Christian nationalism matters a great deal. David, an Ambassador and white evangelical Christian, told us that, "I voted for the man, and

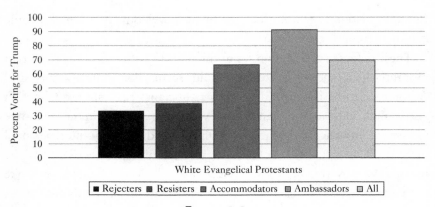

FIGURE 2.2.

FIGURE 2.2.
Voting for Trump Among White Evangelical Protestants Across
Ambassadors, Accommodators, Resisters, and Rejecters
Source: 2017 Baylor Religion Survey.

I'll vote for him tomorrow if I had to. I'm loving what he's doing. I'll support him for as long as he's going to be running for office." David believes Trump is returning America to its Christian roots, and that is why he supports him. But white evangelicals who were Resisters or Rejecters held a decidedly different opinion of Trump. Rick, a white evangelical Christian and Rejecter, stated simply, "I think very little of President Trump. I think he's evil. I think he's full of himself, I think he is selfish, I think he's hateful. And it blows my mind, I think it's self-evident. I've never had to argue with people trying to convince them of something that I just think is self-evident and they just can't see it. That's what frustrating." Clint is a white evangelical pastor who is a Rejecter. He similarly questioned how professing Christians could tolerate Trump's behavior at all.

When you've got a president who has publicly said things. These aren't behind the scenes, I'm not sure what he's going into as he's thinking about voting on policy. He's *publicly* said things, like the "grab your pussy" stuff and just has not conducted himself as a gentleman. I don't expect Trump to have the charisma that Obama had or whatever, but there is a certain amount of just overt kind of terrible behavior . . . just awful things. I don't see how a Christian could . . . for a Christian to look at those things and give [Trump] a pass on that, to me, demonstrates a real amount of suppression of your ethical instincts . . . Either you just don't have them or you're suppressing them because you can't bear to think of Bernie Sanders being president or whatever.

Being an evangelical does not draw Rick or Clint toward Trump. On the contrary, they are offended by Trump's behavior *as Christians*. And Clint believes that professing Christians may either be lacking Christian values entirely or intentionally suppressing them to ensure that someone more committed to restoring their cultural power remains in office. The evidence says as much. Simply put, when it comes to Trump support, speaking in terms of Ambassadors and Accommodators, Resisters and Rejecters, is much more accurate than speaking in terms of "white evangelicals."

THE SWIRLING VORTEX OF "TRUMPOLITICS" AND CHRISTIAN NATIONALISM

Ambassadors, Accommodators, Resisters, and Rejecters all play key roles in understanding Trump's win in 2016 and the support he continues to enjoy. Christian nationalism not only describes a set of views Americans have about their national history; it powerfully predicts their voting behavior. But, as in any election, policies matter, too. "Trumpolitics," or Trump's populist strategy to target a core set of controversial political issues to mobilize his base, continues to play an important role in explaining Trump support. Looking at four such issues, we argue that their connection to Trump travels through Christian nationalism.[25]

TRAVEL BANS, REFUGEES FROM THE MIDDLE EAST, AND TERRORISM

The geopolitical realities of the Middle East are incredibly complicated. The United States is involved in several conflicts in the region, and the war in Iraq now nears its third decade. These wars have resulted in some changes in leadership but have proved costly both in terms of civilian and military lives and in investment. Following the vacuum of leadership resulting from the destabilization of governments and institutions in Libya, Yemen, and Syria, the slew of civil wars and atrocities visited on those living in these regions created the worst refugee crisis in Europe since World War II. Millions of civilians fled the carnage in an effort to gain asylum and some semblance of peace. While many reached Europe, thousands of refugees perished in route; others fell victim to human traffickers. The refugees that survive this trip have not always been welcomed with open arms into various European countries or the United States. While thousands of refugees have been resettled, just as many have been turned away. The argument over how many refugees from the Middle East the United States should accept, or even if they should be allowed to resettle here at all, has been a key political issue since the 2016 election.

During the campaign, Trump and others repeatedly claimed that accepting refugees from the Middle East put Americans at a greater risk of terrorism. As former congresswoman and proponent of Christian nationalism Michele Bachmann claimed, "We bring in all these refugees . . . the largest pipeline for bringing Muslims into the United States. We know, without a doubt, that there is an intentional invasion and an effort to bring radical Islam into the United States . . . the more legislation that we put in to stop all of this immigration from terrorist-oriented countries the American people will say, 'Thank you. It's about time.'"[26] As a candidate, Trump promised that refugees and immigrants from places like Syria and Libya (both Muslim-majority countries) would be denied entry. Trump also suggested screening tests that would include "ideological certification" to ensure that immigrants "share our values and love our people."[27] It was thus unsurprising that soon after he was elected Trump drastically reduced the number of refugees who would be admitted to the United States and issued several executive orders and travel bans aimed at countries that were for the most part majority Muslim.[28]

Trump's continued warnings against refugees, especially those from the Middle East, do not fall on deaf ears. Pairing his promises to restore the cultural and political fortunes of conservative Christians with outright opposition toward cultural outsiders resonates with Ambassadors and Accommodators. Figure 2.3 shows that a greater percentage of Americans in these two groups agree that refugees from the Middle East pose a terrorist threat to the United States. Even when we account for political party and ideology, a host of socio-demographics, and religiosity, the probability of agreeing that refugees from the Middle East pose a terrorism threat increases in lockstep with Christian nationalism.[29]

In fact, across the four orientations to Christian nationalism, beliefs about refugees from the Middle East reveal stark differences between even those Americans who tend to be more supportive of Christian nationalism (Ambassadors and Accommodators) and those who tend to oppose it (Rejecters and Resisters).[30] Just as with Trump support in general, evangelicals who do not adhere to Christian nationalism seem to hold completely different views about Muslim refugees. As Deb, an evangelical and Resister pointed out, "If we were truly a 'Christian nation,' we would be welcoming refugees."

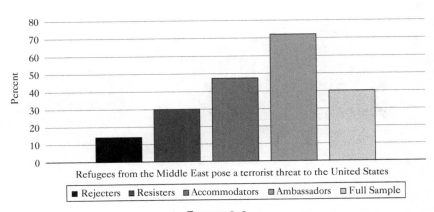

FIGURE 2.3.

Variation in Americans' Agreement with Fear of Muslim Refugees for Ambassadors, Accommodators, Resisters, and Rejecters

Sources: 2017 Baylor Religion Survey.

Christian nationalism also helps us understand why Trump supporters would be so enthusiastic about the idea of imposing a travel ban that not only disproportionately affects Muslims abroad but also impacts American Muslims. These individuals may have family they are now unable to see or who fear that they cannot go back home lest they be denied reentry into the country. Simply put, Americans who adhere more strongly to Christian nationalism are generally more comfortable with restricting the political freedoms and civil liberties of Muslims, whom they deem as a threat to social order.[31] The 2014 General Social Survey (GSS) includes three questions about the extent to which Americans would allow a Muslim clergyman who is openly hostile to the United States to make a public speech, teach at a university, or have a book in a public library. The survey also includes a question about how important Americans feel being a Christian is to being "truly American" (see Figure 2.4). Clearly, as Americans more strongly equate Christian identity with American civic belonging, their willingness to deny the free speech of hostile Muslims increases considerably. Also important, being an evangelical Protestant, a Republican, or political conservative had no discernable influence on any of these attitudes—only Christian nationalism does.[32]

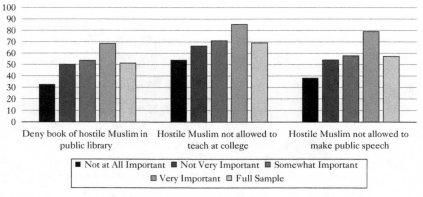

FIGURE 2.4.

Percent Who Would Deny Free Speech to Hostile Muslim Clergymen by How Important Americans Think Being a Christian Is to Being Truly American

Source: 2014 General Social Survey.

What do these findings mean in relation to support for Trumpolitics? It shows that preying on fear regarding terrorism and refugees from the Middle East is ultimately one part of a winning political strategy. Ambassadors and Accommodators are especially drawn to this narrative. Before the 2018 midterm elections, Trump referenced "Middle Easterners" as part of the threat of a migrant caravan that was making its way to the United States–Mexico border. Even though Trump's claim that refugees are a terror threat is objectively false—since 1980 not one person accepted as a refugee has even been implicated in a terror attack—the fears of cultural warfare persist. Even though close to one-third of refugees from the Middle East are actually Christians fleeing persecution, Trump and others believe that the refugee program could operate as a "Trojan horse" for terrorists. The objective realities regarding the terror threat associated with refugees from the Middle East will likely do little to sway the minds of those more committed to Christian nationalism.[33]

The United States Supreme Court and *Roe v. Wade*

From the late 1970s until today, perhaps no other issue has activated religious conservatives as powerfully and consistently as the 1973 *Roe v. Wade* decision legalizing abortion across the United States. This wasn't always the case. As numerous historians have shown, abortion was not a vital voting issue for many evangelicals before the rise of the Religious Right in 1979.[34] However, for the last four decades abortion has been a wedge issue. In the lead-up to the 2016 presidential election, Trump and his conservative Christian supporters routinely pointed to the Supreme Court vacancy as of paramount importance. In an interview with Christian television personality Pat Robertson, a noted promoter of Christian nationalism, Trump warned, "If we don't win this election . . . you'll have a whole different Supreme Court structure."[35]

The underlying reason the Supreme Court vacancy was so important, and why the Supreme Court is always at the forefront of the minds of those on the Christian Right in particular is that it is seen as the place where far-reaching decisions are made. These decisions can either defend a status quo that historically placed white, Christian men at the top of the social order, or it can progressively chip away at that order. Christian nationalists like political operative David Barton, former Republican congresswoman Michele Bachmann, and pastor Robert Jeffress above have long blamed secular, "activist judges" on the Supreme Court for progressive decisions on mandatory prayer and Bible reading in public schools, abortion, and most recently gay marriage.[36] Similarly, founder and former president of Focus on the Family James Dobson recalled that *Roe v. Wade* was put into place by "unelected, unaccountable, and imperialistic judges."[37] Predictably, Americans who share the beliefs of Barton, Bachmann, Jeffress, and Dobson are often quite suspicious of the Supreme Court. In the 2014 GSS, for example, we find that the more someone equates Christian identity with being "truly American," the less confidence they have in the Supreme Court.

Seeing the opportunity to shift the balance of power on the Supreme Court in 2016, Christian Right leaders stressed its importance. Dobson, for example, claimed that, "The next president will nominate perhaps three or more justices whose judicial philosophy will shape our country for generations to come." Evangelical theologian Wayne Grudem claimed that with Clinton as president the Supreme Court would be stocked with liberal judges who would "systematically impose every liberal policy on the nation," including striking down the ban on partial-birth abortion.[38] The Ambassadors we talked to felt similarly. Stanley, an Ambassador living in the South, shared, "The only thing I came to grips with voting that way [for Trump], versus the other [for Clinton] . . . it's around Supreme Court justice seats. That's what it came down to, for me." His choice was almost entirely about *Roe v. Wade*. "That court [the Supreme Court] has, in our world today, some of the biggest power . . . things ongoing for generations to come. *Roe v. Wade* was a big one, because I think that's going to be . . . our generation's slavery. We're just sitting here, and thousands and thousands of lives are being lost."

But as these quotes suggest, the connection between Trump support and concerns about abortion law are not entirely religious. Americans'

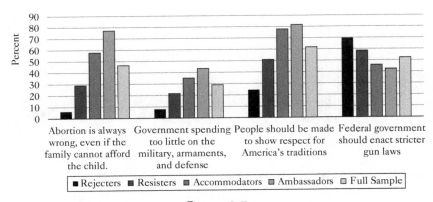

FIGURE 2.5.

Variations in Americans' Agreement with Additional Trumpolitics across Ambassadors, Accommodators, Resisters, and Rejecters

Source: 2017 Baylor Religion Survey.

views about abortion vary widely depending on whether they are a Rejecter, Resister, Accommodator, or Ambassador, *even after* we account for their level of religiosity, religious affiliation, beliefs about the Bible, and their political leanings. In fact, when we examine Americans' support for abortion in cases where the family cannot afford to raise a child (see Figure 2.5), only religious commitment is more predictive of their views than Christian nationalism.[39]

We also examined Americans' views toward abortion across a number of circumstances and how important they feel being a Christian is to being "truly American" using the 2014 GSS (see Figure 2.6). Yet again, as Americans more strongly equate Christian identity with American civic belonging their opposition to abortion increases no matter the situation, even when we account for all other explanations. Interestingly, the only time this isn't true is when the mother's health is in serious danger—Christian nationalism is unrelated. Americans' political ideology and attendance at religious services are the most important predictors in this instance. For all other situations, though, Christian nationalism was consistently one of the strongest predictors.[40]

So why would Christian nationalism still influence abortion attitudes even after the usual suspects like religiosity and political ideology have

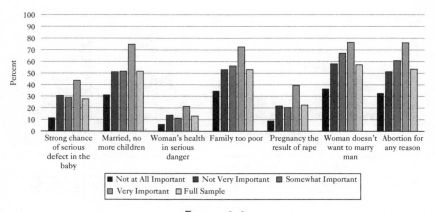

FIGURE 2.6.

Percent of Americans Who Oppose Abortion by How Important
Americans Think Being a Christian Is to Being Truly American

been accounted for? Ultimately, we contend the connection is found in
the identity itself and in Christian nationalism's commitment to male
authority over women's bodies. The latter issue we will take up at length
in chapter 4. But regarding the former, because "American Christian"
identity has become synonymous with an unequivocal pro-life stance,
Ambassadors and Accommodators of Christian nationalism, regardless
of their religious commitment or political leanings, equate a "Christian
society" with a world where abortion is no longer an option.

Knowing this helps explain the confluence of Trump's Christian nationalist rhetoric with promises about the Supreme Court. The Trump
campaign released a list of potential Supreme Court nominees before
the election. Exit polls showed that many more Trump voters than
Clinton voters viewed Supreme Court appointments as the most important factor in their decision.[41]

After winning the election, Trump chose a name from that list, Neil
Gorsuch, who later won Senate confirmation. Trump's usual evangelical supporters and Ambassadors of Christian nationalism were
ecstatic. Dobson was quick to commend Trump for delivering on a critical campaign promise. Dobson also spoke directly to Gorsuch, asking
him "to be unwavering in his commitment to the sanctity of human
life." Tony Perkins wrote that Gorsuch's swearing in was almost as

significant as Trump's.[42] Then, in June 2018, Justice Anthony Kennedy announced his retirement, allowing Trump another chance to nominate a United States Supreme Court Justice. Brett Kavanaugh was later confirmed after a volatile hearing. Not long after, a number of states passed laws criminalizing abortions performed after six weeks, or what their supporters called "fetal heartbeat bills." Anti-abortion advocates hope the court battles over these laws will conclude with the Supreme Court reconsidering *Roe v. Wade*. Those who supported Trump were delighted that the Supreme Court, now with a conservative majority, might now be able to restore America's lost godliness, defending the pre-born and protecting religious liberty.

There's Power in the Blood . . . and in the Flag

In the days leading up to Independence Day, congregations all across the United States celebrate in a variety of ways. Some, like First Baptist Dallas, dedicate an entire Sunday service to honoring the military and the country's freedom. Others band together and produce a special service for their community to attend. The largest congregations plan fireworks, cookouts, and a carnival-style atmosphere to honor America's "birthday." Many others, though, only mention Independence Day in passing, if at all.

We attended a handful of these services. What we saw was generally what you would expect: red, white, and blue everywhere; flags; classic songs celebrating America; the interweaving of Christian and American iconography; and salutes to the military. For the people in certain kinds of congregations, not only is the "Christian nation" narrative unquestioned, but true Christians recognize the freedoms Americans have been granted through a combination of God's grace and the blood of its patriots. Though perhaps not as aggressively as Robert Jeffress, most pastors and other speakers at the God and Country celebrations repeatedly pointed out the sacred nature of giving one's life to defend the United States. Many drew direct comparisons between the sacrifice of Jesus on the cross and the sacrifice of military women and men. For example, at one event, a retired Air Force chaplain prayed during the offering:

We can do nothing but thank thee, God, for the nearly 4 million service members, both men and women, who paid the ultimate sacrifice with their bodies and their blood for our freedoms today. Some of those great American patriots were from our own congregation. Oh Father, we thank you, for they set the support of the freedoms we enjoy this hour. Father, we thank you for Jesus Christ who extends eternal freedom, complete freedom. For the sacred Scripture says, "If Christ shall set you free, you shall be free indeed."

Sociologist Philip Gorski explains that Christian nationalism is heavily connected to the idea of blood, both as a sign of ethno-national purity (thus the connection between Christian nationalism, racism, and xenophobia that we will explore in greater depth in the next chapter) but also in terms of bloody conquest and sacrifice in war.[43] Consequently, parallels like the one drawn in this prayer between Jesus's blood shed for believers and the blood of patriots shed for Americans' freedoms find tremendous resonance.

Surveys affirm this connection, showing that Ambassadors and Accommodators elevate the military and military service to sacred status. There is a powerful link between Christian nationalist beliefs and believing that God's people must fight wars for good (Table I.1) or that truly moral people must serve in the military (Table I.2). Data from the BRS also show that Ambassadors and Accommodators are more likely than Resisters or Rejecters to say the government spends too little on defense (see Figure 2.5).[44] Together these findings give us some indication why Ambassadors and Accommodators supported Trump in 2016 election and continue to support him. As Trump himself proclaimed, "There's nobody bigger or better at the military than I am."[45] Trump repeatedly states his intention to increase spending for the military and defense, and his speeches regularly declare support for veterans. While Trump's "America First" rhetoric led some to worry that a withdrawal from the world stage would lead to a shrinking defense budget, one year into his presidency America's military budget dramatically increased.[46]

But just as Christian nationalism holds sacrifice on behalf of the nation to be sacred, it also connects this divine militarism with the sacred symbols and rituals of American civil religion. Americans' orientations toward Christian nationalism are among the strongest predictors of their propensity to demand that everyone show respect for America's traditions (see Figure 2.5).[47] For some Americans—especially post 9/11—pledging allegiance, standing for the national anthem, and saluting the flag each evoke respect and admiration for the military and those who "paid the ultimate price" for American freedom. Trump himself has claimed, "You have to stand proudly for the national anthem" and has suggested that disrespecting the American flag should cost people their jobs.[48] This is one reason why President Trump and his supporters expressed such outrage as various National Football League (NFL) players knelt in silent protest during the national anthem during the 2016 and 2017 seasons. While the players clearly stated that they were trying to raise awareness of inequalities in police violence toward African American men, Trump and others equated the players' kneeling with disrespect toward military veterans.[49]

Many Ambassadors we interviewed felt equally strongly about respecting the flag and the national anthem, equating failing to do so with dishonoring the military. A veteran and Ambassador named Todd explained, "I took personal offense there. I find that highly offensive. And that's a tough one, because I do think, you know, freedom of speech. But I tie the American flag to the military, and the military is the only reason that we have the freedoms we have. So, I'm personally offended." Likewise, Elena, an Ambassador from central Oklahoma, was particularly scathing:

First of all, Colin Kaepernick is a doofus. If he was a good football player, somebody would've picked him up by now. Him kneeling because of the oppression people are feeling, well, that's just a cop out . . . He doesn't know what true oppression is. If he did, then with his money would do something to help the matter, instead of just kneeling for the flag. You stand at the flag and you kneel at the cross. You do not . . . that's just disrespectful to our veterans who have fought and died for your right to do that. Okay?

There is perhaps no better encapsulation of Christian nationalism than "You stand at the flag and you kneel at the cross."[50]

President Trump was no less scathing in his criticisms of kneeling NFL players. On separate occasions Trump called the players "sons of bitches" and suggested those kneeling "maybe shouldn't be in the country," clearly drawing the boundary of American identity around ritual displays of patriotism.[51] Yet, while Trump received widespread criticism for his vulgarity and attack on free speech, pastor Robert Jeffress—a member of Trump's evangelical advisory board—publicly defended his comments on national television. Like Elena, Jeffress questioned whether the NFL players truly had anything to complain about, explaining, "These players ought to be thanking God that they live in a country where they're not only free to earn millions of dollars every year, but they're also free from the worry of being shot in the head for taking the knee like they would be in North Korea." The irony of these comments is the well-documented fact that unarmed black men *do* stand a much greater chance of being shot by police, the very thing the players were trying to highlight to the broader public.[52] Jeffress later doubled-down on his comments, adding, "All of us should thank God every day we live in a country where we do not have to fear government persecution for expressing our beliefs."[53]

"THOUGHTS AND PRAYERS," BUT NOT GUN CONTROL

"You came through for me and I am going to come through for you!" Donald Trump promised attendees at the 2017 National Rifle Association (NRA) annual convention. On the campaign trail the NRA "came through" for Trump to the tune of $30 million worth of contributions.[54] Part of Trump's appeal to the NRA and other gun rights advocates has been his Christian nationalist rhetoric. Following the February 2018 mass shooting at Stoneman Douglas High School in Parkland, Florida, that killed 17 students and teachers, scores of politicians responded with public statements that their "thoughts and prayers" were with the victims and their families. Yet when the Florida state House of Representatives had the opportunity to consider gun control legislation one week after the Parkland school shooting, they declined.[55] (In the name of public health, however, they did pass a referendum declaring pornography harmful.) Instead, these Florida legislators overwhelmingly passed a bill that required "In God We Trust" to be posted across all Florida public schools in a prominent place. In interviews, the Democratic sponsor of the bill, Kim Daniels, acknowledged that Florida's gun laws should be addressed. However, she and other representatives believed that Florida schools "need light in them like never before" and that God "is the light." According to Daniels, in order to solve gun violence in schools and communities like Parkland, "the real thing that needs to be addressed are issues of the heart."[56]

Two weeks after the Parkland school shooting, state senators in Alabama passed a bill that allowed for the display of the Ten Commandments in public schools. While Republican Gerald Dial had been promoting this bill for years, Dial argued the bill now carried with it an added significance. "I believe that if you had the Ten Commandments posted in a prominent place in school, it has the possibility to prohibit some student from taking action to kill other students . . . If this bill stops one school shooting in Alabama, just one, then it's worth the time and effort we're putting into it," Dial said. These legislators were driven by the belief that only by raising the profile of Christianity in the public sphere could we begin to see a decrease in such despicable acts of violence. Beyond this bill, there were no plans to consider other gun control legislation.[57] Wayne LaPierre—the executive officer of the NRA—also made a spirited case against gun control. While speaking at a conservative political conference, LaPierre claimed that the Second Amendment of the Constitution was "not bestowed by man, but granted by God to all Americans as our American birthright." Thus efforts to restrict Americans' access to firearms was akin to opposing God's will for the United States.

Three months after Parkland there was another mass shooting, this time at a high school in Santa Fe, Texas. One Christian radio host explicitly asked whether "taking God out of schools" was leading to more school shootings. He pointed to the fact that in 1995 a judge had ruled that a Santa Fe high school could not offer a prayer to the Christian God or Jesus in a graduation service. In his view, this directly contradicted the free exercise of religion as protected by the First Amendment. This commentator posited that the "ACLU and the liberal judges that support their misreading of American history have turned many of our public schools into godless wastelands." He wondered whether the Santa Fe school shooting was a consequence of the judge's decision back in 1995. "Thoughts and prayers" he wrote, "are not a trivial distraction, but in the long run a major part of the solution."[58]

These recent responses to school shootings connecting Christian nationalism with an unwillingness to consider stronger gun laws are reflected in national data.[59] In Figure 2.5 it is clear that Rejecters and Resisters are more likely to agree that the federal government should enact stricter gun control legislation, while Ambassadors and Accommodators are not, even after accounting for Americans' political and religious characteristics.[60]

Why is this the case? First, and most obviously, Christian nationalism sacralizes America's founding documents. As LaPierre's quote above suggests, Ambassadors and Accommodators are highly sensitive to any infringements on their God-given Second Amendment rights. Rafael Cruz, pastor and father of Senator Ted Cruz, explains, "Note that the Second Amendment calls keeping and bearing arms a right that 'shall not be infringed.' It assumes that *you already have that right*, because it is intrinsic in the 'unalienable' right to life with which we have been 'endowed by our Creator.' "[61] But just as important, as their enthusiastic support for "wars for good," military spending, and military service would suggest, Ambassadors and Accommodators feel that the solution to societal disorder is not to remove the possibility of violence (which is ultimately impossible because of sin in the world) but to control it with the righteous violence of free, law-abiding citizens. This view is reflected in the mantra, here repeated by Mike Huckabee, "[T]he best way to stop a bad person with a gun is to have a good person with a weapon that is equal or superior to the one that he's using."[62]

Related to this is the *formation* of "bad guys" and "good guys." Christian nationalism sees societal decadence and chaos (including violence) as inevitable when Christian cultural values disappear from America's schools and Americans' hearts. Indeed, in some sense, these instances of gun violence confirm what Christian nationalists believe; they are further evidence of society's moral decay following the removal of prayer and Bible reading from public schools and God's commandments from America's court houses.[63] Consequently, the preferred solution to gun violence is to protect the gun rights of American citizens and encourage the reintroduction of Christian values into the public sphere—both possibilities they believe may be realized only by continuing Trump's presidency.

"WHITE CHRISTIAN AMERICA" AND SUPPORT FOR TRUMPOLITICS

Finally, the current state of our discourse regarding white Christians' support for Trump and his politics would benefit from greater precision. The high levels of support Trump enjoys among white Christians are due to the higher than average levels of Christian nationalism among white Christians. As Figure 2.7 shows, white Christians who are Resisters or Rejecters of Christian nationalism similarly resist and

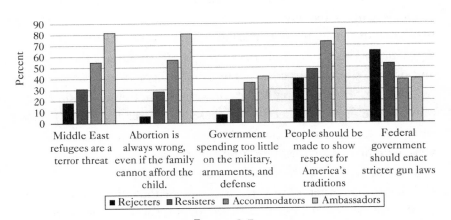

FIGURE 2.7.

White Christians' Views toward Trumpolitics across Christian Nationalism Orientations

Source: 2007 & 2017 Baylor Religion Surveys.

reject Trumpolitics. In other words, it's not "white Christians" who support Trump overwhelmingly, it's a particular subset of white Christians who embrace Christian nationalism.

WHEN IT COMES TO POLITICS, CHRISTIAN NATIONALISM AND RELIGIOUS COMMITMENT ARE NOT THE SAME

There is a fascinating paradox at the heart of Christian nationalism—one that we will return to throughout the book. As we saw in the previous chapter (see Table 1.2), those Americans who most strongly espouse Christian nationalist beliefs also tend to be the most religious as measured by activities like church attendance, prayer, and Scripture reading. Christian nationalism and personal religiosity are strongly correlated, in other words. Yet it would be a mistake to conclude that these two characteristics, because they appear so related, influence Americans' political views in similar ways. In fact, the great paradox is that Christian nationalism and religiosity often influence Americans political views *in the exact opposite direction.*

To illustrate, let's return to three political issues that were powerfully associated with Christian nationalism (see Figures 2.3 and 2.5). As Americans show greater agreement with Christian nationalism, they are more likely to view Muslim refugees as terrorist threats, agree that citizens should be made to show respect for America's traditions, and oppose stricter gun control laws. But as Americans become more religious in terms of attendance, prayer, and Scripture reading, they move in the opposite direction on these issues (see Figure 2.8). These situations are not anomalous. In fact, the crisscrossing pattern we observe here holds true for other political issues.

Why is this important? Obviously it would be a mistake for sociologists or other observers to conclude that "religious commitment" necessarily inclines Americans to hold more conservative political positions. In fact, religious commitment often appears to do the opposite. This should be welcome news for those who fear religion is a barrier to promoting greater tolerance and ushering in what they

84

(a) Refugees from the Middle East pose a terrorist threat to the
United States

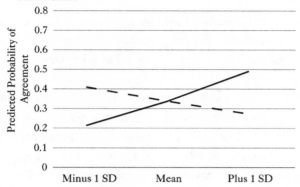

(b) People should be made to show respect for America's traditions

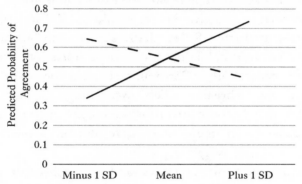

(c) Federal government should enact stricter gun laws.

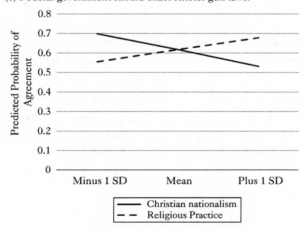

Christian nationalism
Religious Practice

FIGURE 2.8.

Opposing Influences of Christian Nationalism and Religious Practice

believe to be more equitable, humane government policies. Rather, religiosity, and by extension devoutly religious persons, may desire similar outcomes—that is, once other factors like Christian nationalism are taken into account.

But more than this, we want to stress the uniqueness of Christian nationalism as a cultural framework, distinguishing it from "religion" per se. Put simply, Christian nationalism does not encourage high moral standards or value self-sacrifice, peace, mercy, love, justice, and so on. Nor does it necessarily encourage conforming one's political opinions to those that Jesus might have. In a 2018 interview with *The New York Times*, Jerry Falwell Jr. stated plainly, "I don't look to the teachings of Jesus for what my political beliefs should be."[64] Think back on the excerpts we shared from Robert Jeffress's Freedom Sunday sermon. There were no spiritual applications or exhortations to grow in Christian obedience. Rather, Christian nationalist appeals to "Christian foundations" and "Christian beliefs" were more like code words for a way of life that is "ours" (read: white conservative Christians) by divine right and which "the secularists, the humanists, the atheists, the infidels" want to take away.

This distinction helps us understand why Christian nationalist rhetoric reemerges every four years during presidential campaigns or during times of heightened cultural conflict. It helps us understand why Ambassadors of Christian nationalism vote for famously impious and immoral candidates while also consistently taking particular stances on social and political issues. Appeals to someone's religion, in this case Christianity, *may* involve a plea to live out transcendent Christian values of love, mercy, or justice. Appeals to Christian nationalism, by contrast, involve either a proprietary claim or a call to arms, always in response to a perceived threat. In short, Christian nationalism is all about power.

CONCLUSION

Twenty years ago, Christian Smith argued that conservative Christians' calls to "take America back for God" were *really* about religious renewal and personal transformation rather than political power. We beg to differ. Though we certainly agree with Smith that many evangelicals and otherwise committed, conservative Christians are primarily concerned with living out their faith as individuals, Americans who most enthusiastically affirm Christian nationalist ideals seem to put political power above religion. As Rogers Brubaker explains in reference to Europe's own emergent strains of Christian nationalism,

> The Christianity invoked by the national populists . . . is not a substantive Christianity; it is a "secularized Christianity-as-culture" . . . a civilizational and identitarian "Christianism." It is a matter of belonging rather than believing, a way of defining "us" in relation to "them."[65]

This perfectly represents what we observe in American Christian nationalism. Christian nationalism mobilizes Americans to take positions on issues and rally behind candidates that will defend their cultural preferences, preserve their political influence, and maintain the "proper" social order.

We have also seen that while Christian nationalism is most prevalent among white Christians, and specifically white evangelicals, the two are not synonymous and conflating the two is unnecessarily misleading. Indeed, evangelical Rejecters and Resisters likely have more in common politically with unaffiliated Rejecters and Resisters than they do with other evangelicals. Likewise, the source of Christian nationalism's influence in the political realm is not "religious" in essence, since personal religiosity often tends to influence Americans to hold more progressive stances on political issues, once Christian nationalism is taken into account. Rather, Christian nationalism uses Christian language and symbols to demarcate and defend group boundaries and privileges. In the next chapter, we'll demonstrate how Christian nationalism characteristically extends the definitions of "us" and "them" beyond mere religious identities to include other markers of *true* American citizenship.

CHAPTER 3

BOUNDARIES

Ambassadors of Christian nationalism are fond of boundaries—both physical and symbolic—preferably fortified by barriers. Gabe is a straight-shooting 35-year-old youth pastor at an Assemblies of God church in Noble, Oklahoma. Sitting at a tiny table in a cramped Starbucks, Gabe explained with confidence, "our country was founded on Christian values . . . our forefathers, many of them adhered to at least conservative beliefs . . . they all put value in the fact that God was part of this [nation]." Given Gabe's convictions about America's Christian heritage, we asked him how a Christian should think about things like immigration and border walls. He sat pensively for a moment and stated simply, "Well, I think God is a God of borders." When asked to elaborate, he explained this in terms of God wanting protection for innocent people: "I'm probably more conservative than most people on that. I am for the wall. I think it's a great idea. I don't feel like, to me, the wall is not going to keep *good* people out. It's a safety issue." For Gabe, securing the border with a physical barrier is consistent with his understanding of a God who, in his words, favors "structure," "parameters," and "guardrails" that keep the good people safe from menacing influences, whatever or whomever they may be.

Ethan is a Baptist father of three living near Tulsa. Also an enthusiastic Ambassador, Ethan believes "you could go back to the Bible and have strong evidence that our borders should be secure." Referencing the Old Testament book of Nehemiah, which says that the Israelites were charged with rebuilding the walls around Jerusalem, Ethan argued, "You can't read the book of Nehemiah, I don't think, without coming away with the thought that God really wanted that wall to be built . . . How do you reconcile that? It's like 'God is my fortress, God is my strength,' and [people could say] 'Maybe you should just trust in God more, you know? And that will take care of your enemies.' But no, if you look at Nehemiah it's like they actually *built a wall* that would've kept out people that were harassing them." Like Gabe, Ethan sees no ethical conflict with a Christian nation sealing off its borders to outsiders. In fact, the wall merely symbolizes the protection God himself provides for his people. It is *because* "God is our fortress" that America should protect its boundaries.

Prominent Christian nationalists echo Gabe and Ethan's theology. On his radio program, president of the aptly named "WallBuilders" ministry David Barton stressed, "It's God, not man, who establishes the borders of nations . . . When the Most High gave the nations their inheritance, when he divided all mankind, he's the one who set up the boundaries for the nations. National boundaries are set by God; he is the one who drew up the lines for the nations. If you have open borders you say, 'God, you goofed it all up.' " Others, prompted by the political battle over the Mexican border, cite biblical precedent for building a physical wall. Franklin Graham reminded the Christian news site Faithwire, "Jerusalem had walls . . . the pope lives behind the wall." Citing another example, frequent Fox & Friends contributor pastor Robert Jeffress explained in an interview, "The Bible says Heaven itself is gonna have a wall around it. Not everybody is going to be allowed in. So if walls are immoral, then God is immoral." And theologian Wayne Grudem wrote an entire op-ed arguing, "the Bible views border walls as a morally good thing, something for which to thank God. Walls on a border are a major deterrent to evil and they provide clear visible evidence that *a city or nation has control over who enters it*." To all these men, walls are good and godly because they keep the good people (Americans) safe.[1] They keep undesirables (everyone else) out. They are about control.

None of this is new, of course. Walls in centuries past were erected and reinforced with cultural symbols of group membership rather than brick and rebar. In fact, the deliberate exclusion of ethnic and religious outsiders from American civic life is as fundamental to our history as the Declaration of Independence or the Constitution. Indeed, it precedes our very existence. European colonies—famous for expelling persons on the basis of religion alone—felt little obligation to incorporate America's indigenous persons as they would fellow white Europeans since, along with their lack of Christian faith, they allegedly lacked the white man's respect for property rights and hierarchical order.[2] Anti-Catholic prejudice bordering on hysteria played no small role in generating support for independence among American colonists in the early 1770s and would later foment nativist riots driven by opposition to Catholic immigration to the United States.[3] Our very Constitution originally stipulated that black slaves were to be counted as three-fifths of a person. Seventy years later the Supreme Court of the United States doubled down on this idea in the Dred Scott decision of 1857, concluding that black people "are not included, and were not intended to be included, under the word 'citizens' in the Constitution, and can therefore claim none of the rights and privileges which that instrument provides for and secures to citizens of the United States."[4]

What Eurocentrism, anti-Catholicism, xenophobia, and the disenfranchisement of black Americans have in common is that each reflects a general understanding of American civic belonging—namely, that *real* Americans are native-born white Protestants. This ideology has been wholly preserved in contemporary Christian nationalism. Surveys show that, in general, Americans' visions of cultural belonging are expanding to include immigrants, Catholics, and ethno-racial minorities (at least in the past few decades).[5] Yet Americans who embrace Christian nationalism, particularly if they are white, remain committed to the belief that *real* Americans—or at least "the good kind" of Americans—are native-born, white, Christians. Americans who reject or resist Christian nationalism, by contrast, are much more likely to have expansive views of American identity and who should be allowed to come here.

In this chapter we consider how the embrace of Christian nationalism provides the cultural materials used to build walls around American identity, walls that exclude ethnic or religious outsiders. We will also hear how the rejection of this cultural framework leaves Americans much more open to racial and religious diversity. Here we are dealing with something very near the core of Christian nationalism itself. Indeed, some scholars believe endorsing Christian nationalism—again, particularly for white Americans—is *essentially* about white (Christian) supremacy and ethno-religious exclusion.[6] We argue that Christian nationalism is broader than this—it also involves conceptions of gender subordination, sexual morality, and authoritarian control more generally—but it has a powerful influence on Americans' views about ethnic and religious "others." Understanding Christian nationalism is essential to understanding recurrent conflicts over immigration, anti-black prejudice, Islamophobia, anti-Semitism, and even stigma directed toward atheists.

"BAD HOMBRES," "RAPISTS," "TERRORISTS," "GANG MEMBERS"

Because support for Christian nationalism, as we saw above, favors boundaries of all sorts and especially national boundaries, it naturally breeds xenophobia (by which we mean an irrational fear or antipathy regarding immigrants that leads one to exclude them from group membership). Figure 3.1 presents recent data from the General Social Survey showing how the percentage of Americans who affirm negative

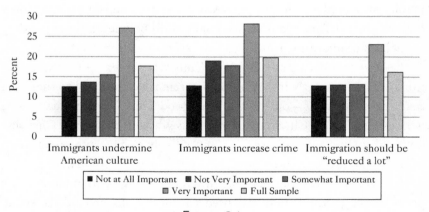

FIGURE 3.1.

Percent of Americans Who Hold Anti-Immigrant Attitudes by Belief in the Importance of Being a Christian to Being Truly American

Source: 2014 General Social Survey.

stereotypes about immigrants and believe the number of immigrants coming into the United States should be "strongly reduced" correlates with how important they think being a Christian is to being "truly American." Clearly, as Americans more closely connect Christian identity with American civic belonging they become more likely to believe that immigrants undermine American culture and increase crime rates. Unsurprisingly, they are also all the more eager to reduce immigration into the United States.[7]

We find an identical pattern when we look at our four orientations toward Christian nationalism (Figure 3.2, left side). Accommodators and Ambassadors of Christian nationalism are much more likely than Rejecters and Resisters to agree that "illegal immigrants from Mexico are mostly dangerous criminals." In fact, the odds of Ambassadors agreeing with this view are six times higher than Rejecters and almost four times higher than Resisters. Ambassadors are even significantly more likely to agree than Accommodators.[8] While none of these percentages approaches a majority, it is nonetheless striking to think that nearly one-quarter of Ambassadors sincerely feel that *most* illegal immigrants from Mexico are dangerous criminals.

Given this propensity to believe negative stereotypes about Mexican immigrants it should be no surprise that Ambassadors like Gabe and

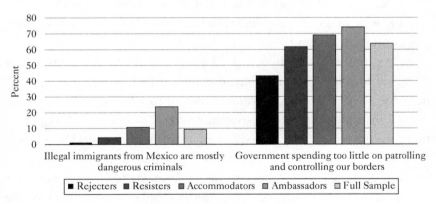

FIGURE 3.2.

Variation in Americans' Agreement with Stereotypes about Illegal Mexican Immigrants and Statements on Border Patrol Spending

Sources: 2017 & 2007 Baylor Religion Surveys.

Ethan wish the borders were better defended. When we look at data from the 2007 Baylor Religion Survey (Figure 3.2, right side), we find that Ambassadors and Accommodators are both more likely than Resisters and Rejecters to believe that the government is spending "too little on patrolling and controlling" our national borders.[9] The operative word in that statement is "controlling." If Americans in stronger agreement with Christian nationalism perceive that outsiders pose a critical threat to law and order, the economy, and American culture, their answer is to control their access with vigilance.

Trump's promises to reign in America's southern border are a key reason Christian nationalists voted so strongly for him and continue to be his most ardent supporters. At the press conference where he announced his candidacy, Donald Trump remarked that, "When Mexico sends its people, they're not sending their best. They're bringing drugs. They're bringing crime. They're rapists. And some, I assume, are good people." Throughout his campaign he returned to this theme, stressing walls and deportation. "We're going to secure the border, and once the border is secured at a later date, we'll make a determination as to the rest," Trump explained at his final presidential debate. "But we have some bad hombres here and we're going to get them out."[10] All of this was to great effect. Numerous polls before and after the November 2016 election showed fear or distrust of immigrants crossing the border illegally was among the strongest predictors of supporting, and eventually voting for, Trump.[11]

Before the 2018 midterms Trump and many in the GOP again appealed to a fear of immigrants coming to the United States and the need for a secure border, this time pointing to a "caravan" of Central Americans making their way north, most of whom were thought to be refugees and were hundreds of miles away from the US–Mexico border.[12] Regardless of the actual threat, Trump's rhetoric about the caravan appealed to the fears of many Ambassadors like Elena, one of our more strident interviewees. Comparing her immigration stance with those of her "lefty" Catholic friend who wanted to let the Central American refugees across the border, Elena argued,

If we don't vet [people] who knows what we'll be letting in? Who's to say that they're all from Honduras? There can be other people that are in that caravan, and we just don't know. Just like there are probably people in that caravan who are not on the up and up, in other words there's probably criminals, pedophiles, gang members, drug dealers, whatever. Why do we want to let that in? The way I look at it as a Christian is, it's very difficult, because I think we need the wall, and because we have to protect ourselves. If you look up Saint Thomas Aquinas, and his stance, and the church's stance on immigration, is we have a right to protect ourselves. Our president, just like our forefathers saw 200 and some odd years ago, have the right to do that . . . I'm protecting my family. As a Christian mother, I will do whatever it takes to protect my children.

Elena first connects the need for a wall of defense around the border with suspicion that there are likely dangerous criminals mixed in with the refugees. Her reference to Thomas Aquinas comes from his *Summa Theologica* in which he argues that the people of Israel were selective about the foreigners they let within their community on the grounds that God did not view other nations equally and some were more quickly assimilated into community life than others.[13] Citing her role as a mother, Elena also argues that Christians have the right to defend those they love from threats. Some Ambassadors, like pastor and Trump's spiritual adviser Paula White, even argue that stronger border security protects undocumented immigrants and refugees as well, since it will deter them from risking life and limb to cross the border. During an interview in which she lauded conditions in a migrant detention center, White explained, "If we are going to be compassionate, we have to have stricter border security and laws."[14]

Resisters and Rejecters also emphasize the role of fear in understanding Ambassadors' and Accommodators' support for walls and border control. Deb, a white married Resister from the Midwest and leader in her church pointed out that "They are fearful of a society that doesn't reflect what they think it should. They are fearful of losing their own power of white middle-class . . . or of having someone below them that makes them feel better about themselves. They are fearful of

God's judgment on us as a nation. Fear is what's being promoted right now. Fear of losing power. Fear of the other." Sharon, a Rejecter from the Southwest who grew up in a very religious home, shared this view. She questions how much of the "wall" rhetoric was actually based on scripture, rather than fear: "It's kind of a Petri dish for unbridled fear of people that are not like us. A fear of the other. And so I don't necessarily think it's based in scripture from what I've heard from folks . . . . I'll be honest with you, I can't square that. I don't know how they rationalize that viewpoint because in my opinion, from what I've learned as a Christian, in my Christian roots growing up, that's totally opposite of anything that Christianity teaches."

The position of the Trump administration toward undocumented immigrants reached a breaking point in the summer of 2018. It was then that the administration's newly instituted policy of separating immigrant children from their parents—introduced in April 2018—began to gain much more media attention. The institution of this policy was basically an effort to deter immigrants from coming, something which both the leaders of the Justice Department and the Department of Homeland Security defended. Jeff Sessions, then attorney general, even cited the New Testament to a group of Christian leaders as justification for the government's practice of familial separation. He claimed, "I would cite you to the Apostle Paul and his clear and wise command in Romans 13, to obey the laws of the government because God has ordained them for the purpose of order. Orderly and lawful processes are good in themselves and protect the weak and lawful." Then Press Secretary Sarah Huckabee Sanders reiterated this claim, stating that, "It is very biblical to enforce the law."[15] For many Ambassadors and Accommodators, these references to the Christian Bible were probably enough to affirm their support for this practice. Lori, an Ambassador from the Midwest, agreed with Sessions' sentiment. She shared that "As a Christian nation we have a higher bar because we are called to higher standards. There's laws and there's reasons why things are in place so that we don't have total chaos . . . we've got to take people in our country the legal way."

While President Trump's dog-whistle references to illegal immigrants throughout his campaign and presidency have often stressed *Latino* criminality, he has also signaled to Americans that those attempting to cross the Mexican border illegally include Muslim terrorists. Trump posted in a January 2019 tweet: "Border rancher: 'We've found prayer rugs out here. It's unreal.' Washington Examiner: People coming across the Southern Border from many countries, some of which would be a big surprise." In light of the "prayer rugs" reference, "many countries" is an unmistakable allusion to Muslim-majority countries, the inhabitants of whom Trump believes might be terrorists. Many Americans have internalized these fears of illegal Muslim immigration.[16] Todd, an army veteran, gun rights enthusiast, and long-time children's Sunday school teacher, explained his own reason for wanting stronger borders.

TODD: [A] lot of the people that are coming through as immigrants right now actually, I believe want to harm the United States violently. . . . This immigration could rip our country completely apart.

SAM: I just want to make sure I heard you right. You feel like most of the people trying to come into our country now *do* want to do us harm?

TODD: Correct.

SAM: Okay, out of curiosity, where do you get that perception from?

TODD: Well, it wasn't *just* . . . don't get me wrong there's probably more people . . . I should backtrack a little bit. Probably more people that just want a better life. But, there's a significant number of serious refugees from the Arab nations that are militant . . . I have a friend who was a state congressman for eight years. He was telling me about the different number of Muslim groups that are here in the state of Oklahoma. There's actually a very large one, the largest one is the northern area. So there's a lot of activity here in just this state. We're in the center of the US. I don't think it's a paranoia, anymore. It's a fact that lots of people have been moved in already. How this plays out, nobody knows.

Why do Americans who embrace Christian nationalism seem so willing to entertain negative stereotypes of ethnic and religious outsiders and prevent their entrance in the country? Why are those who reject or resist Christian nationalism much more open to accepting refugees and immigrants? Part of the answer, we argue, is that Christian nationalism gives divine sanction to ethnocentrism and nativism. Recall that prominent Ambassadors rationalized stronger borders on the grounds that God himself uses walls to protect and preserve his people (Americans, the good guys) from threats. For some, then, Christian theology is inherently compatible with exclusion and protectionism. But from what? Non-Christian influences? Surely not. A higher percentage of Mexicans coming across the border—a growing number of whom are evangelical Protestants—are professing Christians than are the white Americans on the other side.[17] While Ambassadors and Accommodators may not say this explicitly, it is likely that biblical justifications are simply masking ethno-racial understandings of "us" and "them." In effect, Christian nationalism lets them neutralize disputed assumptions about American identity and who belongs by cloaking their views in religious symbolism.

We can see this clearly in how Christian nationalism predicts beliefs about who *real* Americans are. Figure 3.3 shows the percentage of Americans who believe it is "very important" to have been born in

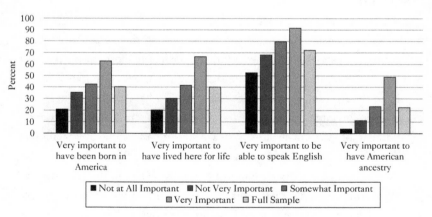

FIGURE 3.3.

Percent of Americans Who Believe in the Importance of American Birth, Lifelong Residence, English Speaking, and American Ancestry to Being Truly American by Belief in the Importance of Being a Christian to Being Truly American

Source: 2014 General Social Survey.

America, lived here one's whole life, speak English, or have American ancestry to be considered "truly American."[18] The trends are strikingly clear. As being a Christian becomes a more important marker of national belonging, the likelihood increases that adults feel that *true* Americans are those who were born here, lived here their whole lives, are able to speak English, and have American ancestry.[19] Stated in reverse, those who see being "Christian" as central to being "American" are highly resistant to the idea that immigrants—even Christians who have been here for years—those who cannot speak English, and those without an American ancestor can be "truly American." They are indelibly "them," not "us."

RACIAL BOUNDARIES AND RACIAL SUBORDINATION IN A CHRISTIAN NATION

The social and political exclusion of black Americans throughout our nation's history was consistently supported through appeals to Christianity.[20] The seeds of this history were planted very early on, as European colonists in North America developed religious and racial categories concurrently. Colonists believed in "hereditary heathenism," which held that religion—like physical characteristics—could be passed down to children. Thus, as historian Jemar Tisby shows, in America race was tightly tethered to religion from the beginning: "From their earliest days in North America, colonists employed religio-cultural categories to signify that European meant 'Christian' and . . . African meant 'heathen.' "[21] Unsurprisingly, then, race-based chattel slavery was often justified through a combination of white supremacy and Christian paternalism. Historian John Fea cites one minister who believed the South "had been called 'to conserve and to perpetuate the institution of slavery as now existing.' It was a duty to 'ourselves, to our slaves, to the world, and to almighty God.' "[22] For others, appeals to Christianity were merely cynical and transparent attempts to sanction the racial hierarchy. Frederick Douglass, for example, famously described the Christianity of the South as, "the justifier of the most appalling barbarity,—a sanctifier of the most hateful frauds,—and a dark shelter under, which the darkest, foulest, grossest, and most infernal deeds of slaveholders find the strongest protection."[23]

As Douglass points out, white Americans' claims to be preserving Christian order, America's Christian heritage, or even "religious freedom" have long served as coverings for what has amounted to the exclusion of nonwhite and especially black Americans.[24] In fact, historians like Randall Balmer trace the very birth of the Religious Right and its brand of Christian nationalism to a reaction to federal efforts to restrict the ability of conservative Christian schools to racially discriminate. During the early 1970s, when the IRS revoked Bob Jones University's tax-exempt status due to their racially discriminatory policies (like forbidding interracial dating), conservative Christian leaders interpreted this as an encroachment on their right to lead their religious academies as they saw fit.[25] Thus, it is no overstatement to suggest that much of the Christian nationalist rhetoric born out of the Religious Right finds its roots in the desire to create boundaries of group membership around race and the right of white Americans to segregate themselves from minorities.

National survey data support this conclusion. Take the issue at the heart of the white conservative reaction that birthed the Religious Right—interracial romance. In the 2007 Baylor Religion Survey, respondents were asked how comfortable they would be if their daughter married an African American. Figure 3.4 shows that the more strongly white Americans embrace Christian nationalism, the more likely they are to say they are "not at all comfortable" with their hypothetical daughter marrying someone who is black. There are even significant differences across the four orientations toward Christian nationalism.[26]

Some of this may be due to explicit prejudice against black Americans. At the very least it clearly represents a preference that Ambassadors have for rigid racial boundaries and a society where racial group members socialize with people of their own race.

Two pieces of evidence support this conclusion. First, the 2007 BRS also asks about how comfortable respondents would be if their daughter married a Latino or an Asian American, and whites who

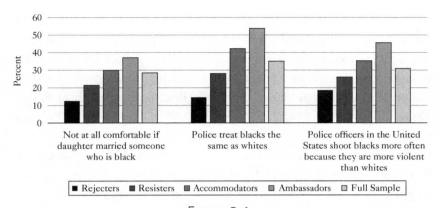

FIGURE 3.4.

Variation in Americans' Attitudes Toward Interracial Marriage and Race and Policing for Rejecters, Resisters, Accommodators, and Ambassadors

Note: Only white respondents included for marriage question.

Source: 2007 & 2017 Baylor Religion Surveys.

reported greater adherence to Christian nationalism were also less comfortable with this arrangement. Thus, the finding holds for racial minority groups generally, not just blacks. Second, we also found in a previous study that white Americans who embrace Christian nationalism were less likely to support other interracial family relationships like transracial adoption, even when no racial group was specified.[27] Most instances of transracial adoption in the United States involve white parents adopting children of color who are quite young. Thus, transracial adoption provides an interesting test case of how white Ambassadors and Accommodators think about interracial families, since cultural or biological "race-mixing" is not necessarily implied, and, in most cases, white parents are exercising authority over minority children (paternalism, quite literally). The fact that Americans who strongly embrace Christian nationalism are less supportive of transracial adoption suggests that interracial families in *any* form violate their preference for maintaining clear racial divisions.

Not only do Ambassadors prefer clear racial boundaries, but because "Christian heritage" has historically been shorthand for "white-dominated society," Christian nationalism is also closely linked with a preference for racial subordination. This is most apparent when nonwhite minorities, and black Americans in particular, attempt to resist structures of racial inequality. For instance, while black men and women have long been victim to unequal treatment at the hands of police, the highly publicized deaths of Eric Garner, Michael Brown, Tamir Rice, Walter Scott, Freddie Gray, Alton Sterling, and Philando Castile between 2014 and 2016 threw a national spotlight on police violence toward black Americans.[28] But even as public demonstrations by organizations like "Black Lives Matter" and NFL athletes like Colin Kaepernick drew greater attention to the issue of anti-black police violence, surveys revealed a severe "perception gap" between how white conservative Christians and most other Americans view black interactions with police. Simply put, white conservative Protestants appear to be the most unwilling to recognize police injustice against blacks.[29]

Take Ethan, for instance. He recognizes that there are certain "problem cops" out there who shouldn't be on the force due to incompetence or outright racism. But he also blames the media for magnifying the extent of racial injustice in policing: "I think there's a little bit of misconception that police are out to get black people . . . there are definitely shooting and killings where there don't need to be, but I think that's kind of magnified in a way. The media will share whatever's news and kind of stir up whatever controversy they can because it keeps people coming back to their news site." So Ethan thinks much of the outrage about police brutality is manufactured for ratings. In other instances, Ethan thinks some of the black men may have even had it coming.

Like the Michael Brown case . . . from what I heard there had been a robbery at the store and the cops arrived on the scene and out bursts this guy and the cops pull their gun and [say] "Hey, you need to stick 'em up." And instead of complying with the officers, he charges at the officers, if I remember right. I don't care if it's a black cop and a white guy is charging at you or if you're a yellow cop and a red guy is charging, I don't care what color you are, if I was a cop in that situation, I just responded to a robbery and this guy is running at me and about to maybe try to take my gun or deck me or something, I'm probably going to pull the trigger. I don't care what color you are. So I tend to think that's probably going through the mind of that cop, you know? But instead of giving him the benefit of the doubt in that situation, it's just "Oh, he's just out to get black people!" You know?

Though Ethan does not accuse Michael Brown of committing the reported robbery, he explains Michael Brown's killing as a result of his failure to comply with the officer. Given several of the inaccuracies present in Ethan's account, his qualification "from what I heard" is notable. Ethan's version of the event implies that Brown's death had nothing to do with race but was simply what (in his mind, justifiably) happens when someone of any color disobeys police and makes them feel threatened. This explanation was echoed in a widely circulated Facebook post by Franklin Graham, noted advocate of Christian nationalism. He stated:

Listen up—Blacks, Whites, Latinos, and everybody else. Most police shootings can be avoided. It comes down to respect for authority and obedience. If a police officer tells you to stop, you stop. If a police officer tells you to put your hands in the air, you put your hands in the air. If a police officer tells you to lay down face first with your hands behind your back, you lay down face first with your hands behind your back. It's as simple as that. Even if you think the police officer is wrong—YOU OBEY . . . Some of the unnecessary shootings we have seen recently might have been avoided. The Bible says to submit to your leaders and those in authority "because they keep watch over you as those who must give an account."[30]

While Graham addresses "Blacks, Whites, Latinos, and everyone else," because the most highly publicized unarmed victims of police shootings since 2013 have been black men, it is clear that he is addressing black men specifically. In Graham's view, backed with a biblical injunction to "submit to your leaders," police have unquestionable, divinely granted authority over their bodies. Consequently, people (read: black men) who are killed by police are killed because they lack "respect for authority and obedience." (We would be remiss if we failed to point out how black men like Philando Castile and Charles Kinsey fulfilled all of Graham's suggestions about obeying authorities and were *still* shot by police.)

Ethan and Franklin Graham, and the many Americans who agree with them (Graham's post was liked close to 200,000 times and shared over 82,000 times), appear to be unaware of the racial disparities in the criminal justice system in the United States. While they would likely acknowledge exceptional incidents, in their view black and white Americans generally receive the same treatment from police, and those who experience deadly police violence are responsible for bringing it upon themselves.

Despite the enthusiastic reception of Graham's post among most of his Facebook viewers, it did draw a pointed response from other Christians, many of whom identify as fellow evangelical Protestants. They pointed out that Graham's post revealed a "lack of empathy and understanding of the depth of sin that some in the body have suffered under the weight of our broken justice system." They also countered Graham's use of the Bible, pointing out to him that he "lifted Hebrews 13:17 out of its biblical context and misappropriated it in a way that encourages believers to acquiesce to an injustice that God hates. That text refers to church leadership, not the secular leadership of Caesar."[31] This response to Graham from those inside his religious tradition suggests that something else is encouraging these divergent views toward racial inequality in policing.

Our quantitative data show these quotes are indicative of broader trends across adherence to Christian nationalism and views toward police treatment of black Americans (see Figure 3.4). Ambassadors and Accommodators are much more likely than Resisters and Rejecters to believe that police treat blacks the same as whites, and that police officers in the United States shoot blacks more often because blacks are more violent than whites (see Figure 3.4).[32] In other words, Americans who embrace Christian nationalism are more likely to disregard racial inequality in policing and place the blame for police violence squarely on the victims.

But why the connection between Christian nationalism and a reluctance to believe black Americans when they decry police injustice? One obvious reason is that Christian nationalism is fundamentally about *preserving* or *returning* to a mythic society in which traditional hierarchical relationships (e.g., between men and women, whites and blacks) are upheld, and authority structures are biblical and just. There is thus every incentive to side with the authority structures (in this case, police) and disregard the claims of minorities as exaggerated, unfounded, or disingenuous.

Another reason is that Christian nationalists associate out-groups with character deficiencies and seek severe penalties on them so as to maintain order. Christian nationalism favors the in-group, which is presumed to be white. In this case, Christian nationalism intensifies in-group bias to see white Americans as good, decent, and law-abiding, and black Americans as probably deserving whatever force the police felt compelled to use.[33] Numerous criminology studies show the more white Americans associate minority status with criminality, the more likely they are to favor extreme and authoritarian forms of control and punishment—even death. For instance, in a study using the 2007 BRS and our Christian nationalism index, sociologist Joshua Davis showed that Christian nationalism was among the strongest predictors that Americans would favor the death penalty, stricter punishment for federal crimes, and a government "crackdown on troublemakers." Davis shows how this latter reference began to emerge in the 1980s as a dog whistle for inner-city black Americans, and thus, it is likely that Christian nationalists are so enthusiastic about the government maintaining law and order by force—and willing to defend the essential fairness of that force—because it is implied that blacks and other disadvantaged minority groups will be the targets.[34]

Christian nationalism thus reinforces boundaries and hierarchical relationships between "us" and "them" *not* exclusively on the basis of birth, or citizenship, or language, and not even primarily religion (since black Americans tend to hold conservative Christian faith more strongly than whites). But as the case of black Americans illustrates, Christian nationalism seeks to preserve white supremacy, in which minorities' access to intimate relationships with whites are limited, and whites maintain hegemonic control over their environment, by force if necessary.

WHICH RELIGIOUS GROUPS POSE A THREAT TO "OUR" VALUES, FREEDOMS, AND SAFETY?

Though ethnic and racial differences are likely the primary way in which Christian nationalism distinguishes "us" from "them," those who are wedded to the idea that America has been and should always be distinctively Christian are keen to favor Christianity over other religions. Likewise, those who resist or reject Christian nationalism are bound to be much more focused on ensuring that secular and non-Christian Americans are welcomed.

An example of the first view, Sarah Palin—a proponent of Christian nationalism—once stated how other faith traditions should be welcomed to America and allowed to peacefully practice whatever religion they choose. However, they must respect that America based its "laws and values on the God of the Bible and the New Testament" and "the Ten Commandments."[35] Expressing a less diplomatic version of this view, Pastor Robert Jeffress proclaims unapologetically: "God apparently has no appreciation for the merits of religious diversity . . . . We have been indoctrinated to believe that religious pluralism . . . is the great strength of our nation. Secularists applaud the Supreme Court's determined efforts to reverse 150 years of American history in which Christianity was elevated above other religions that the Supreme Court had labeled as 'imposters.' " Elsewhere he argues, "[T]he fact that our Constitution demands that everyone have the freedom to embrace any religious beliefs (or no religious beliefs) does not mean that the government cannot demonstrate a preference for Christianity . . . the government can (and for more than 150 years did) show a preference for the Christian faith. A high school principal does not have to have both a Christian and a Muslim student offer a prayer at graduation.

A city mayor is not obligated to balance a nativity scene in the town square with a Jewish menorah."[36]

For many of the Ambassadors and Accommodators we interviewed, the belief that Christianity should be shown preference was often more tacit, and even unrecognized by adherents themselves. For example, those in each of these groups at times affirmed separation of church and state while enthusiastically insisting that the Ten Commandments could be displayed in a courthouse or that public high school football games could be preceded by a Christian prayer over the intercom. They simply did not see the display of biblical symbols or the privileging of Christian religion as an encroachment on anyone else's freedoms. Others, however, like Jeffress, stressed America's responsibility to prioritize Christianity above other religious faiths as an expression that theirs is the one true faith. To do anything less would indicate halfhearted devotion. Ashlyn is a 30-year-old mother of three in suburban Georgia. When asked whether America's commitment to religious freedom required Christians to accommodate religious minorities like atheists or Muslims in public spaces, she explained,

> Because the majority of people do identify as Christians, as far as the [religious] minority is concerned, and this is where I might just sound snobby, but, to me, right is right and wrong is wrong. I know in their minds they believe what they believe is right. But I believe they have been deceived by the Enemy to believe those things. . . . So you can't just say "Okay, well, we're going to promote Christian principles, but we're not going to promote Christianity." Like, to me, they are one in the same. So you either have to lay that down and say "Okay, well, we're just going to be a country that doesn't have any sort of religious affiliation. And we're not going to have a moral compass" . . . Or you say, "Well, we're going to be a Christian nation that has these Christian principles, and we're going to follow those." There's not really a way to do both. You can't be lukewarm. You've got to be one or the other. Like, "Be a nation that follows me, or be a nation that doesn't follow me." But somewhere in the middle, I don't see that working.

Like Jeffress, Ashlyn believes that non-Christian minorities are deceived by Satan, and thus Christians have no obligation to treat their perspective as equally legitimate. Indeed, she feels American Christians cannot divorce promoting "Christian principles" from promoting Christianity itself. God himself sees it as an either/or situation. Either America must unapologetically follow Jesus as a "Christian nation" and encourage others to do the same publicly, or it should be completely secular.

For many Rejecters and Resisters we interviewed, the question of whether to privilege Christianity in the public sphere elicited complicated reactions. One Rejecter's beliefs directly contradicted those of Pastor Jeffress regarding displaying Christian symbols in the public sphere. Sharon claimed, "If you're gonna put up a Christmas tree, I think you need to have a menorah. And I think that when other religious holidays come up, you need to be displaying those too. If you're going to do one, you need to make space for all." Other Rejecters saw the posting of the Ten Commandments as "fundamentally un-American," "very problematic and unconstitutional," and "a clear cut violation of the establishment clause." Among Resisters, there was a bit more equivocation. When asked if displaying the Ten Commandments in courthouses was acceptable, an older gentleman and Resister from the Midwest answered, "I think so, because it's a symbol of our . . . It's part of the religious heritage of the country, very broadly-based," while a younger African American Resister from the South shared, "I really don't think that's okay." The theme of equal opportunity across religions was common among Rejecters and Resisters. The difficulties of actually achieving equality were clear to them, as well. Brett, a white Christian Resister from the South, exemplified this equivocation when asked about prayers before high school football games:

> That's a tough one, because that's kind of a . . . We both live in the South, right? And that's a traditional thing before a lot of these events. And it is true, it excludes certain people. And in an ideal world, I think there's some sort of speech, or some sort of thing that's said that's non-denominational and it's more or less a good statement. Is there anything out there like that right now? Probably not. Ideally, everyone gets their

fair share and gets to say something, I just don't think that's necessarily practical. The answer is yeah, ideally, everyone gets their say and doesn't feel disrespected. Is there a practical way to implement that? Probably not. Could it happen? Probably not.

The flipside of thinking Christian beliefs, values, and institutions should be privileged is perceiving that other religious systems or groups pose a potential threat to those things. Though Jeffress's interpretation of America's religious history is highly selective, he is correct that, historically, many Americans in power perceived (their specific) Christian faith (among other factors like gender, race, and class) as a marker of societal belonging. Consequently, religious "others" were either excluded outright or granted only diminished status. While the largely Protestant populace viewed Roman Catholicism as the primary societal threat for the first 200 years of the nation's history, within the past few decades other religious groups have been cast as outsiders. Recall in Jeffress's quotes near the beginning of this section of the chapter where he cites three groups against which he compares (conservative) Christians: Muslims, Jews, and seculars.

The group most often depicted as a "threat" is Muslims, because of their stereotypical connection with terrorism and the perception that they are ethnically nonwhite.[37] Recall that in chapter 2 we showed that Ambassadors and Accommodators were much more likely to believe that refugees from the Middle East posed a terror threat to the United States. Implicit in that assumption was that refugees from that region were most likely Muslim (even though that is not actually true—many refugees from the Middle East to the United States are Christians), and Muslims are, in their minds, much more likely to be terrorists. So intense is this fear of Muslim refugees that we found it was the third strongest predictor of voting for Donald Trump behind only Republican affiliation and identification with political conservatism.

Antipathy toward Jews may seem surprising given the strong pro-Israel sentiment of prominent promoters of Christian nationalism. Thought leaders who advocate Christian nationalism frequently promote Israel's interests, as they believe America's success depends on its support of "God's people." In May 2018 the United States moved its embassy in Israel from Tel Aviv to Jerusalem. As expected, high-profile Ambassadors of Christian nationalism wasted no time praising the Trump administration. Tony Perkins, head of the conservative political lobby Family Research Council, gushed that moving the embassy was a "major milestone in America's historic relationship with Israel. Under the bold and courageous leadership of President Trump, America is finally putting American interests and the interests of our key allies first. America's foreign policy, as it pertains to Israel, is coming into alignment with this biblical truth." Similarly, former congresswoman Michele Bachmann exclaimed, "We are so grateful to President Donald Trump for his recognition of Jerusalem as Israel's capital. Donald Trump says not only do they [Israel] have a right [to the land], but they have a legal and legitimate right to designate Jerusalem as their capital. That is a powerful statement. We believe, without a shadow of a doubt, that this move will bring not only greater peace to Israel, but greater peace to the region."[38]

Yet, these same men and women clearly separate Israel as a nation from Judaism as a religion. For example, Jeffress, who prayed at the opening ceremony for the U.S. Embassy in Israel, also claimed that, "Not only do religions like Mormonism, Islam, *Judaism*, Hinduism— not only do they lead people away from God, they lead people to an eternity of separation from God in Hell"[39] (emphasis added). In 2015, Michele Bachmann called for the mass conversion of Jews to Christianity to accelerate the second coming of Christ (a remark for which she later apologized). Thus, Christian nationalism can lead people to be quite suspicious of Jewish people even as they advocate for America's political support of Israel.

Lastly, atheists, or the broader term "seculars," are also increasingly cast as a grave threat to America's values and institutions.[40] Drawing from the writing of Francis Schaffer, those on the Religious Right have long argued that two worldviews are at war in the United States: biblical and secular humanist. Rooting out the influence of secular humanism at all levels of government was essential to preserving the American way of life. The documented rise in the unaffiliated from the mid-1990s through today made defining the religious heritage of the country all the more important. In response to a 2016 "Reason Rally" that news organizations claimed was attended by "thousands of atheists," Franklin Graham wrote that the "liberal godless kind of what they call 'reason' should concern every freedom-loving American." Graham went on to assert there was a particular irony that the rally was held near the Lincoln Memorial. Engraved in the memorial is a quote containing the words "this nation UNDER GOD" (emphasis Graham's). Graham explains that Lincoln and many of the founding fathers recognized the role of the Christian God in establishing our rights and freedoms. Graham warns, however, that "now these atheists promoting secularism want to strip God out of America's past, present and future. Here's a warning—If you remove God, you remove God's hand of blessing. That's been shown over and over throughout history."[41]

The connection between Christian nationalism and perceptions of Muslims, Jews, and atheists as threats can be seen clearly in the 2017 BRS. The researchers asked respondents how much respondents agree with these statements:

- (Muslims/Conservative Christians/Jews/Atheists) hold values that are morally inferior to the values of people like me.
- (Muslims/Conservative Christians/Jews/Atheists) want to limit the personal freedoms of people like me.
- (Muslims/Conservative Christians/Jews/Atheists) endanger the physical safety of people like me.

Respondents could strongly disagree, disagree, agree, or strongly agree to all these statements, which we added up together to create a "threat scale" for each group.[42]

As Figure 3.5 clearly demonstrates, Ambassadors are more likely than the other three groups to believe that Muslims and Atheists hold morally inferior values, want to limit their freedoms, or want to endanger their physical safety.[43] In fact, we found that Christian nationalism is the strongest predictor of Americans' attitudes toward these

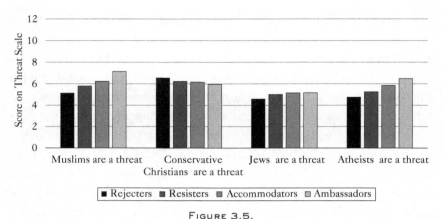

Rejecters, Resisters, Accommodators, and Ambassadors by Perceptions of
Threat Regarding Four Religious Groups
Note: See Footnote 43 for more information about these findings.
Source: 2017 Baylor Religion Survey.

groups. Interestingly, while Jews are much less likely to be viewed as
threatening across the board, the more someone adheres to Christian
nationalism the more likely they are to view Jews as a threat to their
values, freedom, and safety.

When we look at conservative Christians, however, the association
flips completely.[44] Rejecters are most likely to view conservative
Christians as a threat. When comparing the stances toward conservative
Christians among the four orientations toward Christian nationalism,
we actually find that Ambassadors, Accommodators, and Resisters have
essentially identical reactions. Once we account for age, education, political views, and religiosity, these three groups are indistinguishable.
Rejecters, however, are significantly more likely to perceive conservative
Christians as a threat compared to each of these three other groups.[45]
Commenting on the ultimate desires of conservative Christians in the
United States, Sharon—a Rejecter from the Southwest—believes that
"they are looking to push those who don't believe it's a Christian
nation outside of the realm of public life. Absolutely . . . I think they
have every intention of marginalizing anyone that doesn't believe the
way they do." In another interview, one Rejecter shared that a goal of

conservative Christians is to "make people feel like outsiders in their own country," something he views as immoral and against America's most cherished principles. For these two and other Rejecters we spoke with, conservative Christians do not share their values, such as endorsing a pluralistic democratic system that welcomes people of all religions. They see conservative Christians as wanting to restrict their freedoms and those of other non-Christian groups.

The fact that Resisters are more similar to Ambassadors and Accommodators in their views of conservative Christians is also noteworthy. This finding underscores how the four orientations toward Christian nationalism are truly distinct from one another. While Resisters and Rejecters align on many issues, they do not align on all. Americans who merely resist Christian nationalism are much less threatened by conservative Christians or Christianity in general than are Americans who wholly reject Christian nationalism. This sentiment was reflected in some of our interviews with Resisters. Take Stuart, who told us that, "Christianity has to be a viable option for shaping the world . . . Christianity has to be taken seriously. Because of the taste that Christianity has had in our country and what that type of Christianity . . . has meant for disenfranchised communities, there's this knee-jerk backlash to all things Christianity. I think there is a tension there that I can walk in. I can pray openly but not seek to embody a religion that wants to create a Christian nation." For Americans like Stuart, Christianity holds some promise for improving American civil society. As we showed previously, many Resisters identify as Christian. While they resist making Christianity the sole religious influence in the public sphere, they are generally amenable to it and do not see other Christians, even conservative Christians, as threats. The pervasive nature of Christianity throughout American culture perhaps encourages even those who are resistant to Christian nationalism to be less likely to resent the conservative Christians living in their midst.

Clearly, in order to make sense of the religious divides in American society we must account for Christian nationalism. While merely being religious might be one way Americans imagine cultural belonging, these findings demonstrate that for the most part, being "religious" for many

Americans means one must be "Christian." Ambassadors and to a lesser extent Accommodators want Christianity to be privileged in the public sphere and reflected in the national identity, sacred symbols, and public policies of the United States. Ambassadors and Accommodators believe Muslims, Jews, and atheists oppose Christian values and therefore oppose the privileging of Christianity in the public sphere. It appears that even Resisters can be found to agree with Ambassadors and Accommodators on some of these points. In this way, talk of religious liberty and freedom most likely means religious liberty and freedom to be Christian.

WHY IT'S IMPORTANT TO DISTINGUISH BETWEEN CHRISTIAN NATIONALISM AND RELIGIOSITY WHEN IT COMES TO RACIAL AND (MOST) RELIGIOUS BOUNDARIES

Christian nationalism is not unique because it is used to draw boundaries (of the symbolic or physical variety) around group membership. Many cultural frameworks or other social markers, religious or otherwise, are used by groups to draw boundaries between "us" and "them." But Christian nationalism *is* distinct from religiosity in a general sense. The two phenomena share a common tendency to imbue boundaries of group membership with ultimate, cosmic significance, to equate in-group members with divine election and righteousness and see out-group members as hell-bound instruments of the Devil himself. But commitment to Christian nationalism *behaves* differently from private commitment to religion generally speaking, and particularly with regard to where boundaries are drawn.

A number of studies have observed this. Take the issue of immigration, for instance. Political scientist Eric McDaniel and his colleagues, using a measure of Christian nationalism that is similar to ours, showed that the more Americans espoused Christian nationalist views, the more likely they were to hold negative views toward immigrants— exactly as we might expect. However, McDaniel and his co-authors also found that once they took Christian nationalism into account, people who attended church more often seemed to hold more *positive* attitudes toward immigrants. When it came to Americans' openness to immigrants, in other words, Christian nationalism and religious commitment worked in opposite directions. More recently, sociologists Darren Sherkat and Derek Lehman showed that while Americans who connected Christian identity with American cultural membership were more likely to believe immigrant numbers should be reduced, those who attended church more frequently held the opposite view. Again, Christian nationalism seems to promote more rigid ethno-national boundaries, while religious commitment (or at least church attendance) seems to promote greater acceptance of ethnic "others."

This trend also applies to cultural boundaries around religion. Recent work by sociologists Evan Stewart, Penny Edgell, and Jack Delehanty finds opposing effects of Christian nationalism and religious commitment on attitudes toward religious out-groups. Respondents who wanted religion to occupy a central place in public life were more likely to support denying civil liberties to atheists, Buddhists, and Muslims, while private religiosity predicted the opposite in some cases.

This also extends to the *way* we deal with "others" as a society. Recall Joshua Davis's study on punitive attitudes that we discussed earlier. While Christian nationalism seems to incline Americans to be more favorable toward capital punishment, harsher sentences, and the government cracking down on troublemakers (which many may have perceived as a dog-whistle reference to racial minorities), religious commitment influenced Americans' attitudes in the exact opposite direction. Personal religiosity, unlike Christian nationalism, seems to have a softening effect when it comes to the policing of group boundaries.[46]

Our own analyses show this trend repeatedly across a variety of measures of Americans' attitudes toward racial and ethnic minorities. For example, earlier we showed that Americans who adhere more strongly to Christian nationalism are more likely to believe that police treat whites and blacks equally, and that police shoot blacks more often than whites because blacks are relatively more violent. Figure 3.6 illustrates this trend with a solid black line. Yet even while personal religious commitment (which we measure with worship attendance,

(a) Police treat blacks the same as whites

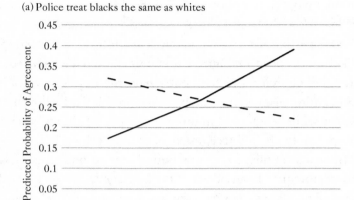

(b) Police officers in the United States shoot blacks more often
because they are more violent than whites

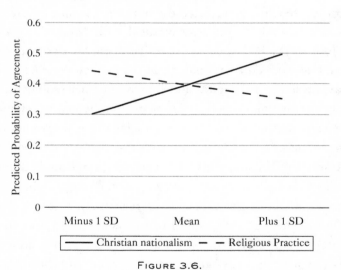

FIGURE 3.6.
Opposing Influences of Christian Nationalism and Religious Practice
Source: 2017 Baylor Religion Survey

scripture reading, and prayer) is positively associated with Christian nationalism, it influences Americans' attitudes regarding the police treatment of blacks in the opposite direction. Notice the dotted line. When we hold all other factors, including Christian nationalism, constant, Americans who are more religious seem to hold more progressive attitudes toward racial injustice in policing, acknowledging police violence against blacks and rejecting the idea that blacks are more violent than whites.

This crisscrossing pattern exists for a number of other situations as well. We find similar results for the following:

- Believing that illegal immigrants from Mexico are mostly dangerous criminals (Christian nationalism positively associated, religious practice negatively associated).
- Believing that immigrants take American jobs (Christian nationalism positively associated, church attendance negatively associated).
- Believing that American birth, American ancestry, ability to speak English, or life-long residence are "very important" for being "truly American" (Christian nationalism positively associated, church attendance negatively associated).
- Being "not comfortable at all" with one's daughter marrying someone who is black, Asian, or Latino (Christian nationalism positively associated, religiosity negatively associated).
- Supporting transracial adoption (Christian nationalism negatively associated, religiosity positively associated).
- Fear of refugees as potential terrorists (Christian nationalism positively associated, religious practice negatively associated).
- Viewing Muslims as a threat (Christian nationalism positively associated, religious practice negatively associated).
- Viewing Jews as a threat (Christian nationalism positively associated, religious practice negatively associated).

There is, however, an interesting caveat to this relationship. When we examine Americans' fear of atheists, individual religious commitment

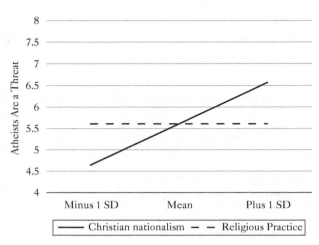

FIGURE 3.7.

Relationship Between Christian Nationalism or Religious Practice with Fear of Atheists

Source: 2017 Baylor Religion Survey.

has no effect on attitudes (see Figure 3.7). Christian nationalism does. This means that Americans who are more religiously active have the same levels of fear of atheists as Americans who do not attend religious services, read their sacred scriptures, or pray. Americans who embrace Christian nationalism, however, are much more likely to believe atheists have inferior values, hope to limit their freedoms, and want to endanger their physical safety. Thus, while greater religiosity is connected with more progressive attitudes toward racial and (most) religious others, this does not hold for Americans' views of atheists. It is likely that seculars or atheists are simply viewed as more of a threat to "religion" per se—as *anti*-religion—in a way that members of other ethnic or even religious communities are not.[47]

CONCLUSION

Christian nationalism idealizes a mythic society in which *real* Americans—white, native-born, mostly Protestants—maintain control over access to society's social, cultural, and political institutions, and "others" remain in their proper place. It therefore seeks strong boundaries to separate "us" from "them," preserving privilege for its rightful recipients while equating racial and religious outsiders with criminality, violence, and inferiority.

Yet, counterintuitively, personal religiosity (which often reinforces group boundaries of its own kind) seems to have the opposite tendency. Nonreligious Americans who seek to foster greater racial and religious inclusion and are committed to religious freedom can (and should be willing to) find co-laborers in the cause among religious Americans who score as Resisters or Rejecters. There is historical precedent there. As historian Randall Balmer points out, devout Baptists were the earliest and strongest supporters of religious liberty in the colonies.[48] In response to the strident Christian nationalism that has come to represent devout Christians in the media, religious Americans, and even particular evangelical Protestant groups like the Baptists Balmer eulogizes, could reclaim their historical support of religious tolerance and the separation of church and state.

But they are not currently the dominant voice. Today "religious liberty" is being redefined to mean something more than the freedom to worship (or not) a particular God or gods in a certain way. Various Christian legal defense organizations and the clients they represent argue that religious liberty is the freedom or right to follow the dictates of one's religion in the public sphere—to "vote one's conscience," influence others to do the same, and establish policies that privilege Christian religious expressions and standards of morality.[49] Because the boundaries of membership and privilege that Christian nationalism draws extend beyond certain religious identities, beliefs, and values to ethnic and racial identities, it is likely that the "religious freedoms" won by these groups serve implicit (or explicit) goals of subordinating groups who are not native-born, white Christians. In the next chapter, we'll extend this discussion to explore how Christian nationalism seeks to defend or reestablish such traditionalist boundaries and hierarchies in the home and the bedroom.

CHAPTER 4

ORDER

Our society has been based upon the belief that the biblical view of traditional marriage and family is the backbone of a healthy social order . . . . The plan of God, nature, and common sense is a man and a woman producing children within the institution of marriage. When that plan is lost . . . a nation is on the road to ruin. World history has proven it over and again. Preserving the traditional family is vital to the future of any great nation.

—Richard G. Lee, *The American Patriot's Bible* (2009)

Preston is a football coach at a private Baptist high school in central Georgia. A white, 38-year-old father of two, he is passionate about his Christian faith, his family, and the young men he coaches, many of whom are African American. He is also an Ambassador of Christian nationalism, agreeing wholeheartedly that prayer and Christian symbols should be reinstituted in public spaces and that God is committed to America's success. Preston's political views are shaped by a commitment to subordinate all of his life to biblical truth. "I would say I'm conservative, yeah. But I'm basically, my truth is what the Bible says to be true and my boundaries are laid out based on [God's] word . . . . From a political standpoint I allow God's word to shape my view of how to live in every way. So for me politically, my political decisions are made based on the shaping of God's word." Beyond the role of faith in politics, our conversation ranged over numerous topics including our nation's challenges regarding racism, immigration, religious freedom, and what he fears is a general decline in character in young people.

Toward the end of this discussion of America's social problems, Preston shared how much he felt "family life" played into America's challenges and future success. His stance was unequivocal:

> [Family life] is 100 percent the reason that we're suffering some of what we're suffering. And it will be the reason that we are able to come up out of it. So if you take a look at different societies, it could be, let's just say the black community . . . I think the family breakdown within the African American population, that family breakdown has its consequences the same way over here when I see kids in more affluent [predominantly white] neighborhoods whose dads are never around because they're out making money, they're not spending time with their family. So these kids have access to money, and now they're out dealing drugs and all kinds of stuff. Dropping out of school. Same reason. It's the breakdown of the family.

Preston locates problems facing both the poorer black communities and affluent white communities with family breakdown and particularly the absence of fathers. Circling back to his earlier statement that the family "will be the reason we are able to come up out of [society's problems]," he elaborated:

> I think it all stems back to headship, leadership, and there's a system of order that was laid out by God in the beginning and having a family knowing that God is first. For me and my family, my wife knows that God is my number one and I'll serve him. And I agree the same should happen from her. And then it's us two and then our kids will see mom and dad love one another. And there's order. The kids are gonna obey their parents. They're gonna have discipline. There's order . . . . And then I go into the community and I start to act better. And then we're better as a nation.

How do we address our national problems? According to Preston, "it all stems back to headship, leadership, and . . . a system of order" in the family. God comes first. Husbands and fathers are dedicated and partner with their wives to raise obedient children. Everyone knows his or her place. Members of these families then go out into the community and "we're better as a nation."

Though Christian nationalism seeks to preserve or reinstitute boundaries in the public sphere (between natives and foreigners, whites and nonwhites, conservative Christians and religious "others") it is Americans' *private* worlds that strong Christian nationalists are most desperate to influence.

This is actually the case for *all* reactionary movements, American Christian nationalism being a textbook example. In his comparison of Christian and Islamic fundamentalism in America and Iran respectively, sociologist Martin Riesebrodt shows that religious movements seeking to return society to its ideal "fundamental" arrangements are best understood as a response to threats to the hierarchical order of the patriarchal family. When economic or cultural circumstances destabilize men's "proper place" as the head of their household and controller of women's bodies, societies are ripe for a fundamentalist resurgence. In *How Fascism Works*, Yale philosopher Jason Stanley explains, "In the fascist imagination, the past invariably involves traditional, patriarchal gender roles . . . . This imagined history provides proof to support the imposition of hierarchy in the present, and it dictates how contemporary society should look and behave." He also demonstrates how a "politics of sexual anxiety" is constantly at play within fascist societies. In decades past, strongmen and demagogues could rouse populist support by stoking fears of interracial sexuality polluting the "pure blood" of the dominant race. More recently, however, fascist movements have targeted "transgender and homosexual individuals . . . to heighten anxiety and panic about the threat to traditional male gender roles." And political theorist Corey Robin explains that "the reactionary mind" is guided by this mantra: "cede the field of the public, if you must, stand fast in the private," for if the traditional, hierarchical order of relationships in the family is overthrown, all societal order would soon follow.[1]

While these authors use labels like "fundamentalism," "fascism," or "reactionary politics," their descriptions align perfectly with what we observe in Christian nationalism. Early Christian nationalist leaders—from Francis Schaeffer, Jerry Falwell Sr., Tim LaHaye, D. James Kennedy, Ralph Reed, James Dobson, Alan Keyes, and Pat Robertson, all the way up to contemporary influencers like Tony Perkins, Ted Cruz, Michele Bachmann, David Barton, Jerry Falwell Jr., Wayne Grudem, Robert Jeffress, Mike Huckabee, and others—all connect America's very survival as a civilization with its adherence to traditional definitions of the family, traditional gender roles, and heterosexuality.[2] As it turns out, so do rank and file Americans who subscribe to Christian nationalist ideology.

UNSETTLED TIMES IN GENDER, SEXUALITY, AND THE FAMILY

Christian nationalism becomes more salient during times of societal unrest. Economic, political, or cultural upheavals cause Americans to fall back on their core identities, traditions, values, and narratives about themselves to bring order out of chaos.[3] In some cases—as with American Christian nationalism—myths, traditions, and identities that were *not* originally part of the nation's core can be manufactured for the purpose of establishing order. While historians are mostly in agreement that the "founding fathers" (at least those that had the greatest hand in forging the nation's founding documents and government) did not view America as an explicitly "Christian nation," in early decades of the 19th century, political leaders drew on a Christian nation narrative to connect the American experiment with a larger divine plan for the world.[4] Historians have documented similar resurgences of Christian nationalism following the Civil War (as Southern whites sought to oppress blacks), the Great Depression (as wealthy capitalists sought to oppose New Deal reforms), World War II (as Americans sought to distinguish themselves from godless communists), and the civil rights movement (as Southern whites sought to oppress blacks yet again).[5]

The economic, demographic, and cultural transitions involving gender, sexuality, and the family have caused yet another societal upheaval. Beginning in the 1960s, the increase in the number of women entering the workforce, legalized abortion, the Pill, a general trend toward sexual freedom, and an expansion of women's roles have completely destabilized Americans' cultural understandings of gender, sexuality, and the family. No longer are there widely agreed upon particular sets of roles for men and women at work or at home. Fewer Americans are getting married, and when they do, it is much later than previous generations. Women outnumber men on graduation days at our colleges and universities and are having fewer children over their lifetimes. And most recently, the legalization of gay marriage in 2015 codified dramatic shifts that had been occurring for decades.[6]

Once again, Christian nationalism has risen up in response. Over the last four decades, a host of conservative religious organizations have emerged to warn Americans of the degradation these transitions will bring. A cursory list highlights how the concept of the family animates these groups: the American Family Association (est. 1977), Focus on the Family (est. 1977), the Family Research Council (est. 1983), and Family Watch International (est. 1999) to name just a few. There are many others. The vision and mission statements of each group underscore the centrality of the nuclear (heterosexual, patriarchal) family in maintaining an orderly and healthy society.

In an interview with Jim Daly, the president of Focus on the Family, Dr. Tony Evans—megachurch pastor and radio personality—stated, "The foundational institution of any society is the family . . . and whoever owns the family owns the future. The breakdown of the family is the single greatest cause of societal chaos and all the civil government in the world . . . can't fix that if the family is not reinstituted *as God designed it to be*."[7] Evans clearly believes that the family is essential to the proper functioning of all societies. Even more importantly, though, he points out that it is only the *right type* of family, the one designed by the Christian God, which ensures a society free from chaos.

This view was shared by many of those we interviewed. Joshua, an Accommodator, pointed out that the family is the basic building block of all societies. He said, "If you're looking at it from a societal standpoint, the breakdown of the family is, in my opinion, probably the single biggest travesty that's hit this country in the past 50 years." When asked how he would define a "strong" family he pointed to the Bible, specifically Matthew 19, "where Jesus describes it as being a man and a woman that cleave to one another and then they have children. So just a man and a woman being married, that's also considered a Christian family, and any children that they may have." Like Preston, Justin believes the "breakdown" of the family is at the heart of our problems. Specifically, he means our country's apparent retreat from the married-heterosexual nuclear family. Others described more explicitly how the decline of the traditional family caused societal problems. One Ambassador, Michael, explained what he saw as a central problem facing poor communities: "A lot of the [wrong] mentalities I think are kind of perpetuated. I mean there's a lot of problems with the country, just the breakdown of the family is a real big one, and that probably has a lot more of an effect on the poverty if the family's broken. The mom's got four or five kids by four or five different men, and none of them are around, but maybe someone else is around now, and there's cycles of poverty that just perpetuate." By "breakdown" Michael seems to mean what he perceives to be poor mothers' unwillingness to have children only within committed marriage relationships, and this, he believes, is a key cause (rather than a consequence) of poverty.

In the many resources conservative religious and political organizations make available, the inherent responsibility of Christians to promote Christian ideals—as these groups define them—in the public sphere is paramount. For example, the stated mission of the Family Research Council is "to advance faith, family, and freedom in public policy and the culture from a Christian worldview." The FRC, and others like it, actively encourage Christians to work to ensure their worldview is represented in civil society. These Christian ideals for the family tend to revolve around a number of issues, including divorce, gay marriage, transgender issues, and gender roles within marriage. As the social institution of the family continues to evolve, Ambassadors, Accommodators, Resisters, and Rejecters respond in myriad ways.

Attitudes toward gender, sexuality, and divorce are all closely related to how strongly Americans want religion—especially Christianity—to be expressed in the public sphere.

A Woman's Proper Place in a Christian Nation

Americans have strong feelings about how to define a family, as well as how families should operate. Gender is central to these understandings. Social scientists find that belonging to particular religious groups, holding certain religious beliefs, and engaging in a variety of religious practices are each associated with how egalitarian, or how traditional, an American's beliefs about gender roles are. And research shows the official and unofficial opinions of religious groups regarding "proper" gender roles change over time.[8]

Christian nationalism is intimately intertwined with Americans' definitions of the family and the proper roles for men and women within the family. The stakes are high, in this view, because having families that conform to God's ideal standard are a vital step toward having a country that he will bless with prosperity. In the early decades of the Christian Right, leaders like Jerry Falwell Sr. excoriated secular feminists and "bored," "lonely," Christian women whom he believed were disgruntled with their God-given roles.[9] While one does find some Christian nationalist writers like Wayne Grudem who directly rebuke "evangelical feminists," most in recent years seek to restore traditional gender roles to American society by challenging *men*, specifically husbands and fathers.[10] In a popular book edited by Grudem and John Piper, pastor Weldon Hardenbrook writes, "Throughout the historical transitions of a variety of cultures, the family existed as a natural society that provided the soul of each nation and that was to be nourished and protected through fatherhood . . . .I humbly but firmly submit that the soul of our nation is in crisis in large part because American men have—from ignorance and for various and sometimes even subconscious reasons—abandoned their God-given role of fatherhood."[11]

Like Hardenbrook, Ambassadors we spoke with connected the absence of men and masculinity in the family with the breakdown of society as a whole. One connected the absence of father figures to various social problems like school shootings and drug abuse and sees broken homes as "a huge issue in this country, even bigger than the wall."[12] Lori explicitly connected the proper order found in patriarchal Christian families to the strengthening of the nation itself.

> I think we need to get back to the foundation where the man is the spiritual [leader of the] household and he's the leader of the family and put it back in the way God had planned family. Obviously if God planned it and ordained it that way, there was a reason and a purpose and I think he knows that that would lead our family units better. We wouldn't have this division and power struggle between a man and a woman. There's so many women out there . . . you think of that famous song, "I am Woman, Hear me Roar." Yes, but if I want [the United States] to be a Christian nation, I want to have the husband as a spiritual leader. I want him to guide and protect and lead my family in the ways of the Lord.

For Lori, it is vitally important that she set aside her own desires, and perhaps her own inclination to lead, and submit to her husband. This is what God has "ordained" and God obviously had a reason for structuring families that way. In order to have a well-functioning society and for the United States to flourish, families across the country should operate as God intended, where men are leaders and women humbly submit to that leadership.

Lori's views are in line with the teachings of numerous religiously conservative family organizations. Many religious conservatives look to groups like Focus on the Family for guidance on how to think about family life, including gender roles. In one publication, Focus on the Family lays out its view on the roles of men and women in marriage and the biblical admonition that a wife should submit to her husband. Though both genders are of equal value to God, they argue, men and women have complementary roles. Focus on the Family goes on to point out that if our society drifts away from male headship and "swing[s] to the other extreme and strip[s] husbands of their authority, we will be disregarding God's plan for marriage and the family, and ultimately courting social disaster."[13] Ambassadors and Accommodators see the proper roles for men and women in similarly traditional terms.

For instance, in Figure 4.1 Panel B we see that in 2017, Ambassadors, Accommodators, Resisters, and Rejecters have very different views of whether men and women should have gender-specific roles in the public and private spheres. The largest differences exist on the question of whether it is God's will that women care for children. We also combined these four questions to create a "gender traditionalism"

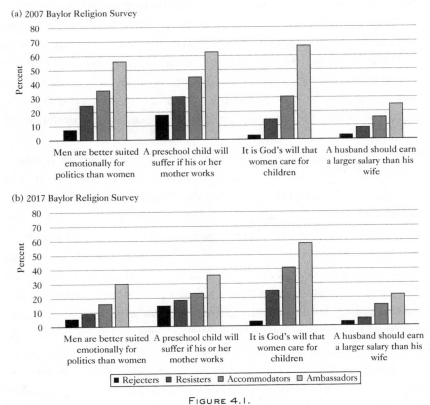

FIGURE 4.1.

Relationship Between Christian Nationalism and Views of Gender Roles from 2007 to 2017

Sources: 2007 & 2017 Baylor Religion Survey.

scale, with higher scores indicating more agreement with traditionalist, patriarchal beliefs. Even when we account for Americans' sociodemographics, politics, and religiosity, Christian nationalism is *the* strongest predictor of more traditionalist attitudes toward gender roles. In fact, there are significant differences between each of the four orientations to Christian nationalism.[14]

What happens when we compare these findings to the earlier Baylor data (Figure 4.1, Panels A and B)? We see evidence that the association between Christian nationalism and Americans' gender attitudes is not quite as strong as it used to be. The most noticeable changes are the percentages of Resisters, Accommodators, and Ambassadors who agree that "Men are better suited emotionally for politics than women" and "A preschool child will suffer if his or her mother works." The differences across categories in 2007 were noticeably greater than in 2017, especially for the first two questions. In fact, when we tested whether Christian nationalism was as strongly related to gender traditionalism in 2017 as it was in 2007, we found that it was not (though, again, it was still the strongest predictor of gender traditionalism in 2017).[15]

What might explain why Christian nationalism is not as strong a predictor of Americans' traditionalist, patriarchal attitudes as it was a decade prior? Part of the answer is that Americans *across the board* were simply less traditional in their view of gender roles in 2017 than they were in 2007. Across every single orientation toward Christian nationalism, fewer Americans agreed with each statement over time. While Ambassadors and Accommodators are still more likely to affirm patriarchal gender roles than Rejecters or Resisters, as Americans' views regarding gender roles have gradually become more progressive, Ambassadors and Accommodators may see this as less of a threat to God's proper order and human society than before. A related possibility is that as more egalitarian gender roles in the family have become more widely accepted, Christian nationalism has seized upon other threats to the stability of traditional, patriarchal order, like homosexuality and transgender people.

From "Sodom and Gomorrah" to Concerns Over Religious Freedom

Americans' attitudes toward homosexuality dramatically shifted over a relatively short period of time. In the early 1970s, more than 7 in 10 Americans believed homosexuality was always wrong; by 2018 that had fallen to 3 in 10. By contrast, only 11 percent of Americans in the early 1970s saw nothing wrong with homosexuality; by 2018 that number exceeded 58 percent.[16] And these shifts in Americans' attitudes have corresponded to growing civil rights recognition for gays and lesbians, culminating in the landmark *Obergefell v. Hodges* (2015) decision that overturned bans on same-sex marriage.

In the decades that Americans have warmed to homosexual relationships, Christian nationalist leaders have prophesied God's impending judgment. In his 1980 jeremiad, *Listen, America!*, Jerry Falwell Sr. lamented the fact that the word *homosexual* was no longer "the zenith of human indecency . . . spoken with contempt," but instead was being normalized. He warned his readers, gravely, "[Homosexuals] are an indictment against America and are contributing to her downfall. History proves that homosexuality reaches a pandemic level in societies in crisis or in a state of collapse. The sin . . . is so grievous, so abominable in the sight of God, that He destroyed the cities of Sodom and Gomorrah because of this terrible sin." Consistent with our earlier argument that Christian nationalists and other reactionary groups associate social order with hierarchal relationships, Falwell traced the scourge of homosexuality to Americans' rejection of gender roles: "We would not be having the present moral crisis regarding the homosexual movement if men and women accepted their proper roles as designated by God. God's plan is for men to be manly and spiritual in all areas of Christian leadership . . . . Women are to be feminine and . . . in the Christian home the woman is to be submissive . . . . Homosexuality is Satan's diabolical attack upon the family, God's order in Creation."

Some more recent authors share Falwell's view that homosexuality is essentially an attack on God's divine order reflected in the family, his foundational institution. Also like Falwell, they believe the celebration of homosexuality reflects a more fundamental trend of moving away from God's divine plan. The 2009 Manhattan Declaration, whose drafters included Christian Right activist Chuck Colson and was signed by Wayne Grudem, James Dobson, Dinesh D'Souza, Jonathan Falwell, and Tony Perkins, stated:

> Vast human experience confirms that marriage is the original and most important institution for sustaining the health, education, and welfare of all persons in a society. Where marriage is honored, and where there is a flourishing of marriage culture, everyone benefits . . . . Where the marriage culture begins to erode, social pathologies of every sort quickly manifest themselves . . . . Unfortunately, we have witnessed over the course of the past several decades a serious erosion of the marriage culture in our country . . . The impulse to redefine marriage in order to recognize same-sex and multiple partner relationships is a symptom, rather than a cause, of the erosion of marriage culture.[17]

In their view, a society in which heterosexual marriages abound is a society in which the health, education, and welfare of all are sustained. But a society in which gay marriage is being championed reflects a culture where God's intention for marriage, and all the societal benefits that go along with it, has eroded and "social pathologies" will inevitably emerge.

Unsurprisingly, national data reveal a strong relationship between Christian nationalism and Americans' attitudes toward same-sex marriage. And these associations have maintained their strength even as public support for same-sex marriage has increased across the board. Figure 4.2 shows data from the 2007 and 2017 Baylor Religion Surveys and the 2004 and 2014 General Social Surveys, each of which asked respondents to indicate whether they agreed at some level that gay couples should be allowed to get married. Looking at both surveys, each a decade apart from its earlier wave, we see the same pattern. In the 2007 and 2017 Baylor Religion Surveys, support for same-sex marriage is highly correlated with Christian nationalism.[18] In the 2004

(a) By Four Orientations to Christian Nationalism

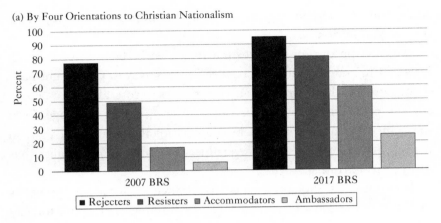

(b) By Importance of Being Christian to Being "Truly American"

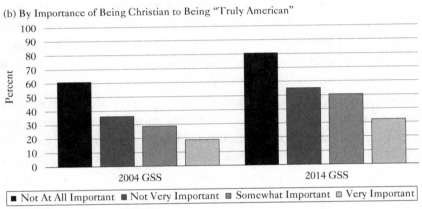

FIGURE 4.2.

Support for Same-Sex Marriage by Time and Christian Nationalism

(a) *Source:* 2007 & 2017 Baylor Religion Surveys.

(b) *Source:* 2004 & 2014 General Social Surveys.

and 2014 General Social Surveys, as Americans feel being a Christian is more essential to American civic belonging, they are less supportive of same-sex marriage. And these trends are just as strong over time. When we performed statistical analyses to see if the relationship between Christian nationalism and attitudes toward gay marriage was weaker or stronger between survey waves, we discovered there was no difference at all. Christian nationalism is just as closely related to

Americans' support for gay marriage in the more recent surveys as it was 10 years prior.[19]

Even so, approval of same-sex marriage clearly *did* increase for each level of Christian nationalism between survey waves. One might have predicted that the liberalization of attitudes across all groups could signal a ratcheting down of the debate over same-sex marriage. Even the staunchest adherents to Christian nationalism may feel that, in many ways, the changes are irreversible. But Christian nationalism has adapted its narrative.

In recent years, thought leaders have shifted from calling Americans to "protect the sanctity of marriage" to framing civil rights for gay couples as a direct assault on religious liberty. This also reflects a paradigmatic response of groups formerly in power (in this case, white conservative Christians) to situations in which they feel that power threatened—namely, to portray oneself as the victim.[20] In his book *A Time for Action*, Rafael Cruz argues "[W]hen homosexual marriage becomes a mandatory civil right, the next obvious step is to enforce this civil right in private businesses, Christian organizations, and even churches. You see, the [2015] decision in favor of homosexual marriage is really a decision *against* religious freedom"[21] (emphasis his). Rafael's son Ted was even more explicit about gay rights representing an attack on Christian values and freedom. He points to Kim Davis, the county clerk who went to jail for refusing to issue a marriage license to a gay couple and subsequently became a Christian nationalist hero:

Christians are somehow singled out. Kim Davis, a Christian, did not want her name to appear on a homosexual marriage license. Under Kentucky law, her faith should have been respected and her name removed . . . . Instead, she was sent to jail, the act of an imperious, arrogant judge wanting to punish a Christian for daring to live according to her faith . . . . What we are really seeing is increasing hostility to religious liberty, and to Christians in particular . . . . These threats are only growing. If we don't stand up and stop them, you and I could be next . . . . Pastors being punished for preaching the Word of God could be next.[22]

The threat is seen as ominous. In their view American Christians and pastors will be the growing target of "hostility" and will soon be prosecuted simply for living out their "religious liberty"—in this case, liberty to discriminate against gays and lesbians by refusing service to them, even as government employees. Christians' response to these threats, counsels Cruz, must be to "stand up and stop them."

An Accommodator from South Carolina, Joshua, expresses a similar concern about religious liberty: "Decorating cakes and obligating people to serve other people, even if they had deep-seated religious opposition to the activity they were asked to engage in, for example, Masterpiece Cakeshop, the Supreme Court case that just came down last year, where it came to him [the baker] participating in a gay wedding ceremony. So on those grounds, I think that's a pretty clear . . . and that's what the Supreme Court ruled, is that that would be a violation of religious liberty." Blake, an evangelical Presbyterian in Georgia, shares some of Joshua's concerns. While he strongly affirms the separation of church and state, believes our culture should accommodate gays and lesbians, and was classified as a rather weak Accommodator on our Christian nationalism scale, he personally feels homosexuality is a sin and fears restrictions on his freedom: "You hear stories of saying like homosexuality is a sin and being prosecuted for a hate crime. That hasn't happened yet, and I'm not sure how far away we are. That would probably be the thing I'm most concerned about is limiting speech, religious speech in that way and considering things hate speech that are Christian, like biblical things. Telling someone they're a sinner and going to hell could be something like that considered hate speech." Thus, while neither Joshua nor Blake want to outlaw gay marriage, they do fear that their freedom as Christians to publicly disapprove of homosexuality—either verbally or simply by not offering service to facilitate same-sex marriage—could be under attack.

Along with same-sex marriage, Americans' growing support for transgender rights—and the challenge this poses for traditional understandings of gender, family, and God's intended order—has also become a talking point for Christian nationalist groups and leaders. Months after the 2016 election, former congresswoman Michele

Bachmann, who now sits on Trump's evangelical advisory board, suggested his win was a "reprieve" from God concerning moves made by the Obama administration toward equality for transgender Americans. Bachmann stated, "I think people just saw no hope that the United States would return to a position of Judeo-Christian morality. We were in a situation where the president of the United States [Obama], on his own, just issued a sheet of paper and said, overnight, every single public school in the country would have to have the girls' bathrooms open to the boys and the boys' bathrooms open to the girls."[23]

The question of how American Christians must respond to transgender issues has become so fraught that in 2017, the Council on Biblical Manhood and Womanhood (founded by Wayne Grudem) issued "The Nashville Statement" to definitively declare what they think biblical Christians ought to believe. Leaders like Grudem, Tony Perkins, and James Dobson were among its initial signatories, quickly followed by a who's who of the Christian Right. Along with affirming essential, God-ordained differences between men and women, the statement declares in Article V, "WE AFFIRM that the differences between male and female reproductive structures are integral to God's design for self-conception as male or female. WE DENY that physical anomalies or psychological conditions nullify the God-appointed link between biological sex and self-conception as male or female." In other words, God intends for the "male" and "female" gender to correspond with reproductive structures; thus, God views being "transgender" as a sin. Brad, an Ambassador, illustrates this view: "Well, God made you a male or a female. He's pretty explicit in that. And so if you're transgender . . . that's just flawed in their thinking."

Because it connects gender distinctions and hierarchy with order, it should be unsurprising that Christian nationalism is particularly at odds with transgender rights. This is made especially visible in Americans' responses to legal controversies over which bathrooms transgender Americans should use.[24] The 2017 Baylor Religion Survey found that 52 percent of Americans believe transgender people should be able to use the bathroom of their choice. Despite this ambivalence in the broader population, however, Aaron, an Accommodator from

Oklahoma, was unequivocal: "Bathrooms? Can a 40-year-old man wake up one morning, declare himself as a herself and walk into a woman's bathroom? No. That is unacceptable. I don't care how many surgeries that individual has had. No."

Aaron's response reflects that of other Americans who ascribe to Christian nationalism (see Figure 4.3). Even when we account for political conservatism, religious practice, and a host of socio-demographic factors, Christian nationalism is the strongest predictor of attitudes on transgender rights.[25] Unsurprisingly, Ambassadors are the group least likely to believe transgender people should be allowed to use the bathroom of their choice, with Accommodators not far behind. Lori, an Ambassador from the Midwest, told us that she did not "think we have to show grace to people that are practicing things that aren't Biblically correct." Another Ambassador we spoke to agreed, "They're born with certain parts, and if they choose to change their parts or add parts than they were born with, then that's their personal choice. But we should definitely not have special laws to allow them . . . they should be identified with how they were born and not with what the decisions they decide to change later on in their life." Another Ambassador, Jay, states simply, "We should care for the sinner, but not mandate that our country celebrate, protect, and promote their sin."

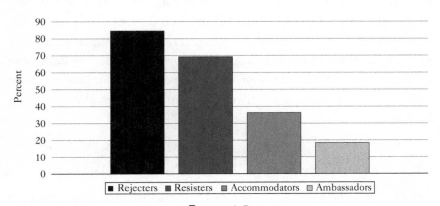

FIGURE 4.3.
Percentage of Americans Who Agree that Transgender People Should Be Allowed to Use the Public Restroom of Their Choice
Source: 2017 Baylor Religion Survey.

Several moves by the Trump administration appear to be in line with the views of Ambassadors and Accommodators. In early 2017 the Departments of Education and Justice reversed protections put in place during the Obama administration that allowed transgender students to use the bathroom of their choice. Then, in the fall of 2018, a leaked Trump administration memo showed that multiple federal agencies were considering a policy to define gender to correspond with one's biological sex at birth. This was widely believed to be aimed at undoing protections from discrimination for transgender Americans.

On the other side of the spectrum, however, we found nearly 70 percent of Resisters and 85 percent of Rejecters agree that transgender people should be able to use the bathroom of their choice.[26] The Freedom From Religion Foundation (FFRF), which strongly rejects the Christian nation narrative, responded to both moves of the Trump administration, labeling them "religiously motivated discrimination." The FFRF argued that the Trump administration and several conservative Christian organizations—like Focus on the Family and the Family Research Council—"are legislating false, biblical ideas about gender essentialism and applying it to public policy. In a secular nation, laws must not be molded by church doctrine." Annie Laurie Gaylor, co-president of the FFRF, reiterated the importance of church–state separation: "This is what you get when you mix religion and government. Our founders recognized that religious dogma turned into national policy can only lead to divisiveness and disaster." Rejecters, and organizations like the FFRF, support the rights of transgender Americans to use the bathroom of their choice because, in their view, the particular interpretations of Christianity supported by Ambassadors and Accommodators should have no place in structuring American civil life.[27]

DO AS WE SAY, NOT AS WE DO—THE CASE OF DIVORCE

Divorce, and the societal ills it was believed to inflict, was central to the platform of the Moral Majority in the late 1970s through the 1980s. While many on the Christian Right acknowledged that divorce was permissible in certain extreme circumstances, they also believed the passing of "no-fault divorce" laws starting in the 1970s made divorce far too easy and subsequently weakened the traditional family. Contemporary Christian nationalist leaders still lament the ease with which one can obtain a divorce in the United States.[28] Framers of the "Manhattan Declaration," for example, called American Christians to repentance for having "too easily embraced the culture of divorce," and recommended that "To strengthen families . . . we must reform ill-advised policies that contribute to the weakening of the institution of marriage, including the discredited idea of unilateral divorce."[29] Some Christian nationalist politicians like Tony Perkins and Mike Huckabee helped institute "covenant marriage" laws in Louisiana and Arkansas, respectively. These laws allow people to voluntarily enter into a marriage of a "stronger" legal status than standard marriage. Covenant marriage requires people to take premarital counseling and only allows divorce in a few circumstances. Notably, few took advantage of this in the states where it was made available.

Consistent with what we might expect given the condemnations of prominent leaders, Christian nationalism is strongly connected to disapproval of divorce and the belief that it should be more difficult to obtain. Looking at the BRS data (Figure 4.4, Panel A) we see that Rejecters, Resisters, Accommodators, and Ambassadors each have very different views on the morality of divorce.[30] While there is clearly more moral acceptance of divorce across the board when children are not in the picture, the trends remain the same whether or not kids are involved. Those who affirm Christian nationalism more strongly are less likely to see nothing wrong with divorce under these circumstances. But we also see that Christian nationalism seems to incline Americans to want to restrict the availability of divorce (Figure 4.4, Panel B). The 2014 General Social Survey asked respondents if they felt divorce in this country should be easier or more difficult to obtain than it is now. We see that as Americans think being a Christian is more important for being "truly American," they are more likely to agree that divorce should be more difficult to obtain.[31]

Despite their condemnation of divorce, however, those on the Christian Right, and Christian nationalists in particular, have an

(a) Agree that Divorce Under Certain Circumstances Is "Not Wrong At All"

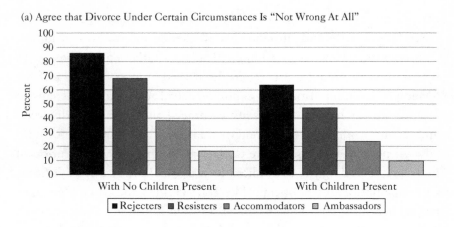

(b) Believes Divorce Laws in U.S. Should Make Divorce More Difficult

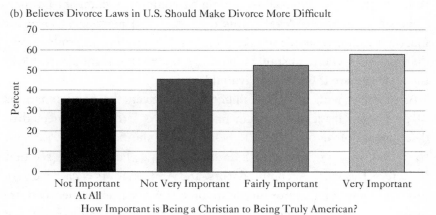

FIGURE 4.4.

Attitudes Toward Divorce by Adherence to Christian Nationalism

(a) *Source:* 2007 Baylor Religion Survey.

(b) *Source:* 2014 General Social Survey.

inconsistent record of applying that standard to their leaders—or themselves. In the 1980 Presidential election, the Moral Majority backed Ronald Reagan, whose first marriage ended in divorce. And, as we showed in Chapter 2, history repeated itself with Ambassadors and Accommodators strongly supporting the election of twice-divorced Donald Trump.

Aside from their willingness to support political leaders who do not exemplify a Christian appreciation for the marriage covenant, our data suggest Accommodators and Ambassadors themselves are no less likely to be divorced than other Americans. In the 2017 Baylor Religion Survey data (see Table 4.1), we see that there are no significant differences in the percent of Rejecters, Resisters, Accommodators, or Ambassadors who are divorced (though there is a higher percentage of Ambassadors who are divorced [15.3%] compared to others, this does not quite attain statistical significance).[32] The same is true across each group for those separated. While Accommodators and especially Ambassadors have moral objections to divorce, they are no more or less likely to divorce than Resisters or Rejecters.[33]

A nearly identical trend emerges in the General Social Survey data when we look at marital status across Americans' views about Christian identity and American civil belonging. In 2014 respondents were asked if they had *ever* been divorced. We found that roughly 29 percent of those who thought being a Christian was very important to being "truly American" had been divorced compared to only 20 percent

Table 4.1. Percent Marital Status of Rejecters, Resisters, Accommodators, and Ambassadors

	Rejecters	Resisters	Accommodators	Ambassadors
Married	49.0	45.2 [b]	56.0	52.2
Divorced	*10.8*	*11.0*	*10.5*	*15.3*
Separated	2.7	2.4	2.2	3.8
Cohabiting	10.2 [b,c]	7.7 [c]	5.0	3.3
Single	24.1 [c]	30.0 [b,c]	19.2 [c]	12.1
Widowed	3.1 [b,c]	3.8 [b,c]	7.1 [c]	13.4

[a] Significant difference compared to Resisters.

[b] Significant difference compared to Accommodators.

[c] Significant difference compared to Ambassadors.

Source: 2017 Baylor Religion Survey.

for everyone else. While these differences were not statistically significant once we accounted for age—older people are more likely to have
been divorced *and* to be Christian nationalists—these findings confirm
that Americans who embrace Christian nationalism are no less likely
to get divorced than other Americans, despite their near-unanimous
condemnation of it.

The point here is not to implicate Christian nationalism in a tendency toward hypocrisy. Rather, we wish to underscore what Christian
nationalism *is* in essence. Despite its ostensible association with family
values and marriage, its primary concern with these issues is not *moral*
in a personal sense, but *political*. Christian nationalism seeks to draw
boundaries around "proper" familial arrangements for the purpose of
maintaining order—perhaps "God's order" to some degree, but mostly
the "traditional order" where families follow the patriarchal, nuclear
norm. Thus, Ambassadors and Accommodators can simultaneously be
extremely concerned with condemning divorce and supporting policies
that limit it *in the abstract*, even while they are no less likely to experience it themselves.

When Christian Nationalism Looks Like Religious Commitment

Christian nationalism, as we have shown, is a powerful predictor of
attitudes toward gender roles in the family, same-sex marriage, transgender rights, and divorce. The pattern is consistent with what we
observed in chapters 2 and 3: those who adhere more strongly to
Christian nationalism (Ambassadors and Accommodators) are more
likely to espouse conservative attitudes toward each issue we have
considered. Also, as in previous chapters, we have shown Christian nationalism has explanatory power above and beyond a number of other
possible explanations. Even when we control for various demographic
factors, political ideology and party identification, and conventional
measures of religion, Christian nationalism is among the strongest
influences on Americans' attitudes about gender, sexuality, and the

family. It also helps us explain why they seek policy interventions supporting their views.

What is quite different here from prior chapters, however, is the comparison of the direction of Christian nationalism's relationship with these issues, and that of personal religiosity more generally. Thus far we have argued that Christian nationalism is something altogether different from religiosity because it seems to influence Americans in the opposite direction. Once we account for Americans' desire to institutionalize Christianity in the public sphere, Americans who are more religious are actually *less* likely to vote for Trump, *less* likely to ostracize immigrants, *less* likely to espouse anti-black prejudice or fear Muslims. Here though, we find the opposite. As Americans exhibit higher levels of religious commitment, even after taking Christian nationalism into account, they are *more* likely to desire more traditional gender roles in the home, oppose same-sex marriage and transgender rights, or have more negative views of divorce. A stronger embrace of Christian nationalism results in much the same.

Figure 4.5 displays some of these relationships. The pattern is clear. Increasing levels of Christian nationalism and increasing levels of personal religiosity result in more conservative attitudes toward sexuality, gender, and divorce. Compare these figures with Figures 2.8 and 3.6. The difference is dramatic.

This raises an important question: Why do religious commitment and Christian nationalism work in a similar direction for gender, sexuality, and divorce, but not for most of the issues we discussed in previous chapters? Most obviously, religion, at least for contemporary Americans, may be more fundamentally related to issues of gender, family, and sexuality in ways that it is not related to ethnic, racial, or national boundaries and hierarchies. Explaining the connection between religion and prejudice, psychologist Gordon Allport famously observed, "However sublime the origins of a religion may be, it rapidly becomes secularized by taking over cultural functions. . . . When religious distinctions are made to do double duty, the grounds for [ethnic or racial] prejudice are laid."[34] Allport argued that while nativism or racism may be completely foreign to a certain religious system originally, one's

(a) Same-Sex Marriage

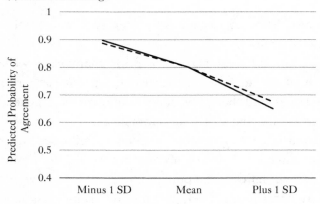

(b) Transgender Americans can use bathroom of their choice

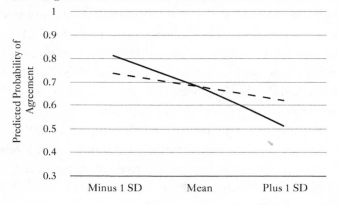

(c) Divorce is not wrong at all when no children are present

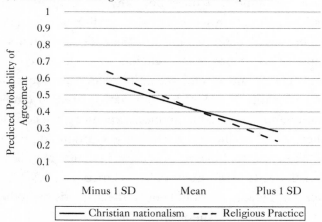

── Christian nationalism   - - - Religious Practice

FIGURE 4.5.

Association Between Gender, Family, and Sexuality Attitudes with
Christian Nationalism and Religious Practice

Source: 2017 Baylor Religion Survey

religious identity often "stands for more than faith" and becomes co-opted to reinforce ethnic, racial, or national boundaries such that to be one of "us" in a religious sense is also to be one of "us" in an ethnic or national sense. This is Christian nationalism—Christianity co-opted in the service of ethno-national power and separation.

Yet unlike ethnic or national distinctions, issues of sexual morality, gender expression, and family formation are likely more *elemental* to religion (again, at least for contemporary Americans). Thus, to be more committed to religion personally is to be more committed to a certain "traditional" model of family life, sexual behavior, or gender, regardless of one's views on Christian nationalism.

Even so, religious commitment and Christian nationalism must be related to issues of family, gender, and sexuality in different ways. We know this because we include both measures in our statistical models, and the two do not cancel one another out. Rather, both remain strong predictors. Here is where our interviews offer some insight. Christian nationalism tends to promote more traditionalist stances on gender, family, and sexuality because of its orientation toward societal "order" and threats to the "proper" arrangements. Jay, an Ambassador and Baptist, explained his opposition to same-sex marriage and transgender rights in these terms: "Believing that sexually immoral lifestyles are both damaging to people's bodies and souls, I do not want my country to celebrate these lifestyles, promote these lifestyles, or mandate that I celebrate and promote these lifestyles." Quoting a less famous part of the Declaration of Independence, which states that "[The king of England] has refused his assent to laws, the most wholesome and necessary for the public good," Jay explains:

> Government is not to be a tyrant and the rules they put in place should be most wholesome and necessary for the public good. Proverbs 29:2 tells us that "When the righteous increase, the people rejoice, but when the wicked rule, the people groan." Wicked laws will bring groaning, so I would not want my country to put in laws that promote sexual sin . . . . When you read the book of Genesis, there are at least two unique times when you see the cry of sin rising to Heaven and God

showing up to judge. In Genesis 4:10 the blood of Abel is crying to God from the ground, and this represents the murder of the innocent. And in Genesis 18:20 you see the outcry of the sexual sin of Sodom and Gomorrah coming to God. So I do believe that America is in a bad place before God and that it is not a good idea to put into our public policy laws that propagate and celebrate abortion or sexual immorality.

While Jay is certainly a religious person, it is his commitment to seeing God's commands regarding homosexuality reflected in American public policy that are most prominently on display here. Opposing homosexuality and transgender rights is about the good of society. Nations that enforce "wicked laws" are not only violating what is "wholesome and necessary for public good," they are inviting God's judgment.

Religious commitment, we argue, is something more personal and less orientated toward societal order and hierarchies. Rather, it reflects a commitment to one's faith community, deity, or system of moral beliefs itself. Those who evidence greater religious commitment, then, even if they are not strong Christian nationalists, may still favor more traditionalist interpretations of gender, family, and sexuality. A Resister, Brian is a "fairly conservative" Christian who considers himself very committed to his evangelical nondenominational church. He also believes homosexuality is sinful, but his perspective differs drastically from Jay's:

I'm working from the basis that homosexuals seeking marriage are not Christians. What I mean is that they are not seeking a life aligned with the Bible to bring God glory. As a Christian I desire for every person to come to faith in Christ, and that certainly extends to the homosexual community. However, I also try not to allow my desire for them to become Christians to lead me to a place where I think mandates and laws should strip [their] American liberties away. Should homosexuals marry? Biblically, no, of course not. As Americans, do I think we should restrict them from marrying? I personally don't care what they do. I think of marriage as a biblical institution. I personally don't see the point when non-Christians marry but hey, knock yourself out.

We certainly don't mean to highlight Brian's quote here as a "more positive" alternative to Jay's. But the differences are important. Brian believes gay men and women are likely not Christians because their homosexuality suggests they are living an unbiblical lifestyle. He also believes the Bible clearly rejects the idea that gay men and women can get married. However, while Jay and Brian would likely both answer the same way on a survey question asking about the *morality* of homosexuality, as a Resister and someone who has reservations about religious mandates curbing the liberties of other Americans, Brian is more ambivalent about the legal status of same-sex marriage. And his concern seems more to be with the religious conversion of gay men and women rather than maintaining societal order by protecting the legal definition of marriage. In other words, Brian's attitudes toward same-sex marriage seemed to be shaped more by his conservative Christian faith than his commitment to the politicization of that faith.

While we do propose that traditionalist conceptions of family, gender, and sexuality are somewhat bound to *contemporary* American religion, this does not mean the association cannot change. There may simply be a cultural lag as American Christianity begins to embrace different expressions of family, gender roles, and even sexuality. Many religious groups, even more liberal denominations, have only recently begun to liberalize in their views toward these issues. Consider same-sex marriage. In 2007 only two of nine large mainline denominations, which are usually considered more liberal, publically supported same-sex marriage, while one favored a traditional legal definition of marriage.[35] In 2019, one of the largest mainline denominations in the United States, the United Methodist Church, was still debating its official stance toward homosexuality. Gender equality has a similar history. While women have officially had access to ordination in various denominations since the 1880s, it was a full century before the percentage of American clergy who were women exceeded five percent.[36] While it takes decades for various religious organizations to liberalize, it takes several more for these shifts to be represented by those in the pews. Compounding this time lag is the reality that, since the mid-1990s, those who may have had more liberal views toward sexuality, divorce, and gender have begun to exit various religious traditions. This was largely due to the influence of the Religious Right and its strident views concerning gender, homosexuality, and divorce. Some Americans decided they would rather not affiliate at all, even if their denomination was not necessarily a part of the Religious Right.[37] Therefore, even those remaining in more liberal denominations and who are religiously active tend to be more conservative on gender, sexuality, and divorce relative to those who left.

CONCLUSION

Focusing on issues of family life, gender, and sexuality allows us to see how Christian nationalism not only seeks to (re)establish order and hierarchy in the public sphere, but perhaps even more so in the private sphere. The hierarchies between men and women, particularly with the patriarchal family, and traditional views of monogamous, heterosexual relationships are highly salient issues for Americans who increasingly feel their cultural influence being not only attenuated but reversed to the point where their own "religious freedom" (to curtail the liberties of sexual or gender minorities or rally opposition to such persons) is now threatened.

And while other religious Americans (even those who are not Ambassadors or Accommodators) might also be morally opposed to homosexuality, transgender rights, and divorce, such opposition is not quite the same as the opposition among Ambassadors and Accommodators, strictly speaking. The connection between religion and traditionalist interpretations of family, gender, and sexuality can be highly personal, but they need not be overtly political. Christian nationalism, however, is political at its core. Threats to the "traditional" (patriarchal, heterosexual, nuclear) family are not just the symptoms of sin in a fallen world. They are threats to the very fabric of American society. Consequently, the solution is not merely converting those souls to faith in Jesus Christ. The solution is the political reinforcement of godly order in covenant marriage laws, the elimination of no-fault divorce, constitutional amendments defining marriage as between a man and a woman, prohibiting homosexual or transgender persons from serving in the military, legislation that require persons to use bathrooms corresponding to their sex at birth, and protecting "religious freedom" to discriminate against sexual and gender minorities.

CONCLUSION

ONE NATION UNDER WHAT?

And [Jesus] continued, "You have a fine way of setting aside the commands of God in order to observe your own traditions."

—Mark 7:9 (NIV)

Throughout its history, America has experienced several transformations—cultural, political, technological, demographic, economic—many of which are interrelated. Like any society in which old orders and regimes are threatened by rapid transition, those who have historically benefited from the status quo not only marshal justifications for the old order, but rally a coordinated response among those who stand to lose the most if that old order topples. At least since the early 1800s, Christian nationalism has provided the unifying myths, traditions, narratives, and value systems that have historically been deployed to preserve the interests of those who wish to halt or turn back changes occurring within American society.

On the surface, Christian nationalist rhetoric seems far more modest. In terms of what is often explicitly stated at "Freedom Sunday" services or in Christian Right literature, we might conclude that Christian nationalism wishes to merely preserve a prominent role for Christianity in Americans' public and private worlds, and to recapture that historic prominence in order to secure God's future blessing. If we were to personally interview David Barton, Tony Perkins, or Robert Jeffress, they would likely claim nothing more.

ne "Christianity" reflected in the myths, narratives, and
of the Christian national*ism* we've described is more than just
.stianity" in general. Rather, it is freighted with a variety of cultural
meanings, all with political implications. *That* Christianity—advocated
by those we call Ambassadors and Accommodators and opposed by
those we call Rejecters and Resisters—seems to be one that paradoxically holds America as sacred in God's sight while viewing its future as
tenuous and bleak. It valorizes conquests in America's name and blood-
shed in its defense. It idealizes relations marked by clear (metaphorical
or physical) boundaries and hierarchies both in the private and public
realms. It baptizes authoritarian rule. It justifies the preservation of
order with righteous violence, whether that be carried out by police
against deserving (minority) criminals, by border agents against pre-
sumptively dangerous (minority) immigrants, or by citizen "good guys"
with guns against rampaging "bad guys" with guns. And it glorifies the
patriarchal, heterosexual family as not only God's biblical standard,
but the cornerstone of all thriving civilizations.

What are we to make of this ideology?

CHRISTIAN NATIONALISM MATTERS

The critical argument of this book, and hopefully most obvious by now,
is that Christian nationalism matters a great deal. More specifically, accounting for the extent to which Americans embrace Christian nationalism is essential if we are to accurately understand Americans' beliefs
and actions across a host of pertinent issues. As a cultural framework,
Christian nationalism provides a lens through which Americans—*all*
Americans, not just Christian nationalists—interpret and experience
their lives. In this way, Christian nationalism is influential across the
entire population because it is not merely embracing Christian nationalism that matters. Rather, it matters whether someone rejects it, resists
it, or even merely accommodates it. We've shown how vote choice and
attitudes toward gun control, immigration, non-Christian religions, racial and ethnic minorities, same-sex marriage, and gender roles, among

others, are all significantly associated with whether someone identifies as an Ambassador, Accommodator, Resister, or Rejecter.

Acknowledging the importance of Christian nationalism also introduces the precision that our public discourse on religion and politics so desperately needs. For the past few years journalists and political commentators have obsessed over why "white evangelicals," voted for President Trump. In reality, however, it is not just being evangelical or even being a white evangelical that truly matters. Rather, it is the degree to which Americans—perceiving current political conflicts through the lens of Christian nationalism—wish to institutionalize conservative "Christian" cultural preferences in America's policies and self-identity. Recognizing the power of Christian nationalism helps us acknowledge not only the diversity within particular religious traditions but also why those of different religious traditions who are Ambassadors tend to vote and act in very similar ways. Evangelicals and mainline Protestants who are Ambassadors are much more alike politically than are Ambassadors and Resisters who are both mainline Protestants. Moreover, Christian nationalism is not bound to any particular religious group. Such findings suggest to us that Christian nationalism is at least one axis upon which the restructuring of American religion has taken place. Public religion matters in the modern world.[1]

This insight is critical to grasp. Christian nationalism is significant because calls to "take America back for God" are not primarily about mobilizing the faithful toward *religious* ends. Some social scientists have argued that when evangelicals appeal to the religious heritage of the United States or work toward privileging Christianity in the public sphere they are focused on encouraging greater religious devotion.[2] We disagree. They are instead seeking to retain or gain power in the public sphere—whether political, social, or religious. Christian nationalism is, therefore, ultimately about privilege. It co-opts Christian language and iconography in order to cloak particular political or social ends in moral and religious symbolism. This serves to legitimate the demands, wants, and desires of those embracing Christian nationalism in the transcendent. If God says the United States should take a particular stance, or pass a specific law, who are we to argue? Christian nationalism is used to defend against shifts in the culture toward equality for groups that have historically lacked access to the levers of power—women, sexual, racial, ethnic, and religious minorities.

CHRISTIAN NATIONALISM IS UNIQUE

While Christian nationalism is closely related to a number of other ideologies and social statuses, it is not synonymous with, reducible to, or a byproduct of any of them. To be sure, Christian nationalism is intimately intertwined with Islamophobia, political conservatism, and gender traditionalism. But it is not just a product or manifestation of these things. It stands on its own and is a unique cultural framework. In other words, in order to accurately examine cultural and social life in the United States, we need to account for Christian nationalism alongside these other important influences. In Appendix A we outline exactly how researchers and pollsters can and should account for Christian nationalism going forward.

We also want to be clear, however, that we are not arguing that Christian nationalism is the root cause of these other ideologies. Again, these things are all intimately intertwined. It is also important to mention that while Christian nationalism is more predictive of Americans' attitudes across a host of issues than their denominational affiliation or race, denominational affiliation and race are still very important. While Christian nationalism is not limited to a particular denomination or racial group, it is more prevalent in some than in others. This means that being a white evangelical in America generally means you are much more likely to be exposed to Christian nationalist ideology—most evangelicals are either Ambassadors or Accommodators. However, not all Ambassadors or Accommodators are evangelicals. And when we make that distinction, we find that it's one's orientation to Christian nationalism that tends to matter most. Ambassadors in different religious traditions look far more alike than people in the same religious tradition who are at opposite ends of the Christian nationalism continuum.

COMMITMENT TO CHRISTIAN NATIONALISM ≠ COMMITMENT TO RELIGION

Third, Christian nationalism and personal religious piety are not one and the same. For the most part we find that the association between Christian nationalism and various hot-button political issues or attitudes toward racial and religious minorities tends to work in the complete *opposite direction* than the association between private religious practice and these same things. While Ambassadors and Accommodators are least likely to support federal gun control legislation, once we account for Americans' embrace of Christian nationalism, those who attend church more often, pray more often, or read their Bible more frequently are more likely to support gun control. Similar to Rejecters and Resisters, Americans who are more religiously active are less likely to fear refugees from the Middle East, or atheists, or Jews. Time and again, when Christian nationalism zigs, religious practice zags.

Regarding questions of gender, sexuality, and the family, however, Christian nationalism and personal religious piety work in the same direction and are equally strong predictors of more conservative attitudes. However, the reasons why strong Christian nationalism and personal religious piety both encourage more traditional views of gender, sexuality, and the family are still distinct. Ambassadors favor traditionalist stances in order to preserve societal order. Religiously active Americans favor traditionalist stances due to a concern for those who they believe are "living in sin" with a hope of eventual conversion. They are not primarily concerned with creating a more Christian nation.

Recognizing how and when Christian nationalism works in a different direction than religious practice is important. First, it allows us to be more accurate when examining the intersection of religion with various issues dominating the public discourse. No one should claim that it is "religious" people writ large who are supporting a certain candidate or policy position. As we mention above, and similar to how many journalists and pundits overgeneralize about evangelicals, some assume that it is merely being religious that makes Americans think and act in particular ways. As we demonstrate time and again, it is the extent to which Americans desire "religion," and specifically a particular ethnocultural strain of Christianity, to be privileged in the public sphere that tells us the most about how they feel about a number of issues. Religious practice is something altogether different. Americans who strongly embrace Christian nationalism do not always report high levels of personal religious piety. While private religiosity and Christian nationalism are strongly correlated, they are not one and the same. In fact, Christian nationalism may serve to bind many disparate groups together, including both the religious and nonreligious.[3]

Furthermore, Rejecters of Christian nationalism include many pious evangelicals. A number of Rejecters we spoke with identified as Christian and reported that religion was very important to them. Some were even working as religious leaders in ministries. Their rejection of Christian nationalism was rooted in their Christian faith and resulted in their having very similar views and goals for American society as those who were not religious who also rejected Christian nationalism. This suggests to us that the *rejection* of Christian nationalism can also serve to unite disparate groups, both religious and nonreligious. Researchers, journalists, and Americans active in civic life must recognize the disparate effects of Christian nationalism and personal religious piety.[4]

THE FUTURE OF CHRISTIAN NATIONALISM IN THE UNITED STATES

POLITICS

What role will Christian nationalism play in the 2020 election? As of this writing (halfway through 2019) there are several things we can say. First, Trump and his supporters will continue to tap into the power of Christian nationalism. As we stated earlier, narratives are very powerful political tools. The narrative that the United States is a Christian nation began as a ploy to create a national identity in the midst of turmoil and change.[5] It has proved useful through a number of historical periods to a variety of different groups, some with opposing ends. As some groups struggle with the increasing diversity of the United States and the increasingly globalized economy, tapping into a shared religious and political-national identity is a powerful way to unite groups to a common cause.

Drawing on Christian nationalist rhetoric will continue to be a savvy political move on Trump's part. Between 2016 and 2020 there will be little if any broad shift across the population regarding the size of Accommodators and Ambassadors. In 2016 these Americans enthusiastically responded to Trump's promises of "stopping the assault on Christianity." For instance, in late 2017 Trump advisor and televangelist Paula White exclaimed, "Isn't it nice to be able to say Merry Christmas and to put Jesus Christ back on the White House lawn? And to have the crusader that we have in our president? And Trump just hasn't put Christ back in Christmas, but he's also put prayer back in the White House, he's put justice back into, and religious freedom back into, our courts."[6] Like Paula White, we do not expect Trump and others to stop claiming that he alone can protect America's Christian heritage when it has worked so well thus far. One example illustrates this perfectly. In early 2019 Trump's favorability was falling as the longest shutdown of the federal government wore on. Three days after it ended, Trump tweeted, "Numerous states introducing Bible Literacy classes, giving students the option of studying the Bible. Starting to make a turn back? Great!"[7] Ambassadors and Accommodators across the country rejoiced and again trusted that President Trump was doing what he could to make America more Christian. Many we interviewed considered it imperative to keep Trump in office to stem the tide of creeping liberalism and secularism. Douglas, a married retiree and Ambassador from the Midwest told us that, "the only thing that concerns me is will he [Trump] be able to do it for another four years after this term is up, because I truly believe it's gonna take him eight years to get this country back on track again."

Second, we expect that any personal moral failings of Trump or his surrogates will continue to do little to sway the minds of his supporters. Ambassadors and Accommodators, both leaders and the rank and file, used words like "antics," or "flaws" or "mistakes" (usually accompanied by caveats like "everyone makes mistakes") when referencing Trump's behavior. Given the consequentialist nature of Christian nationalism, it matters little whether Trump is a pious representative of the Christian faith. Many believe God is bringing about his purposes in the world by working through Trump regardless of Trump's personal failings. As long as Ambassadors and even Accommodators see him as delivering on his promise to restore Christian America, they will continue to support him. Therefore, groups opposing Trump should realize that dwelling on Trump's sexual dalliances, corrupt business practices, or even collusion with a foreign power are not useful tools in the project of changing minds. For a large swath of the American public the only thing that counts is whether they feel as though their religious and national identity is being given preference. As sociologist Gerardo Marti points out, keeping this desired end in mind helps us understand how many religious Americans can support Trump. For these Americans, Trump is "fully orthodox." Ambassadors and many Accommodators want to once again see their political and cultural influence on the ascent, something Trump is happy to deliver. The *personal* orthodoxy of Trump is subordinate to that goal.[8] And how they achieve that end matters little, whether through democratic or more authoritarian means.

Third, if Democrats and those who oppose Trump are unable to espouse a coherent narrative that taps into a powerful national identity, they will have a difficult time defeating Trump in the general election. Sociologist Ruth Braunstein shows how in 2016 Democrats and progressive coalitions were divided in the stories they were telling. Unable to unite behind a persuasive narrative as an alternative to Trump's, they lost the hearts and minds of swing voters.[9] As we presented earlier, almost 60 percent of political Independents are either Resisters or Rejecters of Christian nationalism. These Americans may respond to a narrative of national identity highlighting the importance of religious freedom, rather than Christianity alone, and strength through diversity rather than privileging one religious tradition. The religious history of the United States is peppered with examples of citizens defending the rights of others to worship in a different way (or not) or to a different god or gods (or no god at all). In order to be competitive, the Democratic nominee must not neglect the significance of a unifying national narrative, and one that does not ignore the importance of religion.

Beyond the 2020 presidential election, it is essential to pay attention to how politicians at all levels of federal, state, and local governments use Christian nationalism to engender support and advocate for their particular vision for America. One example is Project Blitz, an initiative created by a coalition of groups on the Christian Right and spearheaded by the Congressional Prayer Caucus Foundation.[10] Project Blitz is a playbook of model legislation from which politicians can easily draw that is focused on promoting and in some cases imposing Christian nationalist interpretations of Christian values at the local, state, and federal level.[11] At root, Project Blitz is a response to the belief that the Christian God is being removed from American culture and that this is shaking the very foundation upon which American society is built.

Project Blitz's model bills are organized into three categories.[12] While Category 1 bills are largely symbolic, Project Blitz organizers see them as laying a foundation for Category 2 or 3 measures that might create more controversy. And as law professor Caroline Mala Corbin recognized, even "traditional" and largely symbolic practices like legislative prayers function to create a religious caste system and bolster symbolic boundaries that exclude non-Christians. Such symbolic boundaries are then translated into social boundaries where the excluded are denied access to the full rights of citizenship, as recent scholarship demonstrates.[13] In fact, Categories 2 and 3 of Project Blitz function on this explicit assumption: the more that Americans generally accept the "Christian heritage" narrative, they will be more likely to accept and support laws and resolutions that formalize the "traditional" social hierarchies we explore throughout this book. Many of these bills have already been proposed and in some cases passed.[14]

The main point here is that Christian nationalism will continue to pervade the political sphere at all levels of government. Even seemingly innocuous moves toward privileging Christianity—things that Accommodators and perhaps even Resisters might shrug at—could be part of a larger effort of political operatives to enshrine Christian nationalist ideology in America's legal and political system.

DECLINING IN SIZE BUT NOT IN IMPORTANCE

In chapter 1 we examined shifts in the relative size of Ambassadors, Accommodators, Resisters, and Rejecters over the past decade. We found that there are indeed fewer Ambassadors today than there were in 2007. There are essentially the same number of Accommodators. Taken together, more than half of Americans reside in these two groups. Both Rejecters and Resisters significantly increased in size, and come close to matching Ambassadors and Accommodators. Using these findings and those from questions asked on other surveys, we predict that Ambassadors will continue to slowly decline in size while Rejecters and Resisters will increase. The significant increase in average age for Ambassadors and the continued disaffiliation of Americans are two of the most important reasons why. An important caveat, however, is that the reliance of Americans on Christian nationalism can wax and wane depending on historical moments. It very well could be that our data come from a period where the cultural context was not as fertile as before. This seems unlikely, though, given the ubiquity of Christian nationalist rhetoric in the political sphere from the lead-up to the 2016 election and after.

It is essential to emphasize that while the relative *size* of Ambassadors may decrease in the coming years, the *importance* of this group will not. More broadly, while there may be shifts in the relative size of each group, the significance of each group will still be of great consequence. In fact, a slow decline in the number of those Americans who fully embrace Christian nationalism will likely serve to increase the relevance of that position. Historian John Fea writes that fear of waning cultural influence was instrumental in evangelical Protestants supporting Trump.[15] As we and others have shown, this fear of waning cultural influence expands far beyond the denominational boundaries of evangelicalism. As Ambassadors and even Accommodators across the country begin to see "their" country disappear, their identities as

"Christian Americans" will grow even more salient. This is why we expect the cultural framework of Christian nationalism to be powerful despite any small shifts in the number of people who embrace it.

IMPLICATIONS FOR CIVIL SOCIETY

Americans who embrace Christian nationalism are much more likely to create, support, and maintain symbolic and social boundaries that exclude non-Christians from full inclusion into American civic life. Many of those we interviewed affirmed the abstract right of all people to live in the United States and either worship according to the dictates of their religion or not worship at all—as long as this was all kept in private. Americans who embrace Christian nationalism drew a distinct line, however, at whether these same people should be allowed to bring their sincerely held beliefs into the public sphere in order to influence civil society.

This forces non-Christians to continually defend their right to exist and advocate for their right to participate in the public sphere. Examples abound. For instance, in early 2019 the federal government moved to allow a South Carolina adoption agency to reject non-Christian or gay couples from service as foster parents.[16] Or recall an effort to oust a Republican county official in Texas because he was Muslim.[17] In both instances, the *religious beliefs* of non-Christian Americans are presumed to hinder their ability to fulfill their duties as American citizens. Non-Christian Americans are viewed as fundamentally deficient. They can never be *truly American.*

Therefore, strong support for Christian nationalism is—without a doubt—a threat to a pluralistic democratic society. As Supreme Court Justice Harry Blackmun once remarked, "A government cannot be premised on the belief that all persons are created equal when it asserts that God prefers some."[18] Christian nationalist ideology is fundamentally focused on gaining and maintaining access to power. It seeks to ensure that one particular group, with a specific vision for the country, enjoys privileged access to the halls of power and has the ability to make the culture in its own image. Because the embrace of Christian nationalism fuses national and religious symbols and identities, it is able to legitimate its desires for the country in the will of the Christian God, bringing the transcendent to bear on everyday realities. This serves to inhibit any chance at compromise. There is no room for disagreement. There is no possibility of alternative viewpoints. Such a stance leads to a devaluation of the democratic process where ideally everyone agrees to play by the same rules. Embracing Christian nationalism, therefore, results in a propensity toward consequentialism, where the ends justify the means. Half-truths, shady practices, and authoritarian measures, if in service to realizing a more "Christian" nation, are deemed necessary to ensure the "right" group stays in power. Strong Ambassadors were more likely to believe that the country would be better off if that "other side" ceased to exist. Strong Ambassadors considered the "other side's" vision of the country completely bankrupt, to be opposed by any means necessary.[19] Strong support for Christian nationalism demands complete allegiance and ultimately desires the silencing and exclusion of its opponents from the public sphere. Such a stance makes it increasingly difficult to engage in good faith conversations about issues or find common ground.

Thankfully, such strong Ambassadors are a minority. Their voices in no way represent a broad coalition of Americans. However, the loudest voices are often the easiest to hear, and the more moderate views and desires of Accommodators or marginal Ambassadors might be lost. Therefore, it seems the Americans who identify as Resisters and Accommodators—who together represent almost two out of three Americans (59 percent)—will have to lead the way in finding common ground where compromise is possible.

IMPLICATIONS FOR CHRISTIANITY IN THE UNITED STATES

Christian nationalism also has something to say about who the "true" Christians are. Clearly, the Christian symbols and language that permeate American Christian nationalism are powerfully resonant to those who affiliate with a Christian tradition. It is easy for these Americans to overlook how Christian nationalism tends to employ these symbols and language toward particular ends—ends that serve a certain segment of the nation first and foremost and that reinforce inequalities between groups that have historically had access to power and those denied that access. Christian nationalism is undeniably concerned with maintaining cultural and political boundaries and hierarchical relationships between "us" and "them." It enjoins Christians to rally behind someone who will "punch the bully" and not ask them to be "a welcome mat which people can stomp their feet on." Christians only have two cheeks, after all.[20]

Given the ubiquity of Christian nationalist ideology, it is no wonder that many—especially younger generations—are leaving Christianity and not looking back. The fusion of the Christian religion with conservative politics played a central role in "The Great Abdicating" in which, since the mid-1990s, the number of Americans who do not affiliate with a religious tradition has increased dramatically.[21] And not only is Christian nationalism turning people away from Christianity, it is creating fissures within the tradition as well.

Christians who reject Christian nationalism point out how its consequences directly contradict dictates found within the Bible. Other interpretive traditions within Christianity call Christians to heed the Old Testament prophets' rebuke of avarice and violence; to follow Jesus in welcoming "the least of these" into their company; and to emulate the self-sacrificial love displayed by Christ on the cross. The kingdom of God, they argue, is broader, more diverse, and will long outlast the kingdoms of this world, including the United States. In this view, fusing national identity with Christianity destroys the witness of the kingdom of God. The desperate quest for power inherent in Christian nationalist ideology is antithetical to Jesus' message. At its core, Christian nationalism is a hollow and deceptive philosophy that depends on human tradition and the basic principles of this world, rather than on Christ.

"TRUE" AMERICANS, "TRUE" CHRISTIANS

The "God and Country" celebrations we visited dramatically underscored the belief that in a "Christian nation" there are "true" Americans as well as "true" Christians. In the services we visited it was not uncommon to see hands raised toward heaven or in dutiful salute, eyes growing misty with emotion or closed in solemn meditation, and voices raised to honor country or to sing praises to a Savior. Participants in these powerful moments of collective effervescence were emphasizing the necessity of *spiritual* citizenship in order to affirm *national* citizenship. These celebrations effectively ask, "How could a citizen *truly* celebrate America without acknowledging the Christian God so instrumental in creating and *even dying for* the United States?" Each assembly asserted that in order to be truly American, one *had* to be Christian—of a certain kind, of course.

As we observed and experienced the "God and Country" worship services we recognized that Christian nationalism goes even further. Those who embrace Christian nationalism insist that the Christian God formed, favors, and sustains the United States over and above the other nations of the world. They proclaim the United States plays a central role in God's plan for the world. But, if the Christian God has truly *"always been on our side,"* America's side, then on whose side are Christians from Iraq, Vietnam, China, England, Afghanistan, or any other country? It serves to reinforce an assumption that *Americans* are favored over and above all other nationalities within the Christian tradition. The rituals, symbols, and celebrations assert not only that in order to be truly American one must be Christian, but that in order to be *truly* Christian one *has to be American*.

Is the United States of America one nation under God? Though Christian nationalism strongly affirms such a view, Americans' diverse responses to this cultural framework challenge any hope of "unity" around our religious heritage and identity. Even so, the historic resonance of Christian nationalist rhetoric; the influence it holds on our social and political views; its ability to re-emerge during times of societal conflict, means that it orients life for *all of us* to some degree. Whether one unequivocally rejects or zealously advocates for Christian nationalism, we're all contending with our legacy as a supposedly "Christian nation."

APPENDIX A
Data and Methods

Our overarching objective in writing about American Christian nationalism was to be as comprehensive as possible without sacrificing important nuance. There are really two goals that we needed to hold in balance. We wanted to be able to generalize our findings to the national population, thus allowing us to talk about Christian nationalism's distribution, trends, and, most importantly, effects in the aggregate. But we also wanted to take into account how individual Americans might elaborate their views on religion in public life in different ways if given the chance. Because no single type of data could accomplish those two goals, we collected and present findings from several different data sources.

QUANTITATIVE SURVEY DATA

While we drew on a variety of quantitative data sources for this book, the majority of quantitative data came from the 2017 Baylor Religion Survey (BRS). We provide more information about the 2017 BRS here because it is not yet publically available. The 2017 BRS (more formally called the Values and Beliefs of the American Public survey) was collected by the Gallup organization. It is the fifth wave of the survey, with prior waves being collected in 2005, 2007, 2010, and 2014. The 2017 BRS was fielded using a pen and paper methodology. It was entirely self-administered and collected via the mail. The collection began on February 2, 2017, when an invitation letter, the survey, a return envelope, and a $1 USD cash incentive was mailed to those in the sampling frame. Reminder postcards were sent out on February 13. On February 28, 2017, a full cover letter, survey, and return envelope was sent to those addresses remaining open. Collection of the surveys finished on March 21, 2017.

The sample was selected using Address Based Sample (ABS) methodology using a stratified sampling design. The ABS method was employed in order to address evolving coverage problems often associated with telephone-based samples. A simple stratified sample design was used to ensure adequate representation among various subpopulations. Gallup constructed post-stratification sampling weights to match the known demographic characteristics of the U.S. adult population by region, gender, age, race/ethnicity, and education.

The initial sampling frame contained 11,000 addresses that included Spanish-speaking only households, as well as residents of Alaska and Hawaii. A total of 1,501 surveys were completed and returned for an overall response rate of 13.5 percent. While a higher response rate is always desirable, this response rate does exceed the average rate for many public opinion polls. Furthermore, researchers highlight that response rates are minimally related to the accuracy of parameter estimates. Finally, surveys that use weights to match population demographics provide accurate data on many political, social, and economic measures.[1]

Below we provide a comparison between the 2017 BRS and the 2016 General Social Survey (GSS), the latter of which is often held up as the gold standard of nationally representative surveys in the United States. While some small differences exist, the overall comparison is quite similar. It is also worthwhile to note that the 2017 BRS has already begun to appear in a number of peer-reviewed articles in a variety of well-respected scholarly outlets.[2]

We are grateful to the Society for the Scientific Study of Religion, the Association for the Sociology of Religion, the (former) College of Business and Behavioral Sciences at Clemson University, and the Department of Sociology, Anthropology, & Criminal Justice at Clemson University for providing grants that offset the cost of including the Christian nationalism questions, as well as the gender traditionalism questions from Chapter 4, on the 2017 BRS.

We also made fairly liberal use of different waves of the GSS, collected by NORC at the University of Chicago. Starting in 1972, the GSS was fielded almost every year, but since 1992, subsequent waves have been fielded every two years. Because NORC makes all GSS data freely available online at www.gss.norc.org where interested readers can find the measures we use and replicate our models with the data provided, we will not elaborate further on the GSS here.

Table A.1. Comparison of the 2017 BRS to the 2016 GSS

	2017 BRS		2016 GSS
Age	49.7	Age	47.6
Women	52.3	Women	54.8
Marital status		Marital status	
Single/never married	21.1	*Single/never married*	27.4
Married	50.2	*Married*	49.9
Nonwhite	35.2	Nonwhite	26.5
Education		Education	
Less than HS	9.0	*Less than HS*	13.5
HS grad	27.0	*HS grad*	29.2
Some college	31.4	*Some college*	26.3
BA	15.3	*BA*	16.8
Post-BA	17.3	*Post-BA*	14.3
Income		Income	
$10,000 or less	9.0	*$9,999 or less*	6.9
$10,001–$20,000	12.4	*$10,000–$19,999*	9.0
$20,001–$35,000	14.3	*$20,000–$34,999*	15.9
$35,001–$50,000	15.4	*$35,000–$49,999*	12.9
$50,001–$100,000	26.2	*$50,000–$109,999*	35.1
$100,001–$150,00	12.4	*$110,000–149,999*	10.3
$150,001 or more	10.6	*$150,000 or more*	10.4
Political Ideology		Political Ideology	
Extremely conservative	3.5	*Extremely conservative*	4.2
Conservative	21.7	*Conservative*	15.8
Leaning conservative	10.2	*Leaning conservative*	14.3
Moderate	37.0	*Moderate*	37.2
Leaning liberal	8.5	*Leaning liberal*	11.3
Liberal	15.8	*Liberal*	12.4
Extremely liberal	3.4	*Extremely liberal*	4.8
Attend religious services		Attend religious services	
Never	27.2	*Never*	25.0
Less than once a year	6.9	*Less than once a year*	5.9
Once or twice a year	12.7	*Once a year*	13.3
Several times a year	11.5	*Several times a year*	11.1
Once a month	4.2	*Once a month*	7.0

Table A.1. Continued

	2017 BRS		2016 GSS
2–3 times a month	8.3	*2–3 times a month*	8.7
About once a week	21.2	*Nearly every week*	4.4
Several times a week	8.0	*Every week*	17.5

Note: All data weighted using *weight* for 2017 BRS and *wtssall* for GSS 2016.

Table A.2. Quantitative Surveys Used to Document Trends in Christian Nationalist Views

Survey	Chapters Cited
1974–2016 Aggregated General Social Surveys	Intro (notes), Ch. 1, Ch. 4 (notes)
1996 General Social Survey	Ch. 1
2003 American Mosaic Project	Ch. 1 (notes)
2004 General Social Survey	Ch. 1, Ch. 4
2007 Baylor Religion Survey	Intro, Ch. 1, Ch. 2, Ch. 3, Ch. 4
2012 Religion, Class, and Culture Survey	Ch. 1
2013 Public Religion Research Institute–Religion News Service Survey	Intro.
2014 General Social Survey	Ch. 1, Ch. 2, Ch. 3, Ch. 4
2017 Baylor Religion Survey	Intro, Ch. 1, Ch. 2, Ch. 3, Ch. 4

We provide the full list of quantitative data sources that we used throughout the book in Table A.2. Though we cite several surveys in chapters that make reference to more general religious trends, here we only list those from which we drew information about Christian nationalist views. Other than the 2017 BRS, all the datasets we cite throughout the book—including how data were collected and relevant questions were asked—are freely available at www.theARDA.com. Under the leadership of Roger Finke, Christopher Bader, and Andrew Whitehead, The Association of Religion Data Archives (ARDA) is an invaluable repository for religion data that can essentially be used like Google for searching out variables and datasets one might need. In fact, researchers can find a host of datasets on the

ARDA that contain at least one measure similar or identical to a measure we use in our Christian nationalism scale.[3]

Hopefully by now our fellow researchers will agree with us that future data collections must account for Christian nationalism. A key question is how to do so. Ideally, future researchers will include the six questions we use in this text in order to account for the variation in Americans' views across the population. This scale is internally consistent and is reliable over time. From 2007 to 2017 we find that these six questions perform quite similarly. Our measure comprises six different questions:

- "The federal government should declare the United States a Christian nation"
- "The federal government should advocate Christian values"
- "The federal government should enforce strict separation of church and state" (which we reverse coded)
- "The federal government should allow the display of religious symbols in public spaces"
- "The success of the United States is part of God's plan"
- "The federal government should allow prayer in public schools."

Respondents were able to either strongly agree, agree, disagree, strongly disagree, or indicate that they were undecided. The third question about the separation of church and state is reverse coded in order to match the other responses. It also ensures respondents were not merely satisficing.

These six questions were first asked in the 2007 wave of the BRS. In order to faithfully compare more recent data collected in 2017 with that collected in 2007, we used the exact same questions, response categories, and overall wording found in the 2007 wave. Table A.3 shows the factor loading scores for each of these questions and Cronbach's alpha coefficient for the scale for both the 2007 and 2017 waves.

We realize, however, that due to space constraints, researchers or pollsters might not be able to include all six measures. If this is the case, we recommend including three so that a Christian nationalism scale can still be created. Looking at the factor loading scores, three measures stand out:

- "The federal government should allow prayer in public schools"
- "The federal government should advocate Christian values"
- "The federal government should declare the United States a Christian nation"

Table A.3. Factor Loading Scores and Cronbach's Alpha Coefficient

	2007	2017
The federal government should declare the United States a Christian nation	.77	.81
The federal government should advocate Christian values	.84	.85
The federal government should enforce strict separation of church and state	.60	.48
The federal government should allow the display of religious symbols in public spaces	.82	.75
The success of the United States is part of God's plan	.76	.82
The federal government should allow prayer in public schools	.87	.84
Cronbach's Alpha Coefficient	.87	.85

One last measure is a very close fourth, almost statistically tied with the third measure above:

- "The success of the United States is part of God's plan"

Using these four measures or any three of them would enable researchers to account for Christian nationalism and ensure they were not overlooking a vital aspect of the influence of religion.

Another option for researchers is to include the following two questions in their survey:

- "In the past, some people have called the United States a Christian nation. Would you characterize the United States as a Christian nation today?" (Yes/No)
- Follow-up, "Would you say that's a good thing, or a bad thing?" (Extremely good thing, very good thing, somewhat good thing, not a very good thing, not a good thing at all)

Our work has provided guidance to other researchers interested in the influence of Christian nationalism. When asked, we recommend that which we share above. We are aware of forthcoming data collections that use some or all of the measures we outline. Other high-visibility data collections are (as of this writing) pre-testing these questions. We hope this trend will continue.

However, if researchers can only include one question, we suggest three options in rank order. Option one is to include one of the above questions. Each taps into whether Americans think the United States *should be* a Christian nation, which is a more important question to answer than *if* the United States is a Christian nation. A large number of surveys include a question about prayer in public schools (see endnote 3 in this appendix), which we find is one of the strongest measures in our index. Another strong contender is to use the second in the list above, "The federal government should advocate Christian values." Knowing the extent to which Americans strongly agree to strongly disagree with either one of these measures is better than having no information at all.

Option two is to use a question we've highlighted throughout this book that appears in the 1996, 2004, and 2014 waves of the GSS. It asks: "Some people say the following things are important for being truly American. Others say they are not important. How important do you think each of the following is? To be a Christian," where respondents can answer with "Very important," "Fairly important," "Not very important," or "Not important at all." This question taps into how Americans think about the symbolic boundaries of American-ness and is useful for establishing whether they think being "Christian" is vital to those boundaries. Like the questions in our scale, it measures whether Americans think Christianity *should be* a vital part of the national identity.

A third option is to use a question we referenced in the Introduction (see Figure I.1). This question asks, "Some people think the United States is a Christian nation and some people think that the United States is not a Christian nation. Which statement comes closest to your view?" Americans could respond in one of four ways:

- "The United States has always been and currently is a Christian nation."
- "The United States was a Christian nation in the past, but is not now."
- "The United States has never been a Christian nation."
- "Don't know."

One of the weaknesses of this question is that it does not account for the strength with which Americans hold these views or if they believe the United States should

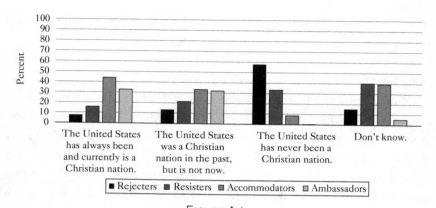

FIGURE A.1.

Percent of Each Possible Response to Whether the United States Is a Christian Nation that are Ambassadors, Accommodators, Resisters, or Rejecters

Source: 2017 Baylor Religion Survey.

be a Christian nation. It also does not allow us to determine if respondents' answers signal that they believe each possible view is a good or bad state of affairs. As Figure A.1 shows, Ambassadors, Accommodators, Resisters, and Rejecters are distributed across each response. Among those Americans who believe that "The United States has always been and currently is a Christian nation," just over 30 percent are Ambassadors, close to 45 percent are Accommodators, 16 percent are Resisters, and almost 8 percent are Rejecters. Only for those Americans who chose the option "The United States has never been a Christian nation" do we see a clear linear relationship with the four possible responses to Christian nationalism. In other work we have found, though, that while this question does not perfectly mirror the Christian nationalism index, it is similarly predictive of Americans' attitudes.[4]

Throughout each chapter all multivariate analyses using the various waves of the BRS or the GSS are performed using multiple imputation data. This includes all of the tables presented throughout the appendix. Multiple imputation techniques allow us to account for missing data in multivariate models and the possibility of biased estimates. The multiple imputation (MI) procedure generates five imputations using multiple Markov Chains based on all variables included in each model, resulting in an overall N of 8,240 (1,648 × 5) for the 2007 BRS and 7,505 (1,501 × 5) for the 2017 BRS. Because the GSS rotate modules across their total sample, the overall N can differ depending on which variable is used. Therefore, the overall N for the 2014 GSS is either 4,130 (826 × 5), 4,375 (875 × 5), or 6,370 (1,274 × 5), again depending on the variables examined. All the multivariate results reported throughout the text or in the appendix are from the MIANALYZE procedure in SAS. This procedure combines all the results from each of the five imputations resulting in overall estimates, standard errors, and significance levels. The standardized coefficients and odds ratios for each model were calculated using these overall estimates. The Proportional Reduction in Error (PRE) and the R-Square model fit statistics reported throughout the text for each model are the average across all five individual iterations. As a sensitivity check, we also ran multivariate models with the non-imputed BRS and GSS datasets, and the relationships and findings we present throughout this book were present in those findings, too.

All of the frequencies and bivariate analyses we report throughout this work do not use the MI datasets because missing data is less of an issue with only one or two variables in view. For all of the regression models presented throughout the appendix, we provide standardized coefficients so readers can compare relative strength of each variable's effect compared to other variables in that model.

Qualitative Data

Because a central goal of ours was to document the powerful connections between Christian nationalist ideology and Americans' views and behaviors regarding the most pressing national issues of the day, we focused much of our attention in the book on national quantitative data. Despite this focus, however, we both agreed that qualitative data would be absolutely essential to flesh out how Ambassadors, Accommodators, Resisters, and Rejecters actually explain their positions, as well as how strong Christian nationalist leaders and citizens talk to one another. Our qualitative data came from two sources primarily: in-depth interviews with 50 American men and women across the Christian nationalism spectrum and from different regions of the country, and participant observation at different events where Christian nationalist ideology would be preached, discussed, or otherwise generally assumed by all in attendance.

INTERVIEWS

SAMPLING AND RECRUITMENT

Because the goal of our quantitative data was to generalize to the broader population of Americans, the surveys we used needed to be "representative," collected among a random sample of Americans. Such is not the goal of qualitative data. Rather, as sociologist Mario Small (2009) points out, "representativeness" in a strict statistical sense is a nearly unattainable goal for in-depth interviews because of issues of limited coverage, selectivity bias, and prohibitively small sample sizes. Consequently, following Small and others, we exchange a "sampling logic" for a "case-study logic" in which each interview is conceived as another case of X (in our case, perspectives on Christian nationalism). Applied to our interviewing strategy, we adopted what Small calls "sequential interviewing." He explains, "The first unit or case [interview] yields a set of findings and a set of questions that inform the next case. If the study is conducted properly, the very last case examined will provide very little new information. The objective is saturation."[5]

We began with the goal of interviewing at least 10 individuals (5 men/5 women) from each of our four categories. To recruit participants we used a combination of purposive, snowball, and convenience sampling. In order to minimize social desirability bias that might come from interviewees crafting their answers because they know what the interviewer thinks politically or religiously, we agreed that we should set as a goal to have at least 1 degree of separation between either of us and the interviewee—friends of friends, or even further removed if possible.

We had each interviewee complete a brief survey that included the six Christian nationalism questions from the 2007 and 2017 BRS that we use to construct our Christian nationalism indexes and categories. From this we were able to locate our interviewees within one of our four categories.

As we show in Table A.4, our final sample of interviewees included 50 individuals. We achieved our goal of interviewing at least 10 individuals from each group, and we ended up speaking with slightly more Ambassadors (15 total interviews) and Accommodators (14 total interviews). We include this material not because we are attempting to argue for the representativeness of our interview sample (because, again, that was not the goal) but rather for the sake of transparency, so that readers can have information about the people we interviewed.

Table A.4. Interview Sample (Percentages)

Interview	Full Sample	Ambassador	Accommodator	Resister	Rejecter
N	50	15	14	11	10
Mean Age	46.4	48.4	47.7	45	43.2
Percent Men	68	67	71	82	50
Percent White	88	87	93	73	100
Region					
South	74	60	93	73	70
Midwest	22	33	7	18	30
Northeast	2	0	0	9	0
West	2	7	0	0	0
Highest Degree					
High school	10	13	21	0	10
Bachelors	42	73	43	36	40
Graduate	38	13	36	64	50
Religion					
Evangelical	56	93	71	27	10
Mainline	14	0	14	36	10
Catholic	8	7	14	9	0
Other	6	0	0	27	10
Unaffiliated	14	0	0	0	70
Religious Importance					
Not at all	10	0	0	0	50
Not very	4	0	0	0	20
Fairly	12	0	7	27	20
Very	74	100	93	73	10
Mean Political Ideology	4.76	6.33	5.93	3.55	2.10

Interviews were digitally recorded and professionally transcribed by a transcription service that signs a confidentiality waiver. We analyzed the interviews using an open-coding procedure, and we also read and coded one another's interviews in order to compare analyses. Despite our open-coding procedure, we would not call our process "grounded" in the sense that we sought to approach the interview data as blank slates. Rather, we came to the data with sensitizing concepts that helped us to make sense of some of the explanations and arguments that kept reoccurring among our interviewees.

Participant Observation

As useful as interviews are in allowing researchers to hear participants' explanations for why they believe or behave a certain way, sociologists are increasingly coming to the conclusion that interviewees' accounts should be corroborated whenever possible with observational data that allows researchers to check for contradictions or information that interviewees might have simply neglected to share. For us, this meant engaging in participant observation at events that gave us a high probability of experiencing Christian nationalist discourse and symbolism up close.

In the Summer of 2018, the authors attended four large events in Texas, Oklahoma, and South Carolina where Christian nationalists and their beliefs were prominently represented. These included the "Freedom Sunday" service at Robert Jeffress's First Baptist Church, Dallas, Texas; the "Freedom Celebration" service at First Moore Baptist Church in Moore, Oklahoma; the "God Bless America, America Bless God" service at Crossings Community Church in Oklahoma City, Oklahoma (which included a message from Republican Senator James Lankford); and the "God & Country Celebration" at Utica Baptist Church in Seneca, South Carolina. The "Celebrate America" service at Rock Springs Baptist Church in Easley, South Carolina was viewed online.

Each of these events were advertised and open to the public (which is why we mention them by name) and provided the opportunity for authors to observe how America's relationship to Christianity was articulated and symbolized in these settings, as well as to have dozens of informal conversations with those in attendance.

Later, in the Fall of 2018 just before November midterm elections, the authors attended services and/or listened to recorded versions of the services at First Baptist Church in Dallas, Texas; Denton Bible Church in Denton, Texas; and Rock Springs Baptist Church in Easley, South Carolina. The authors both took extensive field notes about each event, and often listened to recorded versions of the sermons 2–3 times afterwards.

RECOMMENDATIONS
FOR FUTURE RESEARCH

In addition to what we've shared above, we offer several recommendations for future research. First, while beginning to include measures of Christian nationalism on our polls and surveys is vital, doing so over time is equally important. Chapters 1 and 4 contain analyses that document the change in salience of Christian nationalism over time. Consistently measuring Christian nationalism in subsequent surveys of the American population will allow us to document the ongoing salience of Christian nationalism in the public sphere. It will also help us grow our understanding of *when* and *how* Christian nationalism waxes and wanes. Asked alongside behavioral and attitudinal questions that are consistently included in the same surveys will also broaden our understanding of how closely Christian nationalism is related to what Americans believe and how they act from decade to decade. As we continue to explore the importance of religion in a social context that is ever-changing, we must account for shifts and fluctuations over time in how strongly Americans desire public expressions of religion like Christian nationalism.

A second recommendation is that others examine in greater depth how *certain* Christian nationalist views work differently for Americans in various sociodemographic subgroups. Race and ethnicity is a particularly important prism through which Americans' religious and national views could be refracted onto different social issues. For example, in a recent study we found that black Americans who believe being Christian is very important to being truly American were much more likely than other black Americans to explain black–white inequality in terms of discrimination and lack of access to education. In contrast, whites who believe being Christian is very important to being American were more likely than other whites to blame black Americans themselves.[6] In this case, being black or white completely altered the connection between beliefs about America's Christian identity and explanations for racial inequality.

Historical treatments of the Christian nation narrative demonstrate how integral the question of race can be. Civil rights leaders Frederick Douglass, Dr. Martin Luther King, Jr., and the Rev. William Barber II have each taken seriously the Christian heritage of the United States and the importance of Christianity to American identity. By calling forth that identity and heritage they have demanded the nation live up to the promises of freedom and equality inherent within the Christian religion.[7] The influence of Christian nationalist rhetoric and sentiment in the black community, as well as other racial and ethnic minority groups, could be quite different from what we explore throughout this book. Our modeling accounts for respondents' race and ethnicity, but large, quantitative surveys and methodologies can overlook important nuance. We especially point out the need for more interviews with racial and ethnic minorities about the Christian nation narrative and the religious national identity of the United States. While we were able to converse with a handful of nonwhite Americans, a majority of our interviews were with white Americans, leaving much more left to be done.

A third recommendation is to continue to examine religious nationalism worldwide. Throughout this book we have focused solely on Christian nationalism *in the United States*. In this sense, ours is a case study of the influence and power of religious nationalism in one large and influential country. Widening our gaze to the countries of the world makes clear that the rise of religious nationalism and the desire to closely align national identity with religion—be it Christianity or Hinduism or Islam—is not unique to the United States of America. Indeed, this work is already being done. Political scientists J. Christopher Soper and Joel Fetzer examine religious nationalism in a comparative project and outline various distinct models of church–state arrangements. Various other work highlights how populist movements in Europe similarly co-opt Christian symbols and language in order to cloak their political aims in moral and religious symbolism.[8] It is imperative that our study be read in context with what is taking place in other parts of the world and alongside these and other studies. Keeping multiple sites in view will offer a well-rounded understanding of how cultural frameworks built around religious nationalism influence citizens and various cultural contexts.

APPENDIX B
Tables

Table B.1. OLS Regression Model Predicting Adherence to Christian Nationalism

	β	b	S.E.
Political conservatism	.209	.82***	.08
Identify as "Bible-Believing"	.170	.73***	.11
Bible is the literal word of God [a]	.164	2.52***	.44
Bible is perfectly true, though not literally interpreted [a]	.128	1.71***	.37
Religiously Unaffiliated [b]	−.123	−2.46***	.49
Religious practice [c]	.117	.29***	.06
Believe that the nation is on the brink of moral decay	.115	.62***	.09
Believe that God requires the faithful to wage wars for good	.102	.49***	.08
Believe in "the Rapture"	.094	.54***	.12
Education	−.077	−.33***	.07
Jewish [b]	−.067	−3.18***	.77
Bible contains some human error [a]	.067	1.30***	.36
Republican	.058	.77**	.24
Household income	−.055	−.22**	.08
Other religion [b]	−.049	−1.31**	.44
Female	−.043	−.55**	.19
Black Protestant[b]	.037	1.11*	.54
Married	.033	.44	.24
Don't know [a]	.027	.73	.45
Nonwhite Race	.023	.61	.50

(*continued*)

Table B.1. Continued

	β	b	S.E.
Southern residence	.011	.15	.21
Mainline Protestant[b]	−.008	−.13	.32
Catholic [b]	.004	.06	.28
Age	.003	.001	.01
Intercept	.84		
Adjusted R^2	.673		

Note: Variables Ordered by Highest β to Lowest; β = Standardized coefficient.

*p<.05; **p<.01; ***p<.001.

[a] Compared to believing the Bible is a book of history/legends.

[b] Compared to evangelical Protestants.

[c] A scale made up of three questions asking how frequently respondents attend religious services, prayer, and read their sacred scriptures.

Source: 2007 Baylor Religion Survey (N = 1,648) (MI data).

Table B.2. Ordered Logistic Regression Models Predicting Beliefs about What Makes Someone a Good Person

Question: *How important is it to do the following if one wishes to be a good person?*

	Take care of sick and needy	Actively seek social and economic justice	Consume fewer goods	Have faith in God	Teach others your morals	Convert others to your religious faith	Serve in the military
Christian nationalism	.08	-.11*	-.06	.16***	.37***	.44***	.23***
Religious practice	.26***	.24***	.17***	.38***	.18***	.50***	-.09*
Control variables	√	√	√	√	√	√	√
Intercept 4	.42	.20	-.68	-.81	-1.67***	-3.44***	-3.62***
Intercept 3	3.10***	2.01***	1.18**	.80	.23	-1.66***	-1.82***
Intercept 2	4.40***	3.63***		2.23***	1.60***	.22	-.52
N	1,648	1,648	1,648	1,648	1,648	1,648	1,648

Note: Standardized beta coefficients, p-values, and intercepts are averages across five multiple imputation datasets. "Control variables" include religious tradition, beliefs about the Bible, age, gender, race, educational attainment, household income, region, political ideology, political party, and marital status.

Source: 2007 Baylor Religion Survey (MI data).

Table B.3. Logistic Regression Analyses Predicting Agreement with Various Outcomes Using Christian Nationalism Scale

	Voting for Trump		Middle East Refugees Pose Terror Threat		Abortion when Family Cannot Afford a Child is "Always Wrong"	
	β	OR	β	OR	β	OR
Christian nationalism	.25***	1.07	.35***	1.10	.33***	1.10
Age	.04	1.00	−.02	1.00	−.07*	.99
Female	.04	1.15	−.12*	.65	−.01	.96
Married	−.01	.96	.00	.99	.10*	1.46
White	.20**	2.15	.12**	1.61	.03	1.23
Northeast [a]	—	—	—	—	—	—
Midwest	.04	1.19	.05	1.26	.05	1.22
South	.15	1.74	.09	1.41	.01	1.05
West	.05	1.23	.06	1.29	−.03	.87
Education	−.03	.98	−.11*	.92	−.02	.98
Income	.28***	1.33	.00	1.00	−.17***	.82
City	−.18	.46	−.09	.67	−.04	.81
Suburb [a]	—	—	—	—	—	—
Town	.13	1.65	.01	1.06	−.02	.92
Rural	−.05	.79	−.05	.76	−.05	.79
Political conservatism	.66***	2.22	.59***	2.03	.26***	1.33
Republican	.15*	1.85	.06	1.25	.04	1.15
Independent [a]	—	—	—	—	—	—
Democrat	−.49***	.16	−.11	.66	−.04	.87
Evangelical Protestant [a]	—	—	—	—	—	—
Mainline Protestant	.01	1.08	−.02	.88	−.23***	.35
Black Protestant	−.14	.36	−.12*	.41	−.09	.46
Catholic	.04	1.16	−.01	.96	.08	1.40
Jewish	−.05	.43	.06	2.97	−.03	.69
Other	−.06	.67	−.08	.57	−.02	.89
No affiliation	−.12	.56	.03	1.14	−.06	.71
Biblical literalist	.00	1.02	.00	1.02	.17*	2.08

Table B.3. Continued

	Voting for Trump		Middle East Refugees Pose Terror Threat		Abortion when Family Cannot Afford a Child is "Always Wrong"	
	β	OR	β	OR	β	OR
Religious practice	−.04	.97	−.17**	.89	.37***	1.29
Islamophobia	.23***	1.17	—	—	—	—
Xenophobia	.04	1.32	—	—	—	—
Economic satisfaction	−.03	.95	—	—	—	—
Sexism	.01	1.00	—	—	—	—
Anti-black prejudice	.16*	1.23	—	—	—	—
Intercept	−2.75***		−1.81***		−1.66***	
N	1,501		1,501		1,648	
PRE	.515		.299		.340	

*p<.05; **p<.01; ***p<.001.

[a] Contrast Category.

Source: 2017 Baylor Religion Survey (N = 1,501) & 2007 Baylor Religion Survey (N = 1,648) (MI data).

Table B.4. Logistic Regression Analyses Predicting Extending Free Speech to Hostile Muslim Clergymen

	Allowed to Give Public Speech		Allowed to Teach at College		Allowed to Have Book in Public Library	
	β	OR	β	OR	β	OR
Importance of being Christian to being truly American	−.30***	.64	−.26***	.69	−.22***	.73
Age	.10*	1.01	.09	1.01	.07	1.01
Female	−.12**	.65	−.07	.78	.04	1.17
Married	−.04	.88	.02	1.08	−.03	.91

(*continued*)

Table B.4. Continued

	Allowed to Give Public Speech		Allowed to Teach at College		Allowed to Have Book in Public Library	
	β	OR	β	OR	β	OR
White [a]	—	—	—	—	—	—
Black	.02	1.09	.01	1.08	−.14*	.45
Hispanic	−.14**	.54	−.12*	.60	−.13*	.56
Other race	−.03	.81	−.02	.90	−.05	.72
Northeast [a]	—	—	—	—	—	—
South	.01	1.04	.05	1.23	.10	1.44
Midwest	.11	1.57	.09	1.50	.08	1.42
West	.01	1.04	.04	1.17	.18**	2.12
Education	.13*	1.20	.15**	1.25	.21***	1.34
Income	.02	1.01	.08	1.03	.10	1.03
City	−.01	.96	−.05	.83	−.04	.83
Suburb [a]	—	—	—	—	—	—
Town	−.10	.67	−.06	.79	−.01	.98
Rural	−.06	.69	−.06	.70	−.01	.96
Political conservatism	.06	1.07	−.05	.94	−.01	.99
Republican	−.07	.76	−.17**	.51	−.06	.79
Independent [a]	—	—	—	—	—	—
Democrat	−.11*	.66	−.16**	.57	−.08	.75
Evangelical Protestant[a]	—	—	—	—	—	—
Mainline Protestant	.00	.99	−.08	.65	−.04	.79
Black Protestant	.05	1.43	.00	.97	.06	1.62
Catholic	.02	1.06	−.01	.95	−.05	.83
Jewish	.01	1.15	.02	1.30	−.03	.69
Other	−.05	.68	.00	1.01	−.07	.58
No affiliation	.08	1.39	−.02	.92	.08	1.40
Biblical literalist	−.11*	.65	−.07	.76	−.08	.74
Religious service attendance	−.04	.98	−.03	.98	−.01	.99
Intercept	.17		−.42		−.83	
N	875		875		875	
PRE	.137		.111		.129	

*p < .05; **p < .01; ***p < .001.
[a] Contrast Category.

Source: 2014 General Social Survey (MI data).

Table B.5. Logistic Regression Analyses for Ambassadors, Accommodators, Resisters, and Rejecters (Odds Ratios Shown)

	Model 1	Model 2	Model 3	Model 4
Voting for Trump				
Ambassadors	—	1.28	2.06[†]	2.27[†]
Accommodators	.80	—	1.64[†]	1.83
Resisters	.46[†]	.57[†]	—	1.08
Rejecters	.34[†]	.42[†]	.69	—
Intercept	−1.42*	.1.62*	−2.11**	−2.26***
N	1,501	1,501	1,501	1,501
PRE	.515	.515	.515	.515
Middle East Refugees Pose a Terror Threat				
Ambassadors	—	2.09***	3.00***	4.85***
Accommodators	.54**	—	1.48*	2.45**
Resisters	.36**	.65[†]	—	1.66[†]
Rejecters	.18***	.31***	.47**	—
Intercept	.16	−.44	−.83*	−1.35***
N	1,501	1,501	1,501	1,501
PRE	.299	.299	.299	.299
Abortion when Family Cannot Afford a Child is "Always Wrong"				
Ambassadors	—	1.08	1.83*	4.71***
Accommodators	.98	—	1.72**	4.50***
Resisters	.58*	.60**	—	2.64***
Rejecters	.20***	.20***	.34***	—
Intercept	−.26	−.28	−.82	−1.80***
N	1,648	1,648	1,648	1,648
PRE	.341	.341	.341	.341

[†]p<.10; *p<.05; **p<.01; ***p<.001.

Note: Each model controls for age, gender, marital status, race, region of the country, education, income, size of place, political ideology, political party, religious affiliation, views toward the Bible, and religious practice. The "Voting for Trump" model examines only those respondents who voted in the 2016 election and controls for Islamophobia, racial attitudes, sexism, xenophobia, economic dissatisfaction.

Source: 2017 Baylor Religion Survey (N = 1,501) & 2007 Baylor Religion Survey (N = 1,648) (MI data).

Table B.6. Logistic Regression Analyses Predicting Agreement with Various Outcomes Using Christian Nationalism Scale

	Strong chance of serious defect in the baby		Married, no more children		Woman's health in serious danger		Family too poor		Pregnancy the result of rape		Woman doesn't want to marry man		Abortion for any reason	
	β	OR	β	OR	β	OR	β	OR	β	OR	β	OR	β	OR
Importance of being Christian to being truly American	0.25***	1.45	0.23***	1.39	0.11	1.17	0.19**	1.31	0.20**	1.34	0.22***	1.38	0.22**	1.37
Age	-0.24***	0.98	-0.10†	0.99	-0.11	0.99	-0.07	0.99	-0.16*	0.98	-0.14*	0.99	-0.04	1.00
Female	0.05	1.19	0.01	1.03	0.10	1.45	-0.04	0.87	0.04	1.15	-0.05	0.85	-0.02	0.93
Married	0.01	1.04	0.05	1.18	0.01	1.04	0.05	1.19	0.10†	1.43	0.03	1.13	0.01	1.03
White [a]	—	—	—	—	—	—	—	—	—	—	—	—	—	—
Black	-0.09	0.60	0.06	1.41	-0.04	0.81	-0.02	0.92	0.07	1.46	0.06	1.40	-0.03	0.85
Hispanic	0.12*	1.70	0.02	1.08	0.19*	2.30	0.02	1.10	0.18**	2.23	0.07	1.39	0.05	1.23
Other race	-0.04	0.78	-0.03	0.80	-0.05	0.74	0.06	1.49	0.01	1.07	0.01	1.09	-0.01	0.93
Northeast [a]	—	—	—	—	—	—	—	—	—	—	—	—	—	—
South	-0.11	0.67	0.03	1.14	-0.13	0.62	-0.01	0.98	0.10	1.47	0.08	1.37	0.08	1.34
Midwest	0.01	1.04	-0.02	0.93	-0.09	0.69	0.06	1.29	0.07	1.33	0.09	1.49	0.07	1.37
West	-0.13†	0.59	-0.12†	0.61	-0.19*	0.45	-0.13†	0.58	-0.07	0.74	-0.12†	0.61	-0.09	0.68
Education	-0.04	0.94	-0.09	0.88	-0.17*	0.78	-0.11*	0.86	-0.16*	0.80	-0.13*	0.83	-0.14*	0.82
Income	-0.09	0.97	-0.10†	0.97	-0.13†	0.96	-0.15*	0.95	-0.13†	0.96	-0.16**	0.95	-0.09	0.97
City	-0.06	0.78	-0.11*	0.65	-0.21**	0.42	-0.02	0.91	-0.04	0.85	-0.08	0.73	-0.08	0.73
Suburb [a]	—	—	—	—	—	—	—	—	—	—	—	—	—	—
Town	-0.05	0.83	-0.07	0.75	-0.20*	0.46	-0.01	0.94	-0.05	0.83	-0.05	0.83	0.01	1.05
Rural	0.06	1.42	-0.02	0.87	0.00	1.01	0.06	1.43	0.06	1.42	0.03	1.16	0.03	1.16

Political conservatism	0.29***	1.44	0.24***	1.35	0.19*	1.28	0.15**	1.21	0.27***	1.41	0.16**	1.22	0.21***	1.30
Republican	−0.04	0.85	−0.02	0.91	−0.03	0.88	0.12†	1.58	0.00	0.99	0.08	1.38	0.05	1.23
Independent [a]	—	—	—	—	—	—	—	—	—	—	—	—	—	—
Democrat	−0.13*	0.62	−0.17**	0.55	−0.15†	0.58	−0.12*	0.65	−0.01	0.96	−0.18**	0.52	−0.12*	0.66
Evangelical Protestant [a]	—	—	—	—	—	—	—	—	—	—	—	—	—	—
Mainline Protestant	0.05	1.32	0.04	1.23	−0.05	0.77	−0.01	0.97	0.03	1.17	0.06	1.07	0.06	1.40
Black Protestant	0.06	1.58	−0.08	0.54	−0.26	0.14	−0.10†	0.49	0.03	1.23	−0.05	0.54	−0.05	0.67
Catholic	−0.02	0.92	−0.02	0.92	−0.07	0.74	−0.01	0.95	0.13*	1.72	0.07	0.88	0.00	1.35
Jewish	0.08	3.10	−0.03	0.64	0.12*	6.17	−0.02	0.71	0.11*	4.77	0.00	0.56	0.00	0.99
Other	0.03	1.23	−0.10	2.36	−0.10	0.46	0.09†	1.98	0.09	2.06	0.10†	1.82	0.10†	2.09
No affiliation	−0.08	0.70	−0.02	0.92	−0.01	0.95	−0.04	0.84	0.07	1.33	0.01	0.66	0.01	1.02
Biblical literalist	0.17**	1.93	0.11*	1.53	0.04	1.17	0.11*	1.56	0.06	1.25	0.10*	1.02	0.10*	1.49
Religious service attendance	0.14*	1.10	0.22***	1.15	0.22**	1.15	0.21***	1.15	0.22***	1.15	0.25***	1.14	0.25***	1.17
Intercept	−1.83*		−.69		−1.13		−.08		−2.89***		.733		−1.08†	
N	875		875		875		875		875		875		875	
PRE	.192		.202		.182		.192		.201		.214		.208	

†p<.10; *p<.05; **p<.01; ***p<.001.

[a] Contrast Category.

Source: 2014 General Social Survey (MI Data).

Table B.7. Logistic Regression Analyses Predicting Agreement with Various Outcomes Using Christian Nationalism Scale

	Government is Spending "Too Little" on the Military, Armaments, and Defense		People Should be Made to Show Respect for America's Traditions		Federal Government Should Enact Stricter Gun Laws	
	β	OR	β	OR	β	OR
Christian nationalism	.27***	1.08	.47***	1.14	−.20***	.95
Age	.03	1.00	.09**	1.01	.08*	1.01
Female	−.04	.86	.05	1.20	.16***	1.76
Married	−.01	.96	.03	1.10	−.03	.90
White	.03	1.25	.01	1.04	−.04	.74
Northeast[a]	—	—	—	—	—	—
Midwest	−.13**	.57	−.03	.87	−.10*	.66
South	.08	1.36	−.02	.91	−.15***	.55
West	−.13**	.57	−.04	.85	−.14**	.55
Education	−.07	.92	−.15***	.84	−.04	.95
Income	−.05	.95	.03	1.03	.03	1.03
City	.04	1.21	.01	1.05	−.07*	.67
Suburb [a]	—	—	—	—	—	—
Town	.03	1.10	−.07	.77	−.12**	.64
Rural	.02	1.09	.01	1.06	−.14***	.53
Political conservatism	.28***	1.37	.20***	1.25	−.27***	.73
Republican	.04	1.15	.09*	1.42	−.03	.89
Independent [a]	—	—	—	—	—	—
Democrat	−.02	.91	.11*	1.49	.19***	2.07
Evangelical Protestant [a]	—	—	—	—	—	—
Mainline Protestant	.00	1.00	.07	1.35	.08*	1.40
Black Protestant	−.05	.63	−.01	.90	.09*	2.22
Catholic	.05	1.27	.08	1.45	.11**	1.62
Jewish	.03	1.42	−.03	.65	.07	2.56
Other	.03	1.29	−.06	.62	−.04	.72
No affiliation	.00	1.03	−.08	.64	−.03	.84

Table B.7. Continued

	Government is Spending "Too Little" on the Military, Armaments, and Defense		People Should be Made to Show Respect for America's Traditions		Federal Government Should Enact Stricter Gun Laws	
	β	OR	β	OR	β	OR
Biblical literalist	.08*	1.44	.04	1.19	.09*	1.49
Religious practice	−.13**	.92	−.23***	.85	.15**	1.11
Intercept	−2.21***		−1.45**		1.17*	
N	1,648		1,648		1,648	
PRE	.142		.194		.162	

*p<.05; **p<.01; ***p<.001.

ᵃ Contrast Category.

Source: 2007 Baylor Religion Survey (N = 1,648) (MI data).

Table B.8. Logistic Regression Analyses for Ambassadors, Accommodators, Resisters, and Rejecters (Odds Ratios Shown)

	Model 1	Model 2	Model 3	Model 4
Government is Spending "Too Little" on the Military, Armaments, and Defense				
Ambassadors	—	1.11	1.68*	3.74***
Accommodators	.96	—	1.54*	3.46***
Resisters	.64†	.68*	—	2.31**
Rejecters	.26***	.27***	.41**	—
Intercept	−1.09*	−1.15*	−1.56**	−2.40***
N	1,648	1,648	1,648	1,648
PRE	.142	.142	.142	.142
People Should be Made to Show Respect for America's Traditions				
Ambassadors	—	1.77**	4.33***	8.14***
Accommodators	.63*	—	2.49***	4.73***
Resisters	.25***	.41***	—	1.91**

(continued)

Table B.8. Continued

	Model 1	Model 2	Model 3	Model 4
Rejecters	.13***	.20***	.49***	—
Intercept	1.00*	.53	−.38	−1.03*
N	1,648	1,648	1,648	1,648
PRE	.191	.191	.191	.191

Federal Government Should Enact Stricter Gun Laws

	Model 1	Model 2	Model 3	Model 4
Ambassadors	—	1.11	.71	.47**
Accommodators	.88	—	.63*	.42***
Resisters	1.39	1.57*	—	.65*
Rejecters	2.21**	2.50***	1.60*	—
Intercept	.44	.31	.77	1.20*
N	1,648	1,648	1,648	1,648
PRE	.164	.164	.164	.164

[†]p<.10; *p<.05; **p<.01; ***p<.001.

Note: Each model controls for age, gender, marital status, race, region of the country, education, income, size of place, political ideology, political party, religious affiliation, views toward the Bible, and religious practice.

Source: 2007 Baylor Religion Survey (N = 1,648) (MI data).

Table B.9. Binary Logistic Regression Predicting Agreement with Negative Attitudes Toward Immigrants

	Immigrants Undermine American Culture		Immigrants Increase Crime		Immigration to US Should be "Reduced A Lot"	
	β	OR	β	OR	β	OR
Importance of being Christian to being truly American	.19**	1.32	.12*	1.19	.10†	1.16
Age	−.01	1.00	.09†	1.01	.16**	1.02
Female	.00	.99	−.12**	.66	.07	1.28
Married	−.02	.93	−.01	.95	.02	1.06
White [a]	—	—	—	—	—	—
Black	.07	1.44	−.07	.69	.03	1.19
Hispanic	−.12*	.58	−.10†	.63	−.14*	.54
Other race	.02	1.11	−.04	.80	−.03	.84
Northeast [a]	—	—	—	—	—	—
South	.05	1.21	.13†	1.61	−.04	.86
Midwest	−.05	.82	.01	1.05	−.08	.70
West	−.06	.77	.13†	1.69	−.07	.74
Education	−.12*	.84	−.15**	.80	−.10†	.86
Income	−.05	.99	−.12*	.96	.05	1.02
City	−.03	.89	−.06	.79	−.07	.74
Suburb [a]	—	—	—	—	—	—
Town	.04	1.15	.03	1.11	.07	1.33
Rural	−.03	.86	−.04	.79	.04	1.28
Political conservatism	.08	1.11	.18***	1.25	.14**	1.19
Republican	.08	1.37	−.03	.90	.07	1.29
Independent [a]	—	—	—	—	—	—
Democrat	.08	1.33	−.02	.92	−.06	.80
Evangelical Protestant [a]	—	—	—	—	—	—
Mainline Protestant	−.06	.71	−.10†	.58	−.15*	.44

(continued)

Table B.9. Continued

	Immigrants Undermine American Culture		Immigrants Increase Crime		Immigration to US Should be "Reduced A Lot"	
	β	OR	β	OR	β	OR
Black Protestant	−.14*	.36	−.02	.89	−.05	.68
Catholic	−.07	.76	−.09	.69	−.22**	.42
Jewish	−.01	.92	−.03	.67	−.06	.40
Other	.08	1.80	.04	1.34	−.09	.50
No affiliation	.05	1.24	−.01	.98	−.02	.91
Biblical literalist	.10*	1.48	.04	1.16	−.06	.80
Religious service attendance	−.12*	.93	−.06	.96	−.09	.95
Intercept	−1.80**		−1.55**		−2.70***	
N	1,274		1,274		1,274	
PRE	.078		.091		.098	

†p<.10; *p<.05; **p<.01; ***p<.001.

ªContrast Category.

Source: 2014 General Social Survey (MI Data).

Table B.10. Logistic Regression Analyses Predicting Agreement with Various Outcomes Using Christian Nationalism Scale

	Illegal Immigrants from Mexico are Mostly Dangerous Criminals		The Government is Spending "Too Little" on Patrolling and Controlling Our Borders		"Not at All Comfortable" with Daughter Marrying an African American		Police Officers in the United States Treat Blacks the Same As Whites		Police Officers in the United States Shoot Blacks More Often Because They Are More Violent than Whites	
	β	OR	β	OR	β	OR	β	OR	β	OR
Christian nationalism	.51***	1.16	.14*	1.04	.16**	1.05	.31***	1.09	.23***	1.07
Age	-.09	.99	.16***	1.02	.24***	1.03	-.08*	.99	-.01	1.00
Female	-.06	.80	-.11**	.68	-.08*	.76	.05	1.21	-.14***	.61
Married	-.12	.65	-.05	.84	.06	1.25	-.02	.93	-.11**	.68
White	.19*	2.07	.04	1.39	.12	2.49	—	—	—	—
Black	—	—	—	—	—	—	-.28***	.19	-.02	.86
Hispanic	—	—	—	—	—	—	-.16***	.45	.07	1.45
Other race	—	—	—	—	—	—	-.22***	.27	-.08	.62
Northeast [a]	—	—	—	—	—	—	—	—	—	—
Midwest	.11	1.61	-.03	.87	-.07	.73	.08	1.42	-.01	.97
South	.04	1.18	.09*	1.44	.14**	1.69	.06	1.26	.03	1.12
West	.06	1.27	.10*	1.54	-.13**	.56	.13*	1.71	-.06	.78

(continued)

Table B.10. Continued

	Illegal Immigrants from Mexico are Mostly Dangerous Criminals		The Government is Spending "Too Little" on Patrolling and Controlling Our Borders		"Not at All Comfortable" with Daughter Marrying an African American		Police Officers in the United States Treat Blacks the Same As Whites		Police Officers in the United States Shoot Blacks More Often Because They Are More Violent than Whites	
	β	OR	β	OR	β	OR	β	OR	β	OR
Education	-.27***	.81	-.08*	.91	-.04	.96	-.04	.97	-.11*	.92
Income	-.01	.99	.00	1.00	-.08	.91	.02	1.03	.06	1.06
City	-.07	.75	.00	.98	-.03	.87	.06	1.27	-.03	.90
Suburb [a]	—	—	—	—	—	—	—	—	—	—
Town	-.01	.96	.04	1.18	.09*	1.41	.10	1.46	-.02	.94
Rural	-.06	.74	-.05	.81	.09*	1.51	.03	1.15	-.06	.73
Political conservatism	.20*	1.28	.26***	1.34	.14**	1.17	.26***	1.36	.26***	1.38
Republican	.07	1.31	-.03	.90	.11*	1.52	.09	1.41	-.05	.81
Independent [a]	—	—	—	—	—	—	—	—	—	—
Democrat	-.11	.66	-.10*	.70	.02	1.06	-.13*	.62	-.01	.98
Evangelical Protestant [a]	—	—	—	—	—	—	—	—	—	—
Mainline Protestant	-.05	.78	.03	1.15	.08*	1.43	-.01	.95	.10*	1.69
Black Protestant	.08	1.77	.02	1.22	-.18*	.21	.01	1.05	.02	1.19
Catholic	-.02	.92	.05	1.23	.08	1.43	.04	1.18	.05	1.24

Jewish	−.03	.65	.02	1.26	.08*	2.92	.02	1.52	.11***	6.19
Other	−.01	.93	.02	1.20	−.04	.74	−.02	.84	.03	1.20
No affiliation	−.03	.89	−.08	.64	−.05	.75	.03	1.16	.01	1.03
Biblical literalist	.02	1.12	.06	1.27	.05	1.26	.04	1.22	−.01	.95
Religious practice	−.20*	.87	−.14**	.91	−.13**	.91	−.14*	.91	−.11*	.93
No African American friends	—	—	—	—	.18***	2.08	—	—	—	—
Intercept	−4.80***		.06		−3.40***		−2.01***		−1.18**	
N	1,501		1,648		1,648		1,501		1,501	
PRE	.192		.116		.167		.194		.098	

Source: 2017 Baylor Religion Survey (N = 1,501) & 2007 Baylor Religion Survey (N = 1,648) (MI data).

*p<.05; **p<.01; ***p<.001.

a Contrast Category.

Table B.11. Logistic Regression Analyses for Ambassadors, Accommodators, Resisters, and Rejecters (Odds Ratios Shown)

	Model 1	Model 2	Model 3	Model 4
Illegal Immigrants from Mexico Are Mostly Dangerous Criminals				
Ambassadors	—	1.96**	3.97**	5.96*
Accommodators	.51*	—	2.04†	3.14
Resisters	.21***	.40*	—	1.35
Rejecters	.08***	.15**	.32†	—
Intercept	−2.00**	−2.63***	−3.38***	−3.86***
N	1,501	1,501	1,501	1,501
PRE	.188	.188	.188	.188
The Government is Spending "Too Little" on Patrolling and Controlling Our Borders				
Ambassadors	—	1.14	1.19	1.77*
Accommodators	.92	—	1.05	1.57†
Resisters	.90	.99	—	1.53*
Rejecters	.60†	.65†	.67†	—
Intercept	.60	.51	.48	.07
N	1,648	1,648	1,648	1,648
PRE	.115	.115	.115	.115
"Not at All Comfortable" with Daughter Marrying an African American				
Ambassadors	—	1.35†	1.72*	2.21**
Accommodators	.77	—	1.28	1.66†
Resisters	.60*	.79	—	1.30
Rejecters	.45*	.59†	.75	—
Intercept	−2.51***	−2.77***	−3.02***	−3.28***
N	1,648	1,648	1,648	1,648
PRE	.168	.168	.168	.168

Table B.11. Continued

	Model 1	Model 2	Model 3	Model 4
Police Officers in the United States Treat Blacks the Same as Whites				
Ambassadors	—	1.11	1.66†	2.56*
Accommodators	.94	—	1.53*	2.42**
Resisters	.59*	.63*	—	1.58†
Rejecters	.30***	.32***	.50**	—
Intercept	−.60	−.68*	−1.11***	−1.61***
N	1,501	1,501	1,501	1,501
PRE	.190	.190	.190	.190

Police Officers in the United States Shoot Blacks More Often Because They Are More Violooent than Whites				
Ambassadors	—	1.41	2.25**	2.41*
Accommodators	.76	—	1.63*	1.77*
Resisters	.46**	.59*	—	1.06
Rejecters	.39**	.51*	.82	—
Intercept	.07	−.21	−.70*	.80*
N	1,501	1,501	1,501	1,501
PRE	.098	.098	.098	.098

†$p<.10$; *$p<.05$; **$p<.01$; ***$p<.001$.

Note: Each model controls for age, gender, marital status, race, region of the country, education, income, size of place, political ideology, political party, religious affiliation, views toward the Bible, and religious practice. The third model controls for not having any African American friends.

Source: 2017 Baylor Religion Survey (N = 1,501) & 2007 Baylor Religion Survey (N = 1,648) (MI data).

Table B.12. Logistic Regression Predicting Americans' Views About Being Truly American

	Believes This is "Very Important" to Being Truly American							
	To Have Been Born in America		To Have Lived Here for Life		To Be Able to Speak English		To Have American Ancestry	
	β	OR	β	OR	β	OR	β	OR
Importance of being Christian to being truly American	.38***	1.73	.49***	2.03	.45***	1.91	.68***	2.69
Age	.04	1.00	.12**	1.01	.17***	1.02	.08	1.01
Female	.05	1.21	.02	1.08	.04	1.17	-.04	.86
Married	.04	1.14	-.01	.96	-.04	.88	.05	1.21
White [a]	—	—	—	—	—	—	—	—
Black	.09†	1.64	.15**	2.30	.08	1.53	.04	1.24
Hispanic	.04	1.20	.10*	1.58	.00	1.01	.02	1.07
Other race	.03	1.21	.13***	2.23	.07†	1.52	.10*	1.84
Northeast [a]	—	—	—	—	—	—	—	—
South	.08	1.33	-.12*	.63	-.01	.96	.07	1.30
Midwest	.03	1.13	-.07	.75	.01	1.04	.06	1.31
West	-.04	.86	-.10*	.65	-.04	.86	-.05	.81
Education	-.15***	.81	-.14**	.82	-.09*	.87	-.10†	.87
Income	-.03	.99	-.03	.99	-.01	1.00	-.15**	.95
City	.05	1.23	.07†	1.33	-.01	.94	-.01	.97
Suburb [a]	—	—	—	—	—	—	—	—

	(1) b	(1)	(2) b	(2)	(3) b	(3)	(4) b	(4)
Town	.04	1.19	.03	1.12	-.02	.92	.06	1.25
Rural	.04	1.30	.07†	1.50	-.02	.90	.03	1.17
Political conservatism	.08*	1.11	.10*	1.14	.03	1.04	.09†	1.12
Republican	-.04	.85	.11*	1.55	.12*	1.58	-.02	.93
Independent [a]	—	—	—	—	—	—	—	—
Democrat	-.04	.85	.10*	1.45	-.11*	.68	.01	1.05
Evangelical Protestant [a]	—	—	—	—	—	—	—	—
Mainline Protestant	.01	1.06	.06	1.40	-.09†	.61	.02	1.12
Black Protestant	-.07	.60	-.06	.63	-.09	.51	.04	1.38
Catholic	-.02	.94	.09†	1.42	.02	1.07	.04	1.19
Jewish	-.04	.54	-.03	.69	-.03	.70	-.08	.33
Other	-.02	.85	.05	1.49	.04	1.32	-.04	.72
No affiliation	.00	.99	.10†	1.53	-.12*	.59	.00	1.01
Biblical literalist	-.04	.86	.01	1.02	-.01	.95	.05	1.20
Religious service attendance	-.14**	.92	-.16***	.90	-.15**	.91	-.19***	.89
Intercept	-1.58***		-2.88***		-.36		-3.79***	
N	1,274		1,274		1,274		1,274	
PRE	.123		.166		.157		.248	

†p<.10; *p<.05; **p<.01; ***p<.001.

[a] Contrast Category.

Source: 2014 General Social Survey (MI Data).

Table B.13. OLS Regression Analyses Predicting Scales for Various Religious Groups Using Christian Nationalism Scale

	Muslims Are a Threat		Conservative Christians Are a Threat		Jews are a Threat		Atheists Are a Threat	
	β	SE	β	SE	β	SE	β	SE
Christian nationalism	.29***	.01	−.20***	.01	.14***	.01	.37***	.01
Age	.09***	.00	.05	.00	.08**	.00	.11***	.00
Female	−.07**	.13	.03	.11	−.04	.10	−.08***	.12
Married	−.04	.13	−.08**	.12	−.04	.11	−.01	.12
White	—	—	—	—	—	—	—	—
Black	−.07	.35	.02	.29	.10*	.26	−.03	.30
Hispanic	.01	.18	−.04	.17	.11***	.15	.03	.18
Other race	−.03	.21	−.02	.23	.05*	.16	−.02	.20
Northeast [a]	—	—	—	—	—	—	—	—
Midwest	.08**	.19	.01	.18	.11**	.16	.11***	.19
South	.12***	.18	.01	.16	.09*	.14	.14***	.16
West	.10**	.18	.02	.17	.05	.15	.05	.20
Education	−.11**	.04	−.10**	.03	−.12***	.02	−.09***	.03
Income	.01	.05	.01	.05	−.08*	.04	.00	.04
City	−.04	.15	.02	.15	.02	.13	.01	.17
Suburb [a]	—	—	—	—	—	—	—	—
Town	.00	.15	.02	.14	.00	.11	.01	.16
Rural	.03	.23	.04	.18	.08*	.20	.10***	.21
Political conservatism	.26***	.06	−.15***	.05	.17***	.04	.12***	.05
Republican	.05	.18	.02	.15	.01	.13	.02	.16
Independent [a]	—	—	—	—	—	—	—	—
Democrat	−.04	.15	.08*	.16	−.05	.13	−.02	.14
Evangelical Protestant [a]	—	—	—	—	—	—	—	—
Mainline Protestant	−.03	.22	−.01	.21	−.03	.17	−.01	.20
Black Protestant	.01	.38	−.03	.34	−.05	.29	.04	.35
Catholic	−.03	.17	−.09*	.17	−.07*	.13	−.01	.16
Jewish	.02	.59	.00	.51	−.05	.47	.02	.53
Other	−.02	.24	.00	.26	−.01	.20	.00	.23
No affiliation	.05	.22	.06	.20	.03	.19	−.01	.21
Biblical literalist	.16***	.16	−.04	.18	−.03	.14	.14***	.16

Table B.13. Continued

	Muslims Are a Threat		Conservative Christians Are a Threat		Jews are a Threat		Atheists Are a Threat	
	β	SE	β	SE	β	SE	β	SE
Religious practice	-.10**	.03	-.11**	.03	-.15***	.03	.02	.03
Intercept	4.71***		6.98***		4.52***		3.88***	
N	1,501		1,501		1,501		1,501	
PRE	.402		.214		.153		.449	

*p<.05; **p<.01; ***p<.001; ‡p =.058.

ᵃ Contrast Category.

Source: 2017 Baylor Religion Survey (MI data).

Table B.14. OLS Regression Analyses for Ambassadors, Accommodators, Resisters, and Rejecters (Standardized Coefficients Shown)

	Model 1	Model 2	Model 3	Model 4
Muslims Are a Threat				
Ambassadors	—	.15***	.21***	.29***
Accommodators	-.14***	—	.08**	.17***
Resisters	-.21***	-.08**	—	.08*
Rejecters	-.29***	-.18***	-.11***	—
Intercept	7.05***	6.24***	5.79***	5.24***
N	1,501	1,501	1,501	1,501
PRE	.396	.401	.401	.398
Conservative Christians Are a Threat				
Ambassadors	—	-.05	-.06	-.13**
Accommodators	.06†	—	-.01	-.09*
Resisters	.08†	.02	—	-.08*
Rejecters	.17***	.12**	.11**	—

(continued)

Table B.14. Continued

	Model 1	Model 2	Model 3	Model 4
Intercept	5.87***	6.13***	6.22***	6.64***
N	1,501	1,501	1,501	1,501
PRE	.207	.207	.210	.203

Jews Are a Threat

	Model 1	Model 2	Model 3	Model 4
Ambassadors	—	.00	.04	.15**
Accommodators	.00	—	.05	.18***
Resisters	−.05	−.05	—	.13***
Rejecters	−.19***	−.20***	−.15***	—
Intercept	5.22***	5.22***	5.02***	4.47***
N	1,501	1,501	1,501	1,501
PRE	.164	.164	.163	.159

Atheists Are a Threat

	Model 1	Model 2	Model 3	Model 4
Ambassadors	—	.15***	.26***	.33***
Accommodators	−.14***	—	.13***	.22***
Resisters	−.25***	−.12***	—	.09**
Rejecters	−.34***	−.23***	−.12***	—
Intercept	6.67***	5.89***	5.19***	4.60***
N	1,501	1,501	1,501	1,501
PRE	.434	.440	.440	.436

†p<.10; *p<.05; **p<.01; ***p<.001.

Note: Each model controls for age, gender, marital status, race, region of the country, education, income, size of place, political ideology, political party, religious affiliation, views toward the Bible, and religious practice.

Source: 2017 Baylor Religion Survey (MI data).

Table B.15. OLS Regression Analysis Predicting Gender Traditionalism Scale Using Christian Nationalism Scale

	β	b	SE
Christian nationalism	.29***	.12	.01
Age	.02	.00	.00
Female	−.15***	−.79	.12
Married	.00	.02	.13
Child	.02	.09	.14
White[a]	−.07**	−.40	.14
Northeast [a]	—	—	—
Midwest	−.03	−.16	.18
South	.01	.07	.17
West	−.06*	−.36	.18
Education	−.11***	−.12	.03
Income	−.10***	−.15	.04
Suburb [a]	—	—	—
City	.01	.08	.17
Town	.02	.12	.16
Rural	.03	.21	.20
Political conservatism	.11**	.18	.06
Republican	.08*	.46	.18
Independent [a]	—	—	—
Democrat	−.02	−.09	.15
Evangelical Protestant [a]	—	—	—
Mainline Protestant	−.04	−.27	.20
Black Protestant	−.02	−.25	.29
Catholic	−.04	−.26	.17
Jewish	.02	.57	.54
Other	.03	.34	.24
No affiliation	.03	.21	.23
Biblical literalist	.01	.06	.20
Religious practice	.11**	.11	.03
Intercept	2.64***		
N	1,501		
Adj. R-Square	.325		

*p<.05; **p<.01; ***p<.001.

[a] Contrast Category.

Source: 2017 Baylor Religion Survey (MI data).

Table B.16. OLS Regression Analysis Predicting Gender Traditionalism Scale for Ambassadors, Accommodators, Resisters, and Rejecters (Standardized Coefficients Shown)

	Model 1	Model 2	Model 3	Model 4
Ambassadors	—	.07*	.13***	.25***
Accommodators	−.06†	—	.07*	.22***
Resisters	−.14***	−.08***	—	.14***
Rejecters	−.29***	−.24***	−.17***	—
Intercept	4.70***	4.34***	3.90***	3.03***
N	1,501	1,501	1,501	1,501
Adj. R-Square	.321	.322	.321	.314

†p<.10; *p<.05; **p<.01; ***p<.001

Note: Each model controls for age, gender, marital status, children, race, region of the country, education, income, size of place, political ideology, political party, religious affiliation, views toward the Bible, and religious practice.

Source: 2017 Baylor Religion Survey (MI data)

Table B.17. Logistic Regression Analysis Predicting Agreement that Gays and Lesbians Should be Allowed to Legally Marry using Christian Nationalism Scale

	Agreement that gays and lesbians should be allowed to legally marry		Agreement that transgender people should be allowed to use the restroom of their choice		Divorce w/ no child present is not wrong at all		Divorce w/ child(ren) present is not wrong at all	
	β	OR	β	OR	β	OR	β	OR
Christian nationalism	-.43***	.89	-.39***	.89	-.33***	.91	-.32***	.91
Age	-.13**	.99	-.02	1.00	.09*	1.01	.04	1.00
Female	.13*	1.62	.14***	1.64	.10**	1.43	.17***	1.83
Heterosexual	.05	1.30	-.06	.73	—	—	—	—
Married	-.16***	.56	-.06	.80	-.04	.85	-.09*	.71
White	.15*	1.77	.10*	1.48	.01	1.12	.04	1.33
Northeast [a]	—	—	—	—	—	—	—	—
Midwest	-.09	.67	-.14***	.54	-.06	.78	-.09*	.68
South	-.14	.59	-.21***	.45	-.01	.98	-.06	.81
West	-.14*	.54	-.21***	.42	-.02	.90	-.10*	.64
Education	.13*	1.11	.18	1.15	-.05	.94	-.11**	.87
Income	.10	1.11	-.05	.95	.11*	1.13	.08	1.10
Suburb [a]	—	—	—	—	—	—	—	—
City	-.06	.79	-.04	.84	.03	1.16	.09	1.58

(continued)

Table B.17. Continued

	Agreement that gays and lesbians should be allowed to legally marry		Agreement that transgender people should be allowed to use the restroom of their choice		Divorce w/ no child present is not wrong at all		Divorce w/ child(ren) present is not wrong at all	
	β	OR	β	OR	β	OR	β	OR
Town	-.08	.74	-.01	.95	-.01	.97	.03	1.12
Rural	-.08	.64	-.10*	.58	.08	1.43	.05	1.24
Political conservatism	-.35***	.65	-.28***	.72	-.13*	.86	-.09	.91
Republican	-.12	.62	-.11	.64	-.03	.90	-.11*	.67
Independent[a]	—	—	—	—	—	—	—	—
Democrat	-.04	.86	.12*	1.57	-.01	.96	-.02	.91
Evangelical Protestant[a]	—	—	—	—	—	—	—	—
Mainline Protestant	.11	1.83	.00	1.00	.13**	1.80	.05	1.27
Black Protestant	.00	1.03	.12*	2.37	.11*	2.48	.10*	2.42
Catholic	.08	1.39	.02	1.07	-.06	.77	-.06	.76
Jewish	-.02	.66	-.04	.50	.02	1.38	.03	1.57
Other	-.02	.85	.08	1.76	.05	1.42	.01	1.08
No affiliation	.01	1.04	-.06	.75	.06	1.39	-.01	.97

Biblical literalist	-.11*	.61	-.15*	.50	-.17***	.47	-.12*	.59
Religious practice	-.37***	.77	-.15**	.90	-.50***	.71	-.31***	.81
Intercept	2.80***		2.05***		.85		.02	
N	1,501		1,501		1,648		1,648	
PRE	.389		.311		.316		.218	

Sources: 2017 Baylor Religion Survey (N = 1,501) & 2007 Baylor Religion Survey (N = 1,648) (MI data).

*p<.05; **p<.01; ***p<.001.

[a] Contrast Category.

Table B.18. Logistic Regression Analyses for Ambassadors, Accommodators, Resisters, and Rejecters (Odds Ratios Shown)

	Model 1	Model 2	Model 3	Model 4
Agreement that gays and lesbians should be allowed to legally marry				
Ambassadors	—	.43***	.36***	.26**
Accommodators	2.25**	—	.853	.59
Resisters	2.76**	1.30	—	.74
Rejecters	5.89**	2.78*	2.28*	—
Intercept	.50	1.30**	1.52***	1.96**
N	1,501	1,501	1,501	1,501
PRE	.383	.383	.383	.383
Agreement that transgender people should be allowed to use the restroom of their choice				
Ambassadors	—	.68	.29***	.26***
Accommodators	1.31	—	.41***	.36***
Resisters	3.38***	2.57***	—	.93
Rejecters	4.51***	3.47***	1.42	—
Intercept	−.04	.26	1.20**	1.34**
N	1,501	1,501	1,501	1,501
PRE	.312	.312	.312	.312
Divorce with no children present is not wrong at all				
Ambassadors	—	.67*	.38***	.27***
Accommodators	1.37	—	.55***	.39***
Resisters	2.44***	1.78**	—	.70
Rejecters	3.70***	2.71***	1.53[†]	—
Intercept	−.85	−.54	.03	.39
N	1,648	1,648	1,648	1,648
PRE	.312	.312	.312	.312

Table B.18. Continued

	Model 1	Model 2	Model 3	Model 4
Divorce with child(ren) present is not wrong at all				
Ambassadors	—	.60*	.34***	.27***
Accommodators	1.43†	—	.54***	.43***
Resisters	2.57***	1.77***	—	.78
Rejecters	3.33***	2.31***	1.30	—
Intercept	−1.68***	−1.31**	−.73	−.49
N	1,648	1,648	1,648	1,648
PRE	.213	.213	.213	.213

†p<.10; *p<.05; **p<.01; ***p<.001.

Note: Each model controls for age, gender, marital status, children, race, region of the country, education, income, size of place, political ideology, political party, religious affiliation, views toward the Bible, and religious practice.

Sources: 2017 Baylor Religion Survey (N = 1,501) & 2007 Baylor Religion Survey (N = 1,648) (MI data).

Table B.19. Logistic Regression Analysis of Christian Nationalism and Year Interaction for Agreement that Gays and Lesbians Should be Allowed to Legally Marry and Gender Traditionalism

	Logistic Regression Analysis of Christian Nationalism and Year Interaction for Agreement that Gays and Lesbians Should be Allowed to Legally Marry	OLS Regression Analysis of Christian Nationalism and Year Interaction for Gender Traditionalism Scale
	β	β
Christian nationalism	−.38***	.36***
Year	.57***	−.10*
Christian nationalism*Year	.02	−.10*
Intercept	.61	3.20***
PRE	.441	—
Adj. R-Square	—	.390

*p<.05; **p<.01; ***p<.001.

Note: Models control for age, gender, marital status, children, race, region of the country, education, income, size of place, political ideology, political party, religious affiliation, views toward the Bible, and religious practice.

Sources: 2017 Baylor Religion Survey (N = 1,501) & 2007 Baylor Religion Survey (N = 1,648) (MI data).

Table B.20. Logistic Regression Predicting Wanting to Make Divorce More Difficult

	Model 1	
	β	OR
Importance of being Christian to being truly American	.14*	1.22
Age	−.09[†]	.99
Female	.05	1.18
Married	.03	1.13
White [a]	—	—

Table B.20. Continued

	Model 1	
	β	OR
Black	−.04	.80
Hispanic	−.11†	.61
Other race	.05	1.32
Northeast[a]	—	—
South	.08	1.35
Midwest	.18**	2.19
West	.03	1.15
Education	−.09†	.88
Income	.09	1.03
City	.05	1.22
Suburb [a]	—	—
Town	.07	1.33
Rural	−.02	.90
Political conservatism	.05	1.07
Republican	.14*	1.71
Independent [a]	—	—
Democrat	−.06	.80
Evangelical Protestant [a]	—	—
Mainline Protestant	−.04	.78
Black Protestant	−.06	.63
Catholic	−.17**	.50
Jewish	−.12*	.18
Other	−.04	.74
No affiliation	−.16*	.49
Biblical literalist	−.05	.84
Religious service attendance	.10†	1.06
Intercept	−1.32*	
N	826	
PRE	.120	

†p<.10; *p<.05; **p<.01; ***p<.001.

[a] Contrast Category.

Source: 2014 General Social Survey (MI Data).

APPENDIX C
Interview Guide

Interview Schedule: Christian nationalism in the United Statess
Andrew Whitehead and Samuel Perry—principle investigators
Hello, my name is Andrew Whitehead/Sam Perry and I am conducting research about Americans' beliefs about the religious heritage of the United States and I am interested in your thoughts. The purpose of the research is to better understand our current cultural and political climate. Your participation will involve one informal interview that will last between twenty to thirty minutes. This research has no known risks. This research will benefit the academic community because it helps us to understand how Americans think about the religious heritage of the United States. Please know that I will do everything I can to protect your privacy. Your identity or personal information will not be disclosed in any publication that may result from the study. Notes that are taken during the interview will be stored in a secure location. Would it be all right if I audiotaped our interview? Saying no to audio recording will have no effect on the interview.

BRIEF INTERVIEW QUESTIONNAIRE

1. Age _____
2. Gender _____
3. Race _____
4. Current marital status _____
5. Highest educational degree earned _____
6. What religion/denomination do you consider yourself?
7. How important is religious faith to you? (circle your answer)

   A. Not at all important

   B. Not very important

C. Fairly important

D. Very important

8. How do you consider yourself politically? (circle your answer)

   A. Extremely Liberal

   B. Mostly Liberal

   C. Fairly Liberal

   D. Moderate

   E. Fairly Conservative

   F. Mostly Conservative

   G. Extremely Conservative

9. Please indicate how much you agree with the following statements:

   - *The federal government should declare the United States a Christian nation.*

     Strongly Agree – Mostly Agree – Undecided – Mostly Disagree – Strongly Disagree

   - *The federal government should advocate Christian values.*

     Strongly Agree – Mostly Agree – Undecided – Mostly Disagree – Strongly Disagree

   - *The federal government should enforce strict separation of church and state.*

     Strongly Agree – Mostly Agree – Undecided – Mostly Disagree – Strongly Disagree

   - *The federal government should allow the display of religious symbols in public spaces.*

     Strongly Agree – Mostly Agree – Undecided – Mostly Disagree – Strongly Disagree

   - *The federal government should allow prayer in public schools.*

     Strongly Agree – Mostly Agree – Undecided – Mostly Disagree – Strongly Disagree

   - *The success of the United States is part of God's plan.*

     Strongly Agree – Mostly Agree – Undecided – Mostly Disagree – Strongly Disagree

OPEN-ENDED QUESTIONS

[NOTE: Often, interviewees' responses to the six statements would provoke helpful follow-up questions. One of the interviewers could ask something like, "You said you 'mostly disagreed' that the federal government should enforce a strict separation of church and state. Tell me why you disagreed? Why did you only 'mostly disagree' with that statement?" The following questions were asked to elicit further elaboration from interviewees.]

1. Do you think the United States is a Christian nation? If yes, why? If not, why not?
2. Possible follow up: What does that mean to be a "Christian nation" in your mind?
3. Do you think we as a country are moving away from our religious heritage? In what ways? Is that for the better or for the worse?
4. Do you feel like your religious freedoms have ever come under attack? If so, how so? Have you ever feared that this would happen?
5. How should religion, and perhaps Christianity specifically, shape our nation's policies? Can you think of some specific ways?
6. What do you think about pastors promoting specific political candidates from the pulpit? Why should that be fair game? Or why not?
7. What about those folks who are not Christians or religious at all? What obligations does the US as a Christian nation have to them?
8. [For those who mostly affirm America's Christian heritage] Do you think religious minorities (e.g., Muslims or atheists) might feel excluded from the national culture if it really is Christian? Should they feel that way? Why or why not?
9. [For those who mostly affirm America's Christian heritage] What about people whose activities you disagree with for moral or religious reasons (e.g., gay persons, transgender persons). What should America's relationship to Christianity mean for them?
10. What do you think about teachers/administrators/coaches holding prayer or Bible studies before school starts, or before high school football games? Even if there are lots of non-Christians present? How do you evaluate that?

Should opportunities be given for other religious traditions (e.g., Muslims, Buddhists) to pray or study their scriptures before those events?

11. What about displaying the Ten Commandments in court houses? Also okay? Even if not everyone participating in the legal system is Christian?

12. What do you think Christianity has to say about the way America polices its borders? How should a "Christian nation" think about things like immigration policies and border walls?

13. [For those who mostly affirm America's Christian heritage] Issues surrounding racial inequality and racial injustice have been a hot-button issue, especially in the past few years. What do you think is the most Christian way for America to deal with all the racial issues we have?

14. Do you think life is better for non-Christians for being in a Christian nation or worse in some ways? Maybe both? Why?

15. Do you think the word *theocracy* describes your vision of a Christian nation? Why or why not? If not, why do you think "theocracy" is different from your vision of Christian America?

16. [For professing Christians] How do you as a Christian view Trump? How do you think American Christians ought to view him?

NOTES

PREFACE

1. Brubaker (2017).
2. See sociologist Andrew Lynn's (2020) forthcoming book on evangelical views of work and capitalism.
3. For an excellent example of this mindset, minister Rafael Cruz (2016: 156), father of Texas Senator Ted Cruz, writes, "Godly men wrote the Constitution for a godly nation . . . I believe without a shadow of a doubt that the reason the Declaration of Independence and the Constitution of the United States have lasted over two centuries is that they were divinely inspired and then written by men who had spent time on their knees. These were men of God, seeking revelation from God, and that's what He gave them. Of course, these two documents are not equivalent to the Word of God, but God certainly directed the men who crafted them."
4. Quote from Jerry Falwell Jr., President of Liberty University. Accessed on November 11, 2018. https://www.christianpost.com/news/donald-trump-presidential-election-why-jerry-falwells-jr-wrong-about-endorsement-156440/.
5. Bean (2014); Bonikowski (2016, 2017); Bonikowski et al. (2019); Brubaker (2017); Soper and Fetzer (2018).

INTRODUCTION

1. Kruse (2015: x–xi).
2. For example, data from the General Social Surveys shows that in the early 1970s Republicans and Democrats were virtually identical in their views about prayer and Bible reading in public school.

Approximately 68 percent of Republicans and Democrats alike disagreed with the Supreme Court decision to eliminate state-mandated Bible reading or prayer from schools. By 2016, 69 percent of Republicans still felt that way (a slight increase) compared to only 49 percent of Democrats (a nearly 20 point reduction).

3. Our initial adoption of the term was influenced by Bean (2014); Fea (2016, 2018); and Goldberg (2006), among others. While our understanding of Christian nationalism has been tremendously influenced by Gorski (2017), who often prefers the more general term *religious nationalism*, we feel this obscures the obvious debate regarding the "Christian" character of the nation. This should also underscore that we are not the first to identify the importance of religion, and especially Christianity, to discussions of American nationalism, nor are we claiming such. For example, using advanced statistical methodology, sociologists Bart Bonikowski and Paul DiMaggio (2016) empirically established the importance of religion to national identity, confirming decades of prior work across various fields of study.

4. Three excellent resources for primary source documents discussing Christianity's relationship to American identity and civic life are Conrad Cherry's (1998) *God's New Israel: Religious Interpretations of American Destiny*; Matthew Harris and Thomas Kidd's (2011) *The Founding Fathers and the Debate Over Religion in Revolutionary America: A History in Documents*; and Stephen Prothero's (2012) *The American Bible: How Our Words Unite, Divide, and Define a Nation*. For surveys outlining the history of these debates, see also (listed alphabetically by author) Robert Bellah's (1967) classic article "Civil Religion in America" in *Daedalus* 97(1):1–21 as well as his (1975) book *The Broken Covenant: American Civil Religion in Time of Trial*; Matthew Bowman's (2018) *Christian: The Politics of a Word in America*; Daryl Cornett's (2011) *Christian America? Perspectives on Our Religious Heritage*; John Fea's (2016) *Was America Founded as a Christian Nation?*; Philip Gorski's (2017) *American Covenant: A History of Civil Religion from the Pilgrims to the Present*; Steven Green's (2015) *Inventing a Christian America*; David L. Holmes' (2006) *The Faiths of the Founding Fathers*; Kevin Kruse's (2015) *One Nation Under God: How Corporate America Invented Christian America*; Frank Lambert's (2006) *The Founding*

Fathers and the Place of Religion in America, (2010) *Religion in American Politics*, and his (2014) *Separation of Church & State: Founding Principles of Religious Liberty*; Benjamin Lynerd's (2014) *Republican Theology: The Civil Religion of American Evangelicals*; Matthew Stewart's (2015) *Nature's God: The Heretical Origins of the American Republic*; and Mark Noll, Nathan Hatch, and George Marsden's (1989) dated but still compelling *The Search for Christian America*.

5. Here we are referencing the Thomas Theorem: "If men define situations as real, they are real in their consequences" (Thomas and Thomas 1928: 571–72).

6. Jeffress (2016: 95).

7. A poll conducted in the spring of 2019 found that 47% of registered voters considered Christian nationalism a threat. See Joanna Piacenza's column on the March 2019 Morning Consult poll here: https://morningconsult.com/2019/04/02/roughly-half-the-electorate-views-christian-nationalism-as-a-threat/.

8. Several important scholarly books that have addressed the historic and recent influence of "Christian nationalism" in addition to those we highlighted in note 4 include (alphabetically by author): James Aho's (2016) *Far-Right Fantasy: A Sociology of American Religion and Politics*; Lydia Bean's (2014) *The Politics of Evangelical Identity: Local Churches and Partisan Divides in the United States and Canada*; Ruth Braunstein's (2017) *Prophets and Patriots: Faith in Democracy across the Political Divide*; John Fea's (2018) *Believe Me: The Evangelical Road to Donald Trump*; Corey Robin's (2018) *The Reactionary Mind: Conservatism from Edmund Burke to Donald Trump*; Andrew Seidel's (2019) *The Founding Myth: Why Christian Nationalism is Un-American*; and Jason Stanley's (2018) *How Fascism Works: The Politics of Us and Them*. Excellent journalistic examples would include Michelle Goldberg's (2006) *Kingdom Coming: The Rise of Christian Nationalism*; Chris Hedges' (2006) *American Fascists: The Christian Right and the War on America*; Robert P. Jones's (2016) *The End of White Christian America*, and Katherine Stewart's (2012) *The Good News Club: The Christian Right's Stealth Assault on America's Children* and (2020) *The Power Worshippers: Inside the Dangerous Rise of Christian Nationalism*.

9. Another weakness with this measure is that it gives us no indication how respondents are defining what a Christian nation "is." For instance, some may be thinking about how over half the population in the United States affiliates with a Christian tradition, and so perhaps that makes the United States a "Christian nation." Other respondents might be considering the faiths of the founding fathers or the originating documents.

10. To ensure that strong agreement with the third statement about separation of church and state matched with the other questions, we reverse-coded the responses to this question. See Appendix A for more information about the Christian nationalism scale discussed in this section and used throughout this text. Appendix A also includes information on the statistical validity of the Christian nationalism scale.

11. Several other "Christian nationalism" scales include similar questions. For example, in their analysis of Christian nationalism's influence on Americans' immigration attitudes, political scientist Eric McDaniel and his colleagues (2011; see also Shortle and Gaddie 2015) also construct a scale from Americans' responses to six statements: (1) America holds a special place in God's plan; (2) The vast resources of the United States indicate that God has chosen that nation to lead; (3) The United States was founded as a Christian nation; (4) The government should take steps to preserve the nation's religious heritage; (5) The United States was established to be religiously diverse (reverse coded); and (6) Success of the United States is not a reflection of divine will (reverse coded). Similarly, Merino (2010) uses respondents' agreement with three similar statements: (1) The United States was founded on Christian principles; (2) In the 21st century, the United States is still basically a Christian society; and (3) Our democratic form of government is based on Christianity.

12. For instance, 62% of Americans agree or strongly agree that "the federal government should allow the display of religious symbols in public spaces" (see Figure I.2).

13. We recognize the term *Ambassador* might call to mind thoughts of diplomacy and compromise in addition to a strong sense of promotion, advocacy, and advancement on behalf of a particular group (or nation-state). As we demonstrate in chapter 1, our use of *Ambassador* is more in line with the latter three terms, and much less

with the first two. There were other labels we considered, but each brought its own weaknesses.

14. Bonikowski and DiMaggio (2016) and Delehanty, Edgell, and Stewart (2019) both provide typologies of nationalism more broadly or support for Christian nationalist discourse (which they term *secularized evangelical discourse*), respectively. There are clear overlaps between these various typologies and ours. For instance, Ambassadors and Accommodators of Christian nationalism would likely be "ardent" or at least "restrictive" nationalists according to Bonikowski and DiMaggio, while Rejecters and Resisters might be more likely to be "disengaged" or "creedal" nationalists. The key is that we are focusing specifically on Christianity as the symbolic boundary, while Bonikowski and DiMaggio consider Christianity alongside various other criteria. It is important to also note that in each of these other studies, Latent Class Analysis is used to identify these various groups, while ours is simply identifying each group with a particular range on the scale.

15. Our defining Christian nationalism as a cultural framework dovetails with the broader understanding of "nationalism" used by sociologists Rogers Brubaker and Bart Bonikowski: "nationalism [is a] domain: a heterogeneous set of 'nation'-oriented idioms, practices, and possibilities that are continuously available or 'endemic' in modern cultural and political life" (as cited in Bonikowski and DiMaggio 2016: 952). The ethnocultural, xenophobic, and authoritarian tendencies of Christian nationalism align with some of the other nationalisms found to exist in the popular discourse (see also Bonikowski and DiMaggio 2016; Schildkraut 2011; Smith 1997).

16. Bellah (1967, 1975); Gorski (2017). See also Bonikowski and DiMaggio (2016: 952–53).

17. Namely, those about subduing the earth, sexual/blood purity, military conquest of the Promised Land, God's imminent curses for ritual infidelity, and anticipating cataclysmic global decline.

18. Gorski (2017).

19. Recent analyses of Christian nationalism have raised this distinction between postmillennial and premillennial eschatologies. Michelle Goldberg (2006) and James Aho (2013, 2016) for example, have

connected contemporary Christian nationalist claims with the work of "dominionist" or "reconstructionist" thinkers like R. J. Rushdoony, who was a postmillennialist. Many of the most visible Christian nationalists of today like David Barton, Robert Jeffress, Franklin Graham, as well as the late Tim LaHaye (who co-wrote the very influential *Left Behind* series that popularized many pre-millennialist views), Jerry Falwell, and Adrian Rogers tend toward a premillennialist interpretation. Some, like Ted Cruz's father and preacher, Rafael Cruz, can at times blur the lines between the two, espousing support for dominionism alongside more premillennialist stances. The important point is to recognize that because various beliefs about the end of days have diffused throughout the population, many Americans may hold both postmillennialist and pre-millennialist stances simultaneously with little regard for how they might contradict. However, as we show later, holding to beliefs most associated with premillennial eschatology is one of the leading predictors of Americans' adhering to Christian nationalism.

20. For those interested in exploring the connections between dominionism and modern American Christian nationalism we recommend Julie Ingersoll's fascinating *Building God's Kingdom: Inside the World of Christian Reconstruction* (2015) and Michael McVicar's definitive *Christian Reconstruction: R. J. Rushdoony and American Religious Conservatism* (2015). Journalist Jack Jenkins wrote a series of articles that are each well worth your time that examine the theological tributaries and historical precedence of Christian nationalism (Jenkins 2017a, 2017b, 2017c).

21. Pastor Robert Jeffress (2016: 9) lays out this premillennial perspective clearly in his book *Twilight's Last Gleaming: How America's Last Days Can be Your Best Days*: "Although we can't prevent the ultimate collapse of our nation and destruction of the world, we can postpone it. We have both the ability and responsibility to delay the decay of our nation, even if we can't ultimately reverse it . . . . The motivation for Christians working to delay the coming collapse of our nation is not to preserve our way of life, but to buy more time to share the life-changing gospel of Jesus Christ with as many people as possible before America is swept away by God's judgment."

22. See Appendix Table B.1.

23. See Froese and Mencken (2009) and how Christian nationalism (or what they term *sacralization discourse*) was strongly associated with support for the Iraq War and the Bush administration's fight against the so-called axis of evil.
24. See Appendix Table B.2.
25. See Kruse and Zelizer (2019) for a superb history of the fault lines dividing the American public since the 1970s.
26. For more on how Christian nationalism has permeated the American social context, see Delehanty, Edgell, and Stewart (2019).
27. Altemeyer (2007).
28. In the statistical models featured throughout this text we performed additional analyses in order to account for (where possible) Americans' level of racial prejudice and right-wing authoritarianism alongside Christian nationalism as a robustness check. Consistently, Christian nationalism maintains a distinct and powerful association with a variety of Americans' beliefs and behaviors. This underscores our point that Christian nationalism is not *just* racism or authoritarianism by another name.
29. We also want to make clear that when we say Christian nationalism is distinct from these various other ideologies we are not arguing or implying that Christian nationalism is the originating root cause of them. As we mentioned previously, Christian nationalism certainly overlaps and reinforces these various ideologies, political loyalties, or theological beliefs.
30. Though not always! See chapter 4 for more.
31. Gorski (2017: 3).
32. We do not mean this to provide an "out" or rhetorical maneuver to committed Christians who wish to show their faith in the best possible light, claiming, in effect, "Those [racists, sexists, Trump voters, etc.] aren't *real* Christians like us; they are Christian nationalists." Whether Christian nationalists are *real* Christians is not something we can discern. We only mean to argue that Americans' attitudes and behaviors toward many of the issues we discuss seem to be more strongly influenced by their adherence to Christian nationalism as opposed to, say, the denomination they affiliate with, their views about the Bible, or how faithfully they practice their religion.

CHAPTER 1

1. See the original article with comments from Dallas Mayor Mike Rawlings here: https://www.dallasnews.com/opinion/commentary/2018/06/07/robert-jeffresss-gospel-division-not-represent-dallas.

2. See http://www.dallasobserver.com/news/first-baptist-dallas-getting-20-billboards-thanks-to-clear-channel-10815424.

3. Rejecters are those who score is greater than one standard deviation below the mean on the Christian nationalism scale (0 to 5). Resisters score between the mean on the Christian nationalism scale (11.3) to minus one standard deviation (6). Accommodators score between the mean on the Christian nationalism scale to one standard deviation above the mean (17). Ambassadors scores are over one standard deviation above the mean (18 to 24).

4. See Figure I.3.

5. The most famous words from the Treaty of Tripoli that Patrick is referencing are: "The Government of the United States of America is not, in any sense, founded on the Christian religion." The Treaty of Tripoli was submitted to the United States Senate by President John Adams and ratified unanimously on June 7, 1797. Fea (2011) and Lambert (2006), among others, place this quote and treaty in historical context. It is one of the most popular quotes for those arguing against the Christian nation narrative.

6. Indeed, the socio-demographic characteristics of Rejecters are quite consistent with those of "Religious Nones" and "Secular" Americans identified by sociologists Joseph Baker and Buster Smith (2015).

7. In Tables 1.1, 1.2, and 1.3 we provide significance tests for the means and percentages across each group. The superscript letters designate whether the mean for Rejecters is significantly different from the means for Resisters, Accommodators, or Ambassadors; whether the mean for Resisters is significantly different from the means for Accommodators or Ambassadors; or if the mean for Accommodators is significantly different from the mean for Ambassadors. If there is no superscript letter the difference in the numbers is not statistically significant. This means that the differences could be due to random chance.

8. This parsing of the First Amendment's establishment clause and the free exercise clause is quite consistent with that put forth by popular

Christian nationalist authors and thought leaders like WallBuilder's founder David Barton, pastor Robert Jeffress, radio host Tony Perkins, and theologian Wayne Grudem.

9. The average Christian nationalism scores for the nine census regions are: New England: 8.32; Middle Atlantic: 9.59; South Atlantic: 12.07; East South Central: 13.6; West South Central: 13.24; East North Central: 11.43; West North Central: 12.59; Mountain: 10.54; Pacific: 10.1. We also cross-checked this regional distribution with results from two other national surveys. First, the 2003 American Mosaic Project asked respondents whether they believe the United States is basically a Christian nation and whether they think that is a good thing. We examined the percentage of Americans in each region who affirmed that the United States was indeed a Christian nation and thought this was a good thing. Second, the 1996, 2004, and 2014 General Social Surveys ask respondents how important being a Christian is to being "truly American." We examined the percentage of Americans in each region who thought being a Christian was "very important" to being truly American. For both of these analyses, results were nearly identical to what we found in the 2017 BRS data.

10. For the Christian nation narrative in support of slavery, see Fea (2011) and Noll (2008). For appeals to the Christian nation narrative as an argument against Jim Crow segregation, see Martin Luther King Jr.'s "Letter from a Birmingham Jail" (1963), perhaps the most famous example of the Christian nation narrative being used to challenge whites about the evils of racism. See also Perry and Whitehead (2019).

11. Two well-known self-identified evangelical Rejecters include pastor and author Greg Boyd and Dartmouth professor and historian of American religion Randall Balmer. In a series of sermons and later a book—*Myth of a Christian Nation* (2007)—Greg Boyd forcefully argues that the "kingdom of this world," which would include the United States and its government, should be completely distinct from the "kingdom of God." Boyd posits a series of negative outcomes for "the church" when it becomes too closely entwined with politics and governmental power. Reacting to the marriage between the Religious Right and the Republican Party, Balmer (2006) writes as a "jilted

lover," one who grew up in evangelicalism but can no longer recognize it. The quest for political power—that America was and should again be a Christian nation as the Religious Right sees it—feels completely foreign to him as an evangelical.

12. See Du Mez (2018): https://www.christianitytoday.com/ct/2018/june-web-only/believe-me-donald-trump-john-fea.html. Accessed on February 7, 2019.

13. See Wuthnow (1988); see also Braunstein and Taylor (2017), Stewart, Edgell, and Delehanty (2018), and Delehanty, Edgell, and Stewart (2019).

14. These figures are taken from the 2012 Race, Class, and Culture Survey conducted by the Public Religion Research Institute. This dataset is freely available on www.theARDA.com.

15. These figures are taken from the 2012 and 2016 General Social Surveys, both freely available on www.theARDA.com.

16. Looking back farther to the decade leading up to 2007 to 2017, there is mixed evidence of a decline in the number of Americans who view the United States as a Christian nation. Consider, for example, figures taken from the 1996 Religion and Politics Survey, the 2002 Religion and Public Life Survey, and the 2006 Religion and Public Life Survey conducted by the Pew Research Center (each dataset is freely available on www.theARDA.com). Within these data from 1996 to 2006, the unaffiliated grew from 12 percent (1996) to 16 percent (2006). Sixty-one percent of Americans in 1996 reported that they considered the United States to be a Christian nation. In 2002, this number was also 67 percent. Four years later, in 2006, 67 percent of Americans still considered the United States a Christian nation. During this particular decade the shifts in the relative size of the Christian tradition or nonreligious groups in the United States did not directly portend identical shifts in the acceptance of the Christian nation narrative. It could be that during this time unaffiliated Americans, whose ranks had just begun to grow, had not yet shifted their views toward the Christian nation narrative and supposed religious heritage of the United States. Cultural narratives are difficult to uproot. It should be no surprise that this process appears to have taken some time.

17. Straughn and Feld (2010); Whitehead and Scheitle (2018).

18. Whitehead and Scheitle (2018). See also Bonikowski and DiMaggio (2016) for evidence of shifts in relative size of different responses to nationalism across the United States population.

CHAPTER 2

1. Smith (2000). Over a decade later, sociologist and community activist Lydia Bean (2014: 63) affirmed Smith's argument. Drawing on her observational data from two American evangelical churches, Bean explained: "When church leaders . . . appealed to themes of cultural conflict, Christian nationalism, and 'moral issues,' it was not to achieve immediately political goals. Instead, they used cultural tension to rally the faithful for religious goals: evangelism, community service, lay leadership."

2. See Braunstein and Taylor (2017); Delehanty et al. (2019).

3. For example, see Braunstein (2017, 2018); Hochschild (2016); Polletta (2006); Polletta and Callahan (2017); Smith (2003); Somers (1994).

4. Accessed at: https://www.politico.com/story/2016/12/donald-trump-wisconsin-232605.

5. Hillary Clinton secured 65,844,610 votes to Trump's 62,979,636, for a difference of 2,864,974. See https://www.nytimes.com/2017/05/31/upshot/a-2016-review-why-key-state-polls-were-wrong-about-trump.html.

6. Accessed at: https://www.washingtonpost.com/news/the-fix/wp/2016/12/01/donald-trump-will-be-president-thanks-to-80000-people-in-three-states/?noredirect=on&utm_term=.b4f780b90546. Also see Kennedy et al. (2018) and Johnston et al. (2019). Both studies provide empirical evidence that there was a non-trivial swing in support among non–college educated Americans residing in rustbelt cities from Obama in 2012 to Trump in 2016.

7. See the various predictors of Trump vote found in the following: Bock, Byrd-Craven, and Burkley (2017); Ekins (2017) ; McElwee and Daniel (2017); Rothwell, Hodson, and Prusaczyk (2019); Schaffner et al. (2017); Sides (2017); Stewart (2018); Wayne et al. (2016).

8. See the Afterword written in 2018 added to Hochschild (2016); Jones (2016); McVeigh and Estep (2019).

9. For the PRRI poll, see https://www.prri.org/spotlight/white-evangelical-support-for-donald-trump-at-all-time-high/ch 2015.

10. One famous example of conservative Christians demanding sexual morality from their presidents was James Dobson's open letter to Focus on the Family denouncing Bill Clinton's affair with Monica Lewinsky and arguing that politicians so devoid of morality were not fit to run the country. Dobson would eventually support Donald Trump. See the long letter from Dobson here: http://ontology.buffalo.edu/smith/clinton/character.html. Accessed June 19, 2018.

11. For these quotes, see https://www.washingtonpost.com/politics/surrogates-explaining-away-trumps-sexual-behavior-only-seem-to-make-it-worse/2016/10/13/138a0006-9093-11e6-a6a3-d50061aa9fae_story.html?utm_term=.3032ae99472b. And https://www.washingtonpost.com/local/education/excitement-and-caution-as-liberty-u-awaits-trump-commencement-speech/2017/05/05/4d094138-312f-11e7-8674-437ddb6e813e_story.html?utm_term=.0fac5888727a.

12. See https://townhall.com/columnists/waynegrudem/2016/10/19/if-you-dont-like-either-candidate-then-vote-for-trumps-policies-n2234187.

13. See https://www.nytimes.com/interactive/2016/11/08/us/politics/election-exit-polls.html. Accessed on February 12, 2019.

14. One month before the 2016 Presidential election, sociologist Philip Gorski explained "Trumpism" among white evangelicals: "Trumpism is a *secular form of religious nationalism.* By 'religious nationalism,' I mean a form of nationalism that makes religious identity the litmus test of national belonging. By 'a secular form of religious nationalism,' I mean one that strips religious identity of its ethical content and transcendental reference. In Trumpism, religion functions mainly as a marker of ethnicity . . . In short, the affinity is not really between Trump and Christianity—it's between Trumpism and Christianism. By Christianism, I mean Christianity as a political identity denuded of ethical content" (emphasis his). See https://tif.ssrc.org/2016/10/04/why-do-evangelicals-vote-for-trump/. Accessed on March 13, 2019.

15. Mason (2018). See Robert Jones' comments on the partisan loyalties of white evangelicals here: https://www.vox.com/identities/2018/4/20/17261726/poll-prri-white-evangelical-support-for-trump-is-at-an-all-time-high.

16. See Appendix Table B.3 for full results (see also Whitehead, Perry, and Baker 2018).
17. Gorski (2018); Jones (2016).
18. For more interviews and analysis of Trump voters and numerous examples of Christian nationalism in action, see Angela Denker's *Red State Christians: Understanding the Voters Who Elected Donald Trump*.
19. See Paula White's op-ed: https://www.floridadaily.com/still-a-nation-blessed/. Accessed February 27, 2019.
20. In March 2015 the Public Religion Research Institute (PRRI) began tracking approval ratings for Trump. His favorability ratings among white evangelicals at that point bounced around between 39 and 49 percent. Once it was clear he would win the Republican nomination in mid-2016, those numbers began to climb. As PRRI founder and CEO Robert Jones pointed out, this signals the partisan nature of white evangelicals—they tend to always fall in line with the Republican Party's nominee. See https://www.prri.org/spotlight/white-evangelical-support-for-donald-trump-at-all-time-high/ and https://www.vox.com/identities/2018/4/20/17261726/poll-prri-white-evangelical-support-for-trump-is-at-an-all-time-high.
21. For Pew's polling results, see http://www.people-press.org/2018/06/20/1-views-of-donald-trump/. For Gallup's polling results, see https://news.gallup.com/opinion/polling-matters/235208/things-know-evangelicals-america.aspx?g_source=link_NEWSV9&g_medium=SIDEBOTTOM&g_campaign=item_225380&g_content=5%2520Things%2520to%2520Know%2520About%2520Evangelicals%2520in%2520America. For PRRI's polling results, see https://www.vox.com/identities/2018/10/3/17929696/white-evangelicals-prri-poll-trump-presidency-support.
22. Graham's interview can be found here: https://www.nbcnews.com/politics/donald-trump/evangelist-franklin-graham-defends-trump-against-stormy-daniels-reports-n839496.
23. Perkins's interview can be accessed here: https://www.politico.com/magazine/story/2018/01/23/tony-perkins-evangelicals-donald-trump-stormy-daniels-216498.
24. See Appendix Tables B.3 and B.5 for full results.
25. There are many more that we could have included but do not have space for. Some we have written about elsewhere. Examples include,

but are not limited to, climate change, marijuana, physician-assisted suicide, investment in scientific research, and health care.

26. See https://www.breitbart.com/politics/2017/10/13/exclusive-michele-bachmann-getting-grip-immigration-president-trumps-1-priority/.

27. See Trump's speech at https://www.aljazeera.com/news/2016/09/donald-trump-immigration-arizona-160901005400355.html. Accessed on February 13, 2019.

28. Trump issued several orders (Executive Order 13779 and 13780) that placed limits on travel from certain countries, most of which were majority Muslim. EO 13780 was revised several times, argued over in court, and ultimately upheld by the United States Supreme Court in June 2018.

29. See Table B.3 in Appendix B.

30. These differences are statistically significant. See Table B.5 in Appendix B.

31. For more analysis, see also Dahab and Omori (2018).

32. See Appendix Table B.4.

33. For statistics on the number of fatal terror attacks carried out by refugees, see https://www.cnn.com/2017/01/29/us/refugee-terrorism-trnd/index.html. For statistics on the number of Christian refugees fleeing persecution in the Middle East, see https://www.christianpost.com/news/why-are-2-of-3-white-evangelicals-opposed-helping-refugees-world-relief-director-matthew-soerens-225044/. For Trump's comments about Middle Easterners in the migrant caravan, see https://www.cnn.com/2018/10/22/politics/donald-trump-migrant-caravan-fact-check/index.html.

34. Balmer (2006); FitzGerald (2017); Williams (2010, 2016).

35. See https://www.theguardian.com/us-news/2016/sep/09/trump-demographics-2016-election-republicans-can-win.

36. Barton (2008).

37. See https://www.christianitytoday.com/ct/2016/october/james-dobson-why-i-am-voting-for-donald-trump.html.

38. For Dobson's comments, see https://www.christianitytoday.com/ct/2016/october/james-dobson-why-i-am-voting-for-donald-trump.html. For Grudem's comments, see https://townhall.com/columnists/waynegrudem/2016/10/19/if-you-dont-like-

either-candidate-then-vote-for-trumps-policies-n2234187. Hoping to further drive home the connection between the Supreme Court, abortion, and seeking a future where the United States is a more Christian nation, Grudem wrote:

Which vote is most likely to bring the best results for the nation? In addition, I seek to obey Jesus' command, "You shall love your neighbor as yourself" (Matthew 22:39). This means that I have a moral obligation to seek a good government for my neighbor, and to prevent an anti-Christian liberal tyranny from taking power. If I love my neighbor as myself, then it does matter whether un-born babies are killed or not . . . But the most likely result of not voting for Trump is that we will be abandoning thousands of unborn babies who will be put to death under Hillary Clinton's Supreme Court . . . we will be contributing to a permanent loss of the American system of government due to a final victory of unac-countable judicial tyranny.

39. See Appendix Tables B.3 and B.5. We also examined the association between Christian nationalism and abortion in cases resulting from rape. In those models, Christian nationalism was marginally signif-icant (p=.058) net of all other effects. However, in the models using the 2014 General Social Survey, the Christian nationalism measure was significantly associated with opposition toward abortion in pregnancies resulting from rape, net of all other effects (see Table B.6 and Figure 2.6).

40. See Appendix Table B.6. Christian nationalism was the strongest pre-dictor in one model and the second or third strongest in five models.

41. NBC exit polls: https://www.nbcnews.com/card/nbc-news-exit-poll-future-supreme-court-appointments-important-factor-n680381. CNN exit polls: https://www.cnn.com/election/2016/results/exit-polls/national/president. See also Denker (2019).

42. See Dobson's statement here: http://drjamesdobson.org/news/dr-james-dobson-commends-president-trumps-supreme-court-nomination?memo%5Bsource%5D=FFB. See Perkin's statement here: https://patriotpost.us/opinion/55274-gorsuch-a-justice-for-all.

43. Gorski (2017).

44. See Appendix Tables B.7 and B.8. In Models 1 and 2 in Table B.8, there are no significant differences between Ambassadors and

Accommodators regarding attitudes toward the Government spending "too little" on the military, armaments, and defense.

45. See http://www.foxnews.com/transcript/2015/06/17/donald-trump-running-for-president.html.

46. See https://www.cbsnews.com/news/house-senate-negotiators-land-on-700-billion-deal-for-pentagon/. An interesting caveat to Trump's support of the military is that he is unafraid to attack veterans or those who lost loved ones serving in the military if they in any way oppose him. Trump has repeatedly attacked John McCain, even famously stating that, "I like people who weren't captured," referring to the five and a half years that McCain was a prisoner of war in North Vietnam. Another (in)famous example is Trump's disparagement of Khzir and Ghazala Khan, Gold Star parents who lost their son in the Iraq War. Despite Christian nationalists' love of the military, Trump's propensity to attack veterans and their families if they question him does not appear to influence their support.

47. See Appendix Table B.7. Notice that Christian nationalism has by far the strongest standardized coefficient (.47), almost double the next-highest standardized coefficient (religious practice: −.28). Equally important is that religious practice is significantly and negatively correlated with demanding people show respect to America's traditions. When we compare the four orientations (Appendix Table B.8), each one is significantly different from the other. The odds that Ambassadors agree people should be made to respect America's traditions are two times higher than Accommodators, over four times higher than Resisters, and over eight times higher than Rejecters. Likewise, the odds for Accommodators are two times higher than Resisters and over four times higher than Rejecters. The odds for Resisters are 1.89 times higher than that of Rejecters.

48. For these quotes, see https://www.nbcnews.com/politics/donald-trump/trump-says-nfl-players-who-kneel-during-national-anthem-maybe-n876996 and https://www.theguardian.com/sport/2017/sep/22/donald-trump-nfl-national-anthem-protests.

49. For why players kneel, see https://www.si.com/nfl/2018/05/23/why-do-players-kneel-during-national-anthem. For Trump's and others' attacks on players, see https://www.vox.com/policy-and-politics/2017/9/25/16360264/donald-trump-colin-kaepernick.

50. It is important to note that Kaepernick did "do something with his money" and not "just kneel for the flag." In his first year out of the NFL (2017) he donated one million dollars to various charities focused on social justice. That is over two percent of his total earnings over the course of his professional football career.

51. For Trump's "sons of bitches" remark, see https://www.theguardian.com/sport/2017/sep/22/donald-trump-nfl-national-anthem-protests. For Trump suggesting kneeling players don't belong in the United States, see https://www.nbcnews.com/politics/donald-trump/trump-says-nfl-players-who-kneel-during-national-anthem-maybe-n876996.

52. Anti-black racial bias in police shootings, even after accounting for whether the victim was armed or violent, is well established. See studies conducted by Kahn and Davies (2017); Nix et al. (2017); Ross (2015); Scott et al. (2017). See also the meta-analysis conducted by Mekawi and Bresin (2015).

53. Jeffress's comments can be accessed here: https://www.dallasnews.com/life/faith/2017/09/25/dallas-pastor-robert-jeffress-says-kneeling-nfl-players-thank-god-shot-head. Jeffress's follow-up comments are, again, ironic. Being called out by the President of the United States for exercising free speech would be considered by many to be government persecution.

54. The connection between the NRA and Russian money is of ongoing interest to the FBI and members of Congress. See https://www.theguardian.com/us-news/2019/mar/01/nra-russia-investigations-gun-lobby.

55. See https://www.washingtonpost.com/news/morning-mix/wp/2018/02/21/florida-house-refuses-to-debate-guns-but-declares-porn-dangerous/?utm_term=.2b609600f913.

56. The Kim Daniels comments can be found here: https://www.npr.org/sections/thetwo-way/2018/02/22/588002860/florida-lawmakers-advance-bill-requiring-schools-to-display-in-god-we-trust. Weeks later, Florida governor Rick Scott signed into law a bill that mandates a three-day waiting period for more gun purchases, raises the minimum buying age to 21, and gives police broad powers to confiscate guns from persons deemed to be a threat. It also created a controversial program that will arm some teachers and school staff.

57. Dial's remarks can be found here: http://www.newsweek.com/ten-commandments-alabama-republican-gerald-dial-school-shooting-christian-roy-827195.

58. See the commentary here: https://www.christianheadlines.com/columnists/guest-commentary/is-taking-god-out-of-schools-leading-to-increase-in-school-shootings.html.

59. See our publication with co-author Landon Schnabel, "Gun Control in the Crosshairs: Christian Nationalism and Opposition to Stricter Gun Laws." Available for free download at: https://journals.sagepub.com/doi/full/10.1177/2378023118790189.

60. See Appendix Tables B.7 and B.8. Notice that the Christian nationalism scale has the second largest standardized coefficient in the model in Table B.7. It is also important to notice that religious practice is significantly associated with support for gun control legislation, and in the opposite direction of Christian nationalism. We return to the importance of the religious practice finding later in this chapter.

61. Cruz (2016: 168–69, see also page 23).

62. For Huckabee's interview, see https://www.washingtontimes.com/news/2015/jun/19/huckabee-only-another-gun-wouldve-stopped-roof/. Accessed on February 14, 2019.

63. Some Christian nationalist authors make this quite explicit. See, for example, Cruz (2016) and Jeffress (2016).

64. For the fuller Falwell quote, see https://www.retroreport.org/transcript/the-roots-of-evangelicals-political-fervor/. Accessed on June 26, 2019.

65. Brubaker (2017: 1199).

CHAPTER 3

1. For Barton's comments, see http://religiondispatches.org/professor-david-barton-on-immigration-god-drew-our-borders/. Accessed on January 17, 2019. For Graham's comments, see https://www.faithwire.com/2017/03/31/wake-up-franklin-graham-has-a-tough-message-for-critics-of-trumps-border-wall-and-immigration-policies/. Accessed on January 17, 2019. For Jeffress's comments, see https://www.huffingtonpost.com/entry/

preacher-robert-jeffress-border-wall-trump_us_5c3640d
2e4b00c33ab5f394b. Accessed on January 9, 2019. For Grudem's
comments (2018), see https://townhall.com/columnists/wayne
grudem/2018/07/02/why-building-a-border-wall-is-a-morally-good-
action-n2496574. Accessed on July 4, 2018.

2. Lepore (2018).

3. Kidd (2010: 67) recounts how the Quebec Act of 1774, which
   increased the borders of French Canada down the Ohio River and
   granted religious freedom to the largely Catholic Quebecois became
   interpreted by the Anglo-Protestant colonists as a secret deal between the British Government and "Popery."

4. On the three-fifths stipulation, see Article I, section 3 of the U.S.
   Constitution. On the Supreme Court decision affirming black
   Americans' exclusion from citizenship, see *Dred Scott v. Sanford*, 60
   U.S. at 404–05.

5. For example, studies show that Americans are increasingly willing
   to elect non-Protestants, nonwhites, and even non-heterosexuals to
   high public office. See Edgell et al. (2006); Americans are also increasingly more likely to affirm that immigration should be increased. See
   trends cited in Gallup: https://news.gallup.com/poll/1660/immigra-
   tion.aspx. Accessed on June 17, 2019.

6. See Stewart, Edgell, and Delehanty (2018).

7. See Appendix Table B.9.

8. See Appendix Tables B.10 and B.11.

9. See Appendix Tables B.10 and B.11.

10. See https://www.cnbc.com/2016/10/19/trump-we-have-some-bad-
    hombres-and-were-going-to-get-them-out.html. Accessed on January
    23, 2019.

11. See, for example, an October 2016 poll: http://programs.clearer
    thinking.org/trump_clinton/trump_clinton_analysis.htm?
    fbclid=IwAR2BNzz6vRkkzT-a1aM42kCj_x1cEgL9vf4dZyw
    VslKoltEKwVakmndhfcY. See also exit polls from the *New York
    Times*: https://www.nytimes.com/interactive/2016/11/08/us/poli-
    tics/election-exit-polls.html and CNN: https://www.cnn.com/elec-
    tion/2016/results/exit-polls. All accessed on January 22, 2019.

12. In a speech two months before the 2016 election in Phoenix,
    Arizona, Trump stated that "countless innocent American lives have

been stolen" due to politicians' inability to secure borders and enforce immigration laws. In his speech he went on to mention eight
Americans by name who all died due to someone who was in the
United States illegally. Later, Trump invited 11 people onstage to
share the names of their loved one who was killed by a person who
was not a legal resident of the United States (see https://www.c-span.
org/video/?414550-1/donald-trump-delivers-immigration-policy-
address). Before the 2018 midterms, President Trump routinely
tweeted warnings about an impending "invasion" of migrants and
even deployed soldiers to the border to assist border patrol. He even
referenced "unknown Middle Easterners" that might be mixed in
with the caravan (see https://www.cnn.com/2018/10/22/politics/
donald-trump-migrant-caravan-fact-check/index.html).

13. Elena may have been an avid reader of Thomas's Aquinas's *Summa*,
or she may have learned about his stance from a 2017 Brietbart article
where Aquinas's views on borders were summarized and promoted.
See https://www.breitbart.com/politics/2017/01/31/saint-thomas-
aquinas-opposed-open-borders/. Accessed on January 23, 2019.

14. See http://www1.cbn.com/cbnnews/national-security/2018/july/
these-children-are-being-trafficked-we-must-have-stricter-border-
laws-pastor-paula-white-tours-migrant-detention-facility. Accessed
February 27, 2019.

15. See https://www.usatoday.com/story/news/2018/06/16/jeff-sessions-
bible-romans-13-trump-immigration-policy/707749002/. Accessed
on January 18, 2019.

16. In chapter 2 we found that Americans who more strongly embrace
Christian nationalism are much more likely to believe refugees from
the Middle East pose a terrorist threat.

17. Using the 2003 New Immigrant Survey, Massey and Higgins (2011)
showed that roughly 92% of Mexican immigrants identified as
Christian (82% Catholic, 3% Orthodox, and 7% Protestant),
compared to 81% of U.S. Adults. For the numbers on Mexican
Americans converting to evangelical Christianity, see Mulder, Ramos,
and Marti (2017).

18. See Appendix Table B.12.

19. These questions are all routinely used in studies focused on identifying
the contours of American identity. This literature establishes that for

some Americans these questions are all indicative of a particular view of what it means to be American. Our findings here simply underscore that relationship. See Bonikowski and DiMaggio (2016); Schildkraut (2007, 2014); Theiss-Morse (2009).

20. See Jemar Tisby's *The Color of Compromise: The Truth about the American Church's Complicity in Racism* (2019).

21. Tisby (2019: 36). Here Tisby is drawing on the work of historian Rebecca Anne Goetz (2012).

22. Fea (2018 : 102).

23. Douglass (1967 [1845]: 84–5). The racial boundaries prohibiting blacks' full inclusion into American civic life were incredibly influential to organized religious life as well, tearing apart most major denominations in the mid-1800s and birthing what is today the largest Protestant denomination in the United States (Southern Baptists). See Jones (2016: 166).

24. Baker (2011) and Jones (2016 167–75). Baker and Jones's excellent books provides numerous examples of how race and demands for white superiority structured conservative white Protestant religion and the broader culture from the Civil War throughout the 20th century and into the 21st century. These works show how this legacy is still very much with us today.

25. Balmer (2016: 13–7). From its founding until 1971, Bob Jones University did not admit African Americans as students. Even then, they only admitted married blacks and adopted rules against interracial dating and marriage. This caused BJU to lose its tax-exempt status. It was not until 2000 that BJU changed its interracial dating rule.

26. See Appendix Tables B.10 and B.11. Note in Table B.10 that while Christian nationalism is significantly and positively associated with being "not at all comfortable" with a daughter marrying an African American, religious practice is significantly and negatively associated with being "not at all comfortable." We return to this difference at the end of the chapter.

27. See Perry and Whitehead (2015a, 2015b) for more on these two pieces of evidence.

28. Sociologist Christopher Muller (2012) traces the inequitable treatment of black Americans at the hands of police all the way back to the 1800s.

29. Jones (2016: 150–55).

30. As cited in Jones (2016: 148). See also: https://www.facebook.com/FranklinGraham/posts/listen-up-blacks-whites-latinos-and-everybody-else-most-police-shootings-can-be-/883361438386705/.

31. See "An Open Letter to Reverend Franklin Graham" at https://sojo.net/articles/open-letter-franklin-graham.

32. See Appendix Tables B.10 and B.11. Regarding police treatment Ambassadors and Accommodators are both more likely than Resisters and Rejecters to believe police treat blacks the same as whites. However, there are no significant differences between Ambassadors and Accommodators. Resisters and Rejecters, while being less likely to believe that police treat blacks the same as whites than Ambassadors and Accommodators, are significantly different from one another. Regarding agreement that police shoot blacks more often because they are more violent than whites, Ambassadors and Accommodators are both significantly more likely to agree than Resisters and Rejecters but are not significantly different from each other. The same is true for Resisters and Rejecters—they are not significantly different from each other.

33. As we discussed earlier, these inclinations have historic roots, emerging from early colonists constructing religious and racial categories where white and European was linked to "Christian" while African and black equated to "heathen." See Tisby (2019).

34. See Davis (2018). See also foundational studies like Barkan and Cohn (2005); Baumer, Messner, and Rosenfeld (2003); Unnever and Cullen (2012); Weitzer (2017).

35. See https://www.au.org/blogs/wall-of-separation/palin-palaver-constitution-based-on-bible-former-alaska-governor-tells-o.

36. For these various quotes from Jeffress, see (2016: 51, 93, 95).

37. Dahab and Omori (2018).

38. For Perkin's comments, see http://www.gospelherald.com/articles/71691/20171206/5-christian-leaders-reactions-trump-formally-recognizing-jerusalem-israels-capital.htm. For Bachmann's comments, see https://www.haaretz.com/us-news/.premium-michele-bachmann-apologizes-for-2015-remarks-about-converting-jews-1.6077894. Pastor Robert Jeffress exulted, "President Trump is a modern-day profile in courage . . . It took courage for President Harry S. Truman to

recognize Israel as a nation in 1948, and it took courage for President Donald J. Trump to recognize Jerusalem as the capital of Israel today. He [Trump] is a blessing not only to our nation, but to Israel as well."

39. See https://www.haaretz.com/israel-news/.premium-trump-faith-adviser-who-said-all-jews-go-to-hell-to-speak-at-embassy-1.6078561.

40. Edgell et al. 2006; Edgell et al. 2016.

41. See https://www.facebook.com/FranklinGraham/posts/on-saturday-atheists-gathered-in-dc-at-the-lincoln-memorial-to-hold-what-they-ca/11732311109399735/.

42. In the appendix (see Appendix Tables B.13 and B.14) we present the results of multivariable analyses to examine how threatening Ambassadors, Accommodators, Resisters, and Rejecters perceive Muslims, Conservative Christians, Jews, and Atheists to be.

43. The perception of threat scale is made from three different questions asking the extent to which respondents agreed that [Muslims, Jews, Atheists, Conservative Christians] hold inferior values to theirs; want to restrict their freedoms; or want to endanger their physical safety. Models control for age, gender, race, region, education, income, size of place, political ideology, political party, religious tradition, biblical literalism, and religious practice. Net of all other effects, Christian nationalism is positively and significantly associated with the fear of Muslims and fear of Atheists scales (see Appendix Table B.13). Americans who strongly embrace Christian nationalism are much more likely to fear both. In fact, it is the strongest effect in each of the models. Also, notice that religious practice is significantly and negatively associated with fear of Muslims, but not for fear of atheists. There are also significant differences across the four orientations toward Christian nationalism (see Appendix Table B.14). This means that regarding views toward Muslims or atheists, Americans in any group are significantly different from those in any other group.

44. Yet again, though, Christian nationalism is still the strongest predictor in the entire multivariate model. See Appendix Table B.13.

45. See Appendix Table B.14. Across Models 1 through 3, there are no significant differences between Ambassadors, Accommodators, or Resisters net of all other effects. Rejecters, as you can see in Model 4, are significantly different from all three.

46. For each of the studies referenced in the preceding three paragraphs, see McDaniel et al. (2011); Sherkat and Lehman (2018); Stewart et al. (2018); Davis (2018, 2019).

47. Edgell et al. (2006).

48. In his evangelical lament, Balmer (2006: 69) writes that, "Christianity itself needs more Baptists, women and men willing to reconnect with the scandal of the gospel and not chase after the chimera of state sanction. We need women and men prepared to stand on conviction and articulate the faith in the midst of a pluralistic culture, not by imposing their principles on the remainder of society but by following the example of Jesus and doing what Baptists have always done best: preaching the gospel and not lusting after temporal power and influence."

49. On Christian legal defense organizations, see Bennett (2017), and on the shift in conservatives emphasizing "rights," see Lewis (2017).

CHAPTER 4

1. Reisebrodt (1993); Stanley (2018: 4–5, 127–28); Robin (2018: 24).

2. For early examples of Christian Right fundamentalist leaders connecting the family (and its arch-rival, feminism) with the future of the nation, see Falwell (1980); Jeremiah (1982); and LaHaye (1982).

3. Sociologists highlight how schemas, or interpretive frameworks, are transposable and can be "activated" in response to particular events or contexts (Edgell 2006). Regarding the waxing and waning of Christianity as central to American identity in response to different historical periods, see Whitehead and Scheitle (2018).

4. Green (2015).

5. See Balmer (2006); Fea (2011); Gorski (2017); Kruse (2015); Noll (2008); Tisby (2019).

6. See Jones (2016) and Kruse and Zelizer (2019).

7. Listen at https://www.focusonthefamily.com/media/focus-on-the-family-minute/the-familys-impact-on-society. Accessed on October 17, 2018.

8. The intersection of religion and gender attitudes is a robust literature. There are scores of studies and we know some important ones will

be overlooked here. Those that have influenced our thinking include but are not limited to the following: Bartkowski (2001); Denton (2004); Edgell (2006); Gallagher and Smith (1999); Gallagher (2003); Hempel and Bartkowski (2008) ; Hoffmann and Bartkowski (2008); Peek, Lowe, and Williams (1991); Perry and Whitehead (2016); Petersen and Donnenwerth (1998); Pevey, Williams, and Ellison (1996); Read (2003); Read and Bartkowski (2000); Schnabel (2016); Whitehead (2012).

9. Falwell (1980: 151).

10. See Grudem's (2012) book confronting "evangelical feminism" as an unbiblical slippery slope that leads to liberalism. The broader evangelical turn toward men coincided with the rise of the Promise Keepers movement (Bartkowski 2004) and remains a consistent approach among conservative Christian communities today (e.g., Evans 2012; MacDonald and Getz 2014; Morley 2013). For more, see historian Kristin Kobes DuMez's forthcoming book *Jesus and John Wayne: How White Evangelicals Corrupted a Faith and Fractured a Nation* on the rise of militant masculinity in evangelical Christianity since the 1970s.

11. Hardenbrook (2006: 378).

12. As you may remember from chapter 3, Ambassadors are generally very supportive of walls, which illustrates just how important this particular Ambassador considers the breakdown of the family.

13. See https://www.focusonthefamily.com/family-q-and-a/relationships-and-marriage/submission-of-wives-to-husbands. Accessed on January 28, 2019.

14. See Appendix Tables B.15 and B.16, and Whitehead and Perry (2019).

15. See Appendix Table B.19. The interaction coefficient between year and Christian nationalism is significant and negative, which means that the association between Christian nationalism and gender traditionalism is weaker in 2017 than it was in 2007.

16. For specific numbers, according to the General Social Survey, in 1973, 72.5% of Americans believed homosexuality was always wrong while only 11.2% believed it was not wrong at all. In 2018, 32.0% of Americans believed homosexuality to be always wrong, while 58.3% believe it is not wrong at all.

17. See https://www.manhattandeclaration.org/. Accessed January 29, 2019.
18. For a study using 2007 data, see Whitehead and Perry (2015). For results using 2017 data, see Appendix Tables B.17 and B.18.
19. See Appendix Table B.19.
20. Robin (2018: 191); Stanley (2018: 93–108). See also Andrew Lewis's (2017) book about the transformation of the Religious Right's strategy of opposing certain societal changes by focusing on defending their own "rights" and religious liberties rather than emphasizing morality.
21. Cruz (2016: 110–11).
22. Cruz (2016: 200–02).
23. See https://www.huffingtonpost.com/entry/michele-bachmann-transgender-reprieve_us_58e7eb5ae4b05413bfe2ed5d.
24. Since 2013, courts around the country have considered legal cases primarily surrounding the issue of whether transgender individuals could use the restroom of their choice rather than the restroom that corresponds to their assigned sex. As of 2017, only North Carolina had passed (and subsequently repealed) legislation mandating persons use the bathroom corresponding to the sex identified on their birth certificates. And as of 2018, 18 states and Washington, D. C. had adopted anti-discrimination laws including protections for transgender persons. See https://ballotpedia.org/Transgender_bathroom_access_laws_in_the_United_States. Accessed on September 18, 2019.
25. See Appendix Tables B.17 and B.18.
26. See Appendix Table B.18.
27. For more on the Freedom From Religion Foundation visit: https://ffrf.org/faq. For the responses of the FFRF to the moves made by the Trump administration regarding transgender rights, see https://ffrf.org/news/news-releases/item/28803-removal-of-transgender-protection-laws-violates-state-church-separation and https://ffrf.org/news/news-releases/item/33362-ffrf-condemns-trump-administration-s-discriminatory-transgender-policy.
28. For early reactions on the Christian Right to relaxing divorce laws, see LaHaye (1982: 159–66): Jeremiah (1982: 19–20). For a more contemporary reaction, see Grudem (2010: 220).

29. See https://www.manhattandeclaration.org/. Accessed on January 30, 2019.
30. See Appendix Tables B.17 and B.18.
31. See Appendix Table B.20.
32. For all our nerdy stat friends: The p-values ranged from .059 to .119 when comparing Ambassadors to each other group.
33. We also examined the relationship between marital status and the four postures toward Christian nationalism using the 2007 Baylor Religion Survey. The findings were similar to 2017. The only significant difference regarding rates of divorce were between Resisters and Accommodators, with Resisters reporting significantly lower rates of divorce.
34. Allport (1954: 446).
35. See Van Geest (2007).
36. See Chaves (1997: 15).
37. For studies on this pattern of politics influencing Americans' religious lives, see Bean (2014); Hout and Fischer (2002, 2014); Margolis (2018). For the reasons many Americans began to disaffiliate in the mid-1990s, see Baker and Smith (2015).

CHAPTER 5

1. On the diffusion of Christian nationalism or, as they label it, "secularized Evangelical discourse," see Delehanty, Edgell, and Stewart (2019). On the declining significance of denominational boundaries and the restructuring of American religion, see Wuthnow (1988).
2. Bean (2014); Smith (1998).
3. See Braunstein and Taylor (2017).
4. In order to do so, it is up to future polls and surveys to gather the necessary data. We offer recommendations toward this end in Appendix A.
5. See Braunstein (2018), Green (2015), Haselby (2015), and Kruse (2015).
6. See https://www.christianpost.com/news/paula-white-says-crusader-trump-put-jesus-christ-christmas-prayer-back-in-white-house.html.
7. See https://www.wtsp.com/article/news/politics/president-trump-tweets-support-for-bible-classes-in-public-schools/67-bc0ec6a3-b490-46a9-bf07-7ed352a1e2a1.

8. Marti (2019).

9. Braunstein (2018).

10. The CPCF is related to but not formally affiliated with the Congressional Prayer Caucus. WallBuilders, the organization founded and directed by political operative and Ambassador of Christian nationalism David Barton, and the National Legal Foundation both help direct Project Blitz.

11. The CPCF's webpage identifies the purpose of Project Blitz: "To protect the free exercise of traditional Judeo-Christian religious values and beliefs in the public square, and to reclaim and properly define the narrative which supports such beliefs." Visit the Congressional Prayer Caucus Foundation's Project Blitz webpage for more information: https://cpcfoundation.com/first-freedom-coalition-project-blitz/. Journalist Frederick Clarkson was one of the first to report on Project Blitz and systematically outline its purpose and tactics. Read his reporting here: http://religiondispatches. org/project-blitz-seeks-to-do-for-christian-nationalism-what-alec-does-for-big-business/.

12. Category 1 provides examples of legislation that recognize America's "religious heritage," like passing "In God We Trust" bills. Category 2 are proclamations and resolutions that recognize the importance of religious (Christian) freedom and history. Category 3 are bills protecting "religious liberty," like public policies that favor heterosexual marriages, oppose transgender equality, or allow for discrimination based on religion and sexuality regarding adoption.

13. See Corbin (2019) and Edgell, Stewart, Billups, and Larson (2019).

14. Journalist Kelsey Dallas created an ongoing project that tracks various bills related to religious liberty in America and faith in the public square that allows you to sort by state. You can find her reporting for 2018 here: https://www.deseretnews.com/article/900020906/ interactive-heres-how-139-bills-across-the-country-are-redefining-religious-freedom.html.

15. See Fea (2018).

16. Governor Henry McMaster requested the Trump administration allow the agency to discriminate based on its religious beliefs: "As Americans, our fundamental right to practice religion,

regardless of our faith, will not be in jeopardy under this administration." See https://www.nbcnews.com/feature/nbc-out/
s-c-group-can-reject-gays-jews-foster-parents-trump-n962306.

17. See https://www.foxnews.com/politics/texas-republicans-
overwhelmingly-reject-removal-of-muslim-county-official. Accessed
February 20, 2019.

18. Former Supreme Court Associate Justice Harry Blackmun, *Lee
v. Weisman*, 505 U.S. 577 at 606–07 as cited in Corbin (2019).

19. In Bonikowski et al. (2019), sociologist Bart Bonikowski explains
how populism, nationalism, and authoritarianism can operate as
mutually constitutive concepts. Nationalism combined with populism creates conditions for the politics of nostalgia and resentment,
while populism and authoritarianism enable the framing of the
political opposition as the "morally corrupt enemy of the nation"
allowing for exceptional measures to be taken against them, even
those that violate the norms of democracy. Christian nationalism,
therefore, provides a cultural framework where fear, nostalgia, and
resentment are cultivated, and the pairing of this with populism and
authoritarian tendencies highlights the threat it poses to a pluralistic democracy. See also Goldberg (2006), Hedges (2006), and Seidel
(2019) for the particular threat Christian nationalism may represent
for American democracy.

20. Quotes are from Family Research Council president Tony Perkins
https://www.politico.com/magazine/story/2018/01/23/
tony-perkins-evangelicals-donald-trump-stormy-daniels-216498.

21. See Hout and Fischer (2002, 2014); Margolis (2018). According to
the General Social Survey, in 1990 around 8 percent of Americans
identified as unaffiliated with any religious tradition. By 2000 14 percent identified in this way, and in 2018 23.3 percent of Americans
were unaffiliated. See Baker and Smith (2015) for the definitive study
of "The Great Abdicating" and American secularism.

APPENDIX A

1. American Association for Public Opinion Research (2008), Pew
Research Center (2012), and Singer 2006.

2. See Perry, Davis, and Whitehead (2019); Perry and Whitehead (2019); Whitehead, Perry, and Baker (2018); Whitehead and Perry (2019).

3. A number of data sources that contain at least one question similar or identical to those we use in our Christian nationalism scale are available for free from the Association of Religion Data Archives (www.theARDA.com). Questions pertaining to school prayer account for a majority of these sources: 1996 American Jewish Committee Religious Right Survey; 1948–2004 American National Election Studies Cumulative Data File; 2000 American Rabbi Study; 1964 and 1981 Anti-Semitism in the United States Surveys; 2005 and 2007 Baylor Religion Surveys; 1987 Church and Community Project; 2000–2001 Cooperative Clergy Project; 1997 Detroit Area Study: Social Change in Religion and Child Rearing; 1991 Effective Christian Education: A National Study of Protestant Congregations; 1998 and 1999–2000 ELCA-Episcopal Church Clergy Study; 1997 Endtime Family (Children of God) Survey; 1976–2016 General Social Surveys; 1996 God and Society in North America; 1984 Harris Business-Week Survey; 2008 The Henry Institute National Survey of Religion and Public Life; January 2013 PRRI Religion & Politics Tracking Poll; 1981, 1982, 1984, and 1985 Middletown Area Studies; 1989 Mennonite Church Member Profile; 2005 National Study of Youth and Religion; 1988 and 2012 Nebraska Annual Social Indicators Survey; July 2005 News Interest Index/Religion Overflow Survey; 1983 and 1984 Notre Dame Study of Catholic Parish Life; 1975–1995 Project Canada Surveys; 2012 Race, Class, and Culture Survey; 2002–2003 Religion and Diversity Survey; 1996 Religion and Politics Survey; 2002, 2004, and 2006 Religion and Public Life Surveys; 1994 Religion in Italy Survey; 1996 Religious Influence and Identity Survey; 1967–1969 Salt Lake City and San Francisco Surveys of Mormons; Spring 1994 Southern Focus Poll; 1996 State of Disunion Survey; 1997, 2000, 2001, 2004, and 2005 State of the First Amendment Surveys; 2000 Survey of Clergy in Indianapolis; 1963 Survey of Northern California Church Bodies; 1999 Survey of Religion and Community Life in Indianapolis; 1987 Williamsburg Charter Survey on Religion and Public Life; 1996 Winthrop University Student Religion Survey.

4. See Footnote 7 in Whitehead, Perry, and Baker (2018).
5. Small (2009: 24–5). See also Yin (2018).
6. Perry and Whitehead (2019).
7. Wilson-Hartgrove (2018).
8. See Bonikowski (2016, 2017); Bonikowski et al. (2019); Brubaker (2017); Soper and Fetzer (2018).

BIBLIOGRAPHY

Aho, James. 2013. "Christian Heroism and the Reconstruction of America." *Critical Sociology* 39(4): 545–60.

Aho, James. 2016. *Far-Right Fantasy: A Sociology of American Religion and Politics*. New York, NY: Routledge.

Allport, Gordon W. 1954. *The Nature of Prejudice*. Reading, MA: Addison-Wesley.

American Association for Public Opinion Research. 2008. "Do Response Rates Matter?" https://www.aapor.org/Education-Resources/For-Researchers/Poll-Survey-FAQ/Response-Rates-An-Overview.aspx.

Baker, Joseph O., and Buster Smith. 2015. *American Secularism: Cultural Contours of Nonreligious Belief Systems*. New York, NY: New York University Press.

Baker, Kelly J. 2011. *Gospel According to the Klan: The KKK's Appeal to Protestant America, 1915–1930*. Lawrence, KS: University of Kansas Press.

Balmer, Randall. 2006. *Thy Kingdom Come: How the Religious Right Distorts the Faith and Threatens America—An Evangelical's Lament*. New York, NY: Basic Books.

Barkan, Steven E., and Steven F. Cohn. 2005. "Why Whites Favor Spending More Money to Fight Crime: The Role of Racial Prejudice." *Social Problems* 52(2): 300–14.

Bartkowski, John P. 2001. *Remaking the Godly Marriage: Gender Negotiation in Evangelical Families*. New Brunswick, NJ: Rutgers University Press.

Bartkowski, John P. 2004. *The Promise Keepers: Servants, Soldiers, and Godly Men*. Piscataway, NJ: Rutgers University Press.

Barton, David. 2008. *Original Intent: The Courts, the Constitution, and Religion*. Aledo, TX: WallBuilder Press.

Baumer, Eric P., Steven F. Messner, and Richard Rosenfeld. 2003. "Explaining Spatial Variation in Support for Capital Punishment: A Multilevel Analysis." *American Journal of Sociology* 108(4): 844–75.

Bean, Lydia. 2014. *The Politics of Evangelical Identity Local Churches and Partisan Divides in the United States and Canada.* Princeton, NJ: Princeton University Press.

Bellah, Robert N. 1967. "Civil Religion in America." *Daedalus* 96(1): 1–21.

Bellah, Robert N. 1975. *The Broken Covenant: American Civil Religion in a Time of Trial.* New York, NY: Seabury Press.

Bennett, Daniel. 2017. *Defending the Faith: The Politics of the Christian Conservative Legal Movement.* Lawrence, KS: University of Kansas Press.

Bock, Jarrod, Jennifer Byrd-Craven, and Melissa Burkley. 2017. "The Role of Sexism in Voting in the 2016 Presidential Election." *Personality and Individual Differences* 119(1): 189–93.

Bonikowski, Bart. 2016. "Three Lessons of Contemporary Populism in Europe and the United States." *The Brown Journal of World Affairs* 23(1): 9–24.

Bonikowski, Bart. 2017. "Ethno-nationalist Populism and the Mobilization of Collective Resentment." *The British Journal of Sociology* 68(S1): 181–213.

Bonikowski, Bart, and Paul DiMaggio. 2016. "Varieties of American Popular Nationalism." *American Sociological Review* 81(5): 949–80.

Bonikowski, Bart, Daphne Halikiopoulou, Eric Kaufmann, and Matthijs Rooduijn. 2019. "Populism and Nationalism in a Comparative Perspective: A Scholarly Exchange." *Nations and Nationalism* 25(1): 58–81.

Bowman, Matthew. 2018. *Christian: The Politics of a Word in America.* Cambridge, MA: Harvard University Press.

Boyd, Gregory A. 2007. *The Myth of a Christian Nation: How the Quest for Political Power Is Destroying the Church.* Grand Rapids, MI: Zondervan.

Braunstein, Ruth. 2017. *Prophets and Patriots Faith in Democracy across the Political Divide.* Oakland, CA: University of California Press.

Braunstein, Ruth. 2018. "A (More) Perfect Union? Religion, Politics, and Competing Stories of America." *Sociology of Religion* 79(2): 172–95.

Braunstein, Ruth, and Malaena Taylor. 2017. "Is the Tea Party a 'Religious' Movement? Religiosity in the Tea Party Vs. the Religious Right." *Sociology of Religion* 78(1): 33–59.

Brubaker, Rogers. 2017. "Between Nationalism and Civilizationism: The European Populist Moment in Comparative Perspective." *Ethnic and Racial Studies* 40(8): 1191–226.

Chaves, Mark. 1997. *Ordaining Women: Culture and Conflict in Religious Organizations.* Cambridge, MA: Harvard University Press.

Cherry, Conrad. 1998. *God's New Israel: Religious Interpretations of American Destiny.* Chapel Hill, NC: The University of North Carolina Press.

Corbin, Caroline Mala. 2019. "Christian Legislative Prayers and Christian Nationalism." *Washington and Lee Law Review* 75. Available at: https://papers.ssrn.com/sol3/papers.cfm?abstract_id=3333378.

Cornett, Daryl C. 2011. *Christian America?: Perspectives on Our Religious Heritage.* Nashville, TN: B&H Publishing Group.

Cruz, Rafael. 2016. *A Time for Action: Empowering the Faithful to Reclaim America.* Washington, DC: WND Books.

Dahab, Ramsey, and Marisa Omori. 2018. "Homegrown Foreigners: How Christian Nationalism and Nativist Attitudes Impact Muslim Civil Liberties." *Ethnic and Racial Studies* 42(10): 1727–46.

Davis, Joshua T. 2018. "Enforcing Christian Nationalism: Examining the Link Between Group Identity and Punitive Attitudes in the United States." *Journal for the Scientific Study of Religion* 57(2): 300–17.

Davis, Joshua T. 2019. "Funding God's Policies, Defending Whiteness: Christian Nationalism and Whites' Attitudes Towards Racially-Coded Government Spending." *Ethnic and Racial Studies* 42(12): 2123–42.

Delehanty, Jack, Penny Edgell, and Evan Stewart. 2019. "Christian America? Secularized Evangelical Discourse and the Boundaries of National Belonging." *Social Forces* 97(3): 1283–306.

Denker, Angela. 2019. *Red State Christians: Understanding the Voters Who Elected Donald Trump.* Minneapolis, MN: Augsburg Books.

Denton, Melinda Lundquist. 2004. "Gender and Marital Decision Making: Negotiating Religious Ideology and Practice. *Social Forces* 82: 1151–80.

Douglass, Frederick. 1967 [1845]. *Narrative of the Life of Frederick Douglass, An American Slave.* Public Domain.

Du Mez, Kristin Kobes. 2018. "Fear, Power, Nostalgia, and the 81 Percent." *Christianity Today.* Accessed at: https://www.christianitytoday.com/ct/2018/june-web-only/believe-me-donald-trump-john-fea.html.

Edgell, Penny. 2006. *Religion and Family in a Changing Society.* Princeton, NJ: Princeton University Press.

Edgell, Penny, Joseph Gerteis, and Douglas Hartmann. 2006. "Atheists as 'Other': Moral Boundaries and Cultural Membership in American Society." *American Sociological Review* 71(2): 211–34.

Edgell, Penny, Douglas Hartmann, Evan Stewart, and Joseph Gerteis. 2016. "Atheists and Other Cultural Outsiders: Moral Boundaries and the Non-religious in the United States." *Social Forces* 95(2): 607–38.

Edgell, Penny, Evan Stewart, Sarah Catherine Billups, and Ryan Larson. 2019. "The Stakes of Symbolic Boundaries." *The Sociological Quarterly.* DOI: 10.1080/00380253.2019.1625736.

Ekins, Emily. 2017. "The Five Types of Trump Voters: Who They Are and What They Believe." A Research Report from the Democracy Fund Voter Study Group. Accessed at: https://www.voterstudygroup.org/publication/the-five-types-trump-voters.

Evans, Tony. 2012. *Kingdom Man: Every Man's Destiny, Every Woman's Dream.* Carol Stream, IL: Tyndale House Publishers.

Falwell, Jerry. 1980. *Listen America!* Garden City, NY: Doubleday.

Fea, John. 2011. *Was America Founded as a Christian Nation? A Historical Introduction.* Revised Edition. Louisville, KY: Westminster John Knox Press.

Fea, John. 2018. *Believe Me: The Evangelical Road to Donald Trump.* Grand Rapids, MI: Eerdmans.

FitzGerald, Frances. 2017. *The Evangelicals: The Struggle to Shape America.* New York, NY: Simon & Schuster.

Froese, Paul, and F. Carson Mencken. 2009. "A U.S. Holy War? The Effects of Religion on Iraq War Policy Attitudes." *Social Science Quarterly* 90(1): 103–16.

Gallagher, Sally K. 2003. *Evangelical Identity and Gendered Family Life.* New Brunswick, NJ: Rutgers University Press.

Gallagher, Sally K., and Christian Smith. 1999. "Symbolic Traditionalism and Pragmatic Egalitarianism: Contemporary Evangelicals, Family, and Gender." *Gender and Society* 13: 211–33.

Goetz, Rebecca Anne. 2012. *The Baptism of Early Virginia: How Christianity Created Race*. Baltimore, MD: Johns Hopkins University Press.

Goldberg, Michelle. 2006. *Kingdom Coming: The Rise of Christian Nationalism*. New York, NY: W.W. Norton.

Gorski, Philip. 2017. *American Covenant: A History of Civil Religion from the Puritans to the Present*. Princeton, NJ: Princeton University Press.

Gorski, Philip. 2018. "Christianity and Democracy after Trump." Political Theology Network. Accessed at: https://politicaltheology.com/christianity-and-democracy-after-trump/.

Green, Steven K. 2015. *Inventing a Christian America: The Myth of the Religious Founding*. New York, NY: Oxford University Press.

Grudem, Wayne. 2010. *Politics According the Bible: A Comprehensive Resource for Understanding Modern Political Issues in Light of Scripture*. Grand Rapids, MI: Zondervan.

Grudem, Wayne. 2012. *Evangelical Feminism and Biblical Truth: An Analysis of More Than 100 Disputed Questions*. Wheaton, IL: Crossway.

Hardenbrook, Weldon. 2006. "Where's Dad? A Call for Fathers with the Spirit of Elijah." In *Recovering Biblical Manhood and Womanhood*, edited by John Piper and Wayne Grudem, pp. 378–87. Wheaton, IL: Crossway.

Harris, Matthew, and Thomas Kidd. 2011. *The Founding Fathers and the Debate over Religion in Revolutionary America: A History in Documents*. New York, NY: Oxford University Press.

Haselby, Sam. 2015. *The Origins of American Religious Nationalism*. New York, NY: Oxford University Press.

Hedges, Chris. 2006. *American Fascists: The Christian Right and the War on America*. New York, NY: Free Press.

Hempel, Lynn M., and John P. Bartkowski. 2008. "Scripture, Sin and Salvation: Theological Conservatism Reconsidered." *Social Forces* 86(1): 1647–74.

Hochschild, Arlie Russell. 2016. *Strangers in Their Own Land: Anger and Mourning on the American Right*. New York, NY: The New Press.

Hoffmann, John P., and John P. Bartkowski. 2008. "Gender, Religious Tradition, and Biblical Literalism." *Social Forces* 86(3): 1245–72.

Holmes, David L. 2006. *The Faiths of the Founding Fathers*. New York, NY: Oxford University Press.

Hout, Michael, and Claude Fischer. 2002. "Why More Americans Have No Religious Preference: Politics and Generations." *American Sociological Review* 67(2): 165–90.

Hout, Michael, and Claude Fischer. 2014. "Explaining Why More Americans Have No Religious Preference: Political Backlash and Generational Succession, 1987–2012." *Sociological Science* 1: 423–47.

Ingersoll, Julie. 2015. *Building God's Kingdom: Inside the World of Christian Reconstruction.* New York, NY: Oxford University Press.

Jeffress, Robert. 2016. *Twilight's Last Gleaming: How America's Last Days Can Be Your Best Days.* Franklin, TN: Worthy Publishing.

Jenkins, Jack. 2017a. "Why Christian Nationalists Love Trump." *ThinkProgress.* Available at: https://thinkprogress.org/trumps-christian-nationalism-c6fe206e4occ/.

Jenkins, Jack. 2017b. "Historians of Christian Nationalism are Alarmed by Its Appearance in American Pulpits." *ThinkProgress.* Available at: https://thinkprogress.org/history-christian-nationalism-e3303b46c3bc/.

Jenkins, Jack. 2017c. "How Trump's Presidency Reveals the True Nature of Christian Nationalism." *ThinkProgress.* Available at: https://thinkprogress.org/christian-nationalism-religion-research-b8f9cdc16239/.

Jeremiah, David. 1982. *Before It's Too Late: Crises Facing America.* Nashville, TN: Thomas Nelson Publishers.

Johnston, Ron, Ryne Rohla, David Manley, and Kelvyn Jones. 2019. "Voting for Trump and the Electoral Mosaics of US Metropolitan Areas: Exploring Changing Patterns of Party Support by Neighborhood." *Cities* 86: 94–101.

Jones, Robert P. 2016. *The End of White Christian America.* New York, NY: Simon & Schuster.

Kahn, Kimberly Barsamian, and Paul G. Davies. 2017. "What Influences Shooter Bias? The Effects of Suspect Race, Neighborhood, and Clothing on Decisions to Shoot." *Journal of Social Issues* 73(4): 723–43.

Kennedy, Courtney, Mark Blumenthal, Scott Clement, et al. 2018. "An Evaluation of the 2016 Election Polls in the United States." *Public Opinion Quarterly* 82(1): 1–33.

Kidd, Thomas. 2010. *God of Liberty: A Religious History of the American Revolution.* New York, NY: Basic Books.

King, Jr., Martin Luther. 1963. "Letter from a Birmingham Jail." *Christian Century*, June 12.

Kruse, Kevin. 2015. *One Nation Under God: How Corporate America Invented Christian America*. New York, NY: Basic Books.

Kruse, Kevin, and Julian Zelizer. 2019. *Fault Lines: A History of the United States Since 1974*. New York, NY: W.W. Norton.

LaHaye, Tim. 1982. *The Battle for the Family*. Old Tappan, NJ: Revell.

Lambert, Frank. 2006. *The Founding Fathers and the Place of Religion in America*. Princeton, NJ: Princeton University Press.

Lambert, Frank. 2008. *Religion in American Politics: A Short History*. Princeton, NJ: Princeton University Press.

Lambert, Frank. 2014. *Separation of Church & State: Founding Principle Religious Liberty*. Macon, GA: Mercer University Press.

Lepore, Jill. 2018. *These Truths: A History of the United States*. New York, NY: W.W. Norton.

Lewis, Andrew R. 2017. *The Rights Turn in Conservative Christian Politics: How Abortion Transformed the Culture Wars*. New York, NY: Cambridge University Press.

Lynerd, Benjamin T. 2014. *Republican Theology: The Civil Religion of American Evangelicals*. New York, NY: Oxford University Press.

MacDonald, James, and Gene A. Getz. 2014. *Act Like Men: 40 Days to Biblical Manhood*. Chicago, IL: Moody Publishers.

Margolis, Michele F. 2018. *From Politics to the Pews: How Partisanship and the Political Environment Shape Religious Identity*. Chicago: University of Chicago Press.

Martí, Gerardo. 2019. "The Unexpected Orthodoxy of Donald J. Trump: White Evangelical Support for the 45th President of the United States." *Sociology of Religion* 80(1): 1–8.

Mason, Lilliana. 2018. "Ideologues Without Issues: The Polarizing Consequences of Ideological Identities." *Public Opinion Quarterly* 82(1): 866–87.

Massey, Douglas S., and Monica Espinoza Higgins. 2011. "The Effect of Immigration on Religious Belief and Practice: A Theologizing or Alienating Experience?" *Social Science Research* 40(5): 1371–89.

McDaniel, Eric L., Irfan Nooruddin, and Allyson Faith Shortle. 2011. "Divine Boundaries: How Religion Shapes Citizen's Attitudes toward Immigrants." *American Politics Research* 39(1): 205–33.

McElwee, Sean, and Jason McDaniel. 2017. "Economic Anxiety Didn't Make People Vote Trump, Racism Did: New Data Provide a Compelling Answer to this Vexing Question." The Nation. May 8. https://www.thenation.com/article/economic-anxiety-didnt-make-people-vote-trump-racism-did/.

McVeigh, Rory, and Kevin Estep. 2019. *The Politics of Losing: Trump, the Klan, and the Mainstreaming of Resentment.* New York, NY: Columbia University Press.

McVicar, Michael. 2015. *Christian Reconstruction: R. J. Rushdoony and American Religious Conservatism.* Chapel Hill, NC: The University of North Carolina Press.

Mekawi, Yara, and Konrad Bresin. 2015. "Is the Evidence from Racial Bias Shooting Task Studies a Smoking Gun? Results from a Meta-Analysis." *Journal of Experimental Social Psychology* 61: 120–30.

Merino, Stephen M. 2010. "Religious Diversity in a 'Christian Nation': The Effects of Theological Exclusivity and Interreligious Contact on the Acceptance of Religious Diversity." *Journal for the Scientific Study of Religion* 49(2): 231–46.

Morley, Patrick. 2013. *How God Makes Men: Ten Epic Stories.* Colorado Springs, CO: Multnomah.

Mulder, Mark T., Aida I. Ramos, and Gerardo Martí. 2017. *Latino Protestants in America: Growing and Diverse.* Lanham, MD: Rowman & Littlefield.

Muller, Christopher. 2012. "Northward Migration and the Rise of Racial Disparity in American Incarceration, 1880–1950." *American Journal of Sociology* 118(2): 281–326.

Nix, Justin, Justin T. Pickett, Scott E. Wolfe, and Bradley A. Campbell. 2017. "Demeanor, Race, and Police Perceptions of Procedural Justice: Evidence from Two Randomized Experiments." *Justice Quarterly* 34(7): 1154–83.

Noll, Mark A. 2008. *God and Race in American Politics: A Short History.* Princeton, NJ: Princeton University Press.

Noll, Mark A., Nathan O. Hatch, and George M. Marsden. 1989. *The Search for Christian America.* Colorado Springs, CO: Helmers & Howard.

Peek, Charles W., George D. Lowe, and L. Susan Williams. 1991. "Gender and God's Word: Another Look at Religious Fundamentalism and Sexism." *Social Forces* 69: 1205–21.

Perry, Samuel L., and Andrew L. Whitehead. 2015a. "Christian Nationalism and White Racial Boundaries: Examining Whites' Opposition to Interracial Marriage." *Ethnic and Racial Studies* 38: 1671–89.

Perry, Samuel L., and Andrew L. Whitehead. 2015b. "Christian Nationalism, Racial Separatism, and Family Formation: Attitudes toward Transracial Adoption as a Test Case." *Race and Social Problems* 7: 123–34.

Perry, Samuel L., and Andrew L. Whitehead. 2016. "Religion and Non-traditional Families in the United States." *Sociology Compass* 10(5): 391–403.

Perry, Samuel L., and Andrew L. Whitehead. 2019. "Christian America in Black and White: Racial Identity, Religious-National Group Boundaries, and Explanations for Racial Inequality." *Sociology of Religion* 80(3): 277–98.

Perry, Samuel L., Andrew L. Whitehead, and Joshua T. Davis. 2019. "God's Country in Black and Blue: How Christian Nationalism Shapes White Americans' Views about Police Treatment of Blacks." *Sociology of Race and Ethnicity* 5(1): 130–46.

Petersen, Larry R., and Gregory V. Donnenwerth. 1998. "Religion and Declining Support for Traditional Beliefs about Gender Roles and Homosexual Rights." *Sociology of Religion* 59: 353–71.

Pevey, Carolyn, Christine L. Williams, and Christopher G. Ellison. 1996. "Male God Imagery and Female Submission: Lessons from a Southern Baptist Ladies' Bible Class." *Qualitative Sociology* 19: 173–93.

Pew Research Center. 2012. "Assessing the Representativeness of Public Opinion Surveys." http://www.people-press.org/2012/05/15/assessing-the-representativeness-of-public-opinion-surveys/#.

Polletta, Francesca. 2006. *It Was Like a Fever: Storytelling in Protest and Politics*. Chicago, IL: University of Chicago Press.

Polletta, Francesca, and Jessica Callahan. 2017. "Deep Stories, Nostalgia Narratives, and Fake News: Storytelling in the Trump Era." *American Journal of Cultural Sociology* 5(3): 392–408.

Prothero, Stephen. 2012. *The American Bible: How Our Words Unite, Divide, and Define a Nation*. New York, NY: HarperOne.

Read, Jen'nan. 2003. "The Sources of Gender Role Attitudes among Christian and Muslim Arab-American Women." *Sociology of Religion* 64: 207–22.

Read, Jen'nan Ghazal, and John P. Bartkowski. 2000. "To Veil or Not to Veil? A Case Study of Identity Negotiation among Women in Austin, Texas." *Gender and Society* 14: 395–417.

Riesbrodt, Martin. 1993. *Pious Passion: The Emergence of Modern Fundamentalism in the United States and Iran.* Berkeley, CA: University of California Press.

Robin, Corey. 2018. *The Reactionary Mind: Conservatism from Edmund Burke to Donald Trump.* New York, NY: Oxford University Press.

Ross, Cody T. 2015. "A Multi-Level Bayesian Analysis of Racial Bias in Police Shootings at the County-Level in the United States, 2011–2014." *PLoS ONE* 10(11): e0141854.

Rothwell, Valerie, Gordon Hodson, and Elvira Prusaczyk. 2019. "Why Pillory Hillary? Testing the Endemic Sexism Hypothesis Regarding the 2016 U.S. Election." *Personality and Individual Differences* 138(1): 106–8.

Schaffner, Brian F., Matthew MacWilliams, and Tatishe Nteta. 2018. "Understanding White Polarization in the 2016 Vote for President: The Sobering Role of Racism and Sexism." *Political Science Quarterly* 133(1): 9–34.

Schildkraut, Deborah J. 2007. "Defining American Identity in the Twenty-first Century: How Much 'There' Is There?" *The Journal of Politics* 69(3): 597–615.

Schildkraut, Deborah. 2011. *Americanism in the Twenty-First Century: Public Opinion in the Age of Immigration.* New York, NY: Cambridge University Press.

Schildkraut, Deborah J. 2014. "Boundaries of American Identity: Evolving Understandings of 'Us'." *Annual Review of Political Science* 17: 441–60.

Schnabel, Landon. 2016. "Gender and Homosexuality Attitudes Across Religious Groups from the 1970s to 2014: Similarity, Distinction, and Adaptation." *Social Science Research* 55: 31–47.

Scott, Kendra, Debbie S. Ma, Melody S. Sadler, and Joshua Correll. 2017. "A Social Scientific Approach toward Understanding Racial Disparities in Police Shooting: Data from the Department of Justice (1980–2000)." *Journal of Social Issues* 73(4): 1–22.

Seidel, Andrew L. 2019. *The Founding Myth: Why Christian Nationalism is Un-American.* New York, NY: Sterling.

Sherkat, Darren E., and Derek Lehman. 2018. "Bad Samaritans: Religion and Anti-Immigrant and Anti-Muslim Sentiment in the United States." *Social Science Quarterly* 99(5): 1791–804.

Shortle, Allyson F., and Ronald Keith Gaddie. 2015. "Religious Nationalism and Perceptions of Muslims and Islam." *Politics and Religion* 8: 435–457.

Sides, John. 2017. "Race, Religion, and Immigration in 2016: How the Debate Over American Identity Shaped the Election and What It Means for a Trump Presidency." A Research Report from the Democracy Fund Voter Study Group. Accessed at: https://www.voterstudygroup.org/publication/race-religion-immigration-2016.

Singer, Eleanor. 2006. "Special Issue on Nonresponse Bias in Household Surveys." *Public Opinion Quarterly* 70: 639–810.

Small, Mario. 2009. "'How Many Cases Do I Need?' On Science and the Logic of Case Selection in Field-Based Research." *Ethnography* 10(1): 5–38.

Smith, Christian. 1998. *American Evangelicalism: Embattled and Thriving*. Chicago, IL: University of Chicago Press.

Smith, Christian. 2000. *Christian America? What Evangelicals Really Want*. Berkeley, CA: University of California Press.

Smith, Christian. 2003. *Moral, Believing Animals: Human Personhood and Culture*. New York, NY: Oxford University Press.

Smith, Rogers. 1997. *Civic Ideals: Conflicting Visions of American Citizenship in U.S. History*. New Haven, CT: Yale University Press.

Somers, Margaret R. 1994. "The Narrative Constitution of Identity: A Relational and Network Approach." *Theory and Society* 23(5): 605–49.

Soper, J. Christopher, and Joel S. Fetzer. 2018. *Religion and Nationalism in a Global Perspective*. New York, NY: Cambridge University Press.

Stanley, Jason. 2018. *How Fascism Works: The Politics of Us and Them*. New York, NY: Random House.

Stewart, Evan. 2018. "Public Religion and the Vote for Donald Trump: Evidence from Panel Data." Paper Presented at the American Sociological Association Annual Conference in Philadelphia, PA. August 11–14. Accessed at: https://convention2.allacademic.com/one/asa/asa18/index.php?cmd=Online+Program+View+Session&selected_session_id=1395004&PHPSESSID=s1im6vehgvajsll3viptdq6et3.

Stewart, Evan, Penny Edgell, and Jack Delehanty. 2018. "The Politics of Religious Prejudice and Tolerance for Cultural Others." *The Sociological Quarterly* 59(1): 17–39.

Stewart, Katherine. 2012. *The Good News Club: The Christian Right's Stealth Assault on America's Children*. New York, NY: PublicAffairs.

Stewart, Katherine. 2020. *The Power Worshippers: Inside the Dangerous Rise of Religious Nationalism*. New York, NY: Bloomsbury Publishing.

Stewart, Matthew. 2015. *Nature's God: The Heretical Origins of the American Republic*. New York, NY: W.W. Norton.

Straughn, Jeremy Brooke, and Scott L. Feld. 2010. "America as a 'Christian Nation'? Understanding Religious Boundaries of National Identity in the United States." *Sociology of Religion* 71(3): 280–306.

Theiss-Morse, Elizabeth. 2009. *Who Counts as an American? The Boundaries of National Identity*. New York, NY: Cambridge University Press.

Thomas, W.I., and D.S. Thomas. 1928. *The Child in America: Behavior Problems and Programs*. New York, NY: Knopf.

Tisby, Jemar. 2019. *The Color of Compromise: The Truth about the American Church's Complicity in Racism*. Grand Rapids, MI: Zondervan.

Unnever, James D., and Francis T. Cullen. 2012. "White Perceptions of Whether African Americans and Hispanics are Prone to Violence and Support for the Death Penalty." *Journal of Research in Crime and Delinquency* 49(4): 519–44.

Van Geest, Fred. 2007. "Changing Patterns of Denominational Political Activity in North America: The Case of Homosexuality." *Review of Religious Research* 49(2): 199–221.

Wayne, Carly, Nicholas Valentino, and Marzia Oceno. 2016. "How Sexism Drives Support for Donald Trump." *The Washington Post*. October 23. https://www.washingtonpost.com/news/monkey-cage/wp/2016/10/23/how-sexism-drives-support-for-donaldtrump/?utm_term=.2917164186bo.

Weitzer, Ronald. 2017. "Theorizing Racial Discord over Policing Before and After Ferguson." *Justice Quarterly* 34(7): 1129–53.

Whitehead, Andrew L. 2012. "Gender Ideology and Religion: Does a Masculine Image of God Matter?" *Review of Religious Research* 54(2): 139–56.

Whitehead, Andrew L., and Samuel L. Perry. 2015. "A More Perfect Union? Christian Nationalism and Support for Same-Sex Unions." *Sociological Perspectives* 58(3): 422–40.

Whitehead, Andrew L., and Samuel L. Perry. 2019. "Is a "Christian America" a More Patriarchal America? Religion, Politics, and Traditionalist Gender Ideology." *The Canadian Review of Sociology* 56(2): 151–77.

Whitehead, Andrew L., Samuel L. Perry, and Joseph O. Baker. 2018. "Make America Christian Again: Christian Nationalism and Voting for Donald Trump in the 2016 Presidential Election." *Sociology of Religion* 79(2): 147–71.

Whitehead, Andrew L., and Christopher P. Scheitle. 2018. "We the (Christian) People: Christianity and American Identity from 1996 to 2014. *Social Currents* 5(2): 157–72.

Whitehead, Andrew L., Landon Schnabel, and Samuel L. Perry. 2018. "Gun Control in the Crosshairs: Christian Nationalism and Opposition to Stricter Gun Laws." *Socius* 4: 1–13. https://journals.sagepub.com/doi/full/10.1177/2378023118790189.

Williams, Daniel K. 2010. *God's Own Party: The Making of the Christian Right*. New York, NY: Oxford University Press.

Williams, Daniel K. 2016. *Defenders of the Unborn: The Pro-Life Movement before Roe v. Wade*. New York, NY: Oxford University Press.

Wilson-Hartgrove, Jonathan. 2018. *Reconstructing the Gospel: Finding Freedom from Slaveholder Religion*. Downers Grove, IL: InterVarsity Press.

Wuthnow, Robert. 1988. *The Restructuring of American Religion*. Princeton, NJ: Princeton University Press.

Yin, Robert K. 2018. *Case Study Research and Applications: Design and Methods*. Sixth Edition. Thousand Oaks, CA: SAGE.

INDEX

For the benefit of digital users, indexed terms that span two pages (e.g., 52–53) may, on occasion, appear on only one of those pages.

Tables and figures are indicated by *t* and *f* following the page number.